THE ART OF PSYCHOTHERAPY

Case Studies from the
Family Therapy Networker

Edited by
Richard Simon
Laura Markowitz
Cindy Barrilleaux
Brett Topping

JOHN WILEY & SONS, INC.

New York • Chichester • Weinheim • Brisbane • Singapore • Toronto

Published by John Wiley & Sons, Inc.
Published simultaneously in Canada.

This publication is designed to provide accurate and authoritative information in regard to the subject matter covered. It is sold with the understanding that the publisher is not engaged in rendering professional services. If professional advice or other expert assistance is required, the services of a competent professional person should be sought.

Library of Congress Cataloging-in-Publication Data:

   The art of psychotherapy: Case studies from the Family therapy
networker / edited by Richard Simon . . . [et al.].
      p.   cm.
   Includes index.
   ISBN 0-471-19131-0 (pbk. : alk. paper)
   1. Family psychotherapy—Case studies.   2. Marital psychotherapy—
Case studies.   I. Simon, Richard, 1949–   . II. Family therapy
networker.
   RC488.5.C3675   1999
   616.89′156—dc21   98-42306

Printed in the United States of America.

10 9 8 7 6 5 4 3 2 1

Acknowledgments

This book represents the work of some of the finest therapists in our field. We are grateful to the authors of the 26 case studies in this book, not only for their clinical sensitivity and skill, but for daring to offer such an intimate view of their experiences in the consultation room. The other essential ingredient in this book is the refreshing candor and clinical savvy of the commentators, equally willing to discuss the strengths and blind spots in these cases. While sparks sometimes flew in the back-and-forth of case commentaries, there is little of the numbing tameness of ordinary case discussions to be found in this book. We believe readers of this volume will derive the benefit of a variety of viewpoints that few case books can rival.

After the cases were written, and the commentators had their say and the authors had their last word, there was plenty left to do to get these case studies ready for publication in the *Networker* and, eventually, to find their way into this book. In the unrelenting collaboration that makes the *Networker* possible, it can often be difficult to separate out any single person's precise contribution. Certainly, over the years, the four of us have spent countless hours discussing how to make sure each case comes across as powerfully on the page as possible. While senior editor Mary Sykes Wylie and former managing editor Karen Sundquist have moved on to other assignments at the *Networker*, both have been instrumental in the demanding editing and continuing discussions that have shaped our case studies department. In addition, we would like to express our appreciation of the *Networker*'s creative consultant, Dick Anderson, for many of the case titles. Dick's flair for crystallizing complex ideas into inviting titles has been a staple of the *Networker* for almost two decades. We also want to thank editorial assistants Rose Levine and Cheryl Stanley, and proofreaders Karen Craft and Andrea Peterson for their painstaking attention to detail that took the far-ranging dialogue that inspired this book and brought it into a coherent and readable form.

Finally, we want to express our deepest appreciation of all to the clients discussed in this book for their resourcefulness and grit. Ultimately, this book celebrates the human capacity to learn and change. However exacting the art of psychotherapy may be, without clients' pivotal contributions of heart and mind, even the most skilled therapist can accomplish nothing.

R.S.
L.M.
C.B.
B.T.

Editors

Richard Simon, PhD, is the editor of the *Family Therapy Networker*, author of *One on One: Interviews with the Shapers of Family Therapy* and principal editor of *The Evolving Therapist*.

Laura Markowitz is a senior editor of the *Family Therapy Networker* and is editor of *In the Family: The Magazine for Lesbians, Gays, Bisexuals and Their Relations*.

Cindy Barrilleaux has been an editor for the *Family Therapy Networker* for 15 years and has also edited fiction and nonfiction books.

Brett Topping has been managing editor of the *Family Therapy Networker* for three years, and was previously an editor at the Library of Congress and director of publications for the National Museum of Women in the Arts.

Contributors

Mary Jo Barrett, MSW, is the director of training and consultation at the Center for Contextual Change, and on the faculties at the University of Chicago and Chicago Center for Family Health. She has coauthored *Treating Incest* and *The Systemic Treatment of Incest*.

Susan Bogas, PhD, is in private practice in Princeton, New Jersey. She is the author of "An Integrative Treatment Model for Children's Attentional and Learning Problems," *Family Systems Medicine,* 11(4), 1993.

Michele Bograd, PhD, is a licensed psychologist in Arlington, Massachusetts. She is coeditor of *Reflections on Feminist Family Therapy Training* and *Feminist Perspectives on Wife Abuse,* editor of *Feminist Approaches for Treating Men in Family Therapy,* and a contributing editor to *Family Therapy Networker.*

Lois Braverman, MSW, is a clinical social worker in private practice and founding editor of *The Journal of Feminist Therapy.* She is also editor of the book *Women, Feminism and Family Therapy.*

Emily M. Brown, LCSW, is director of the Key Bridge Therapy and Mediation Center in Arlington, Virginia, and author of *Patterns of Infidelity and Their Treatment.*

Bruce Buchanan, MA, MS, is a couples and family therapist with Centra, P.C., a private practice group in Philadelphia and southern New Jersey. He is former training director at the Philadelphia Child Guidance Center and the Penn Council for Relationships.

Lee Combrinck-Graham, MD, is a child and adolescent psychiatrist who has published several books on children in family contexts. She works as a consultant and psychiatrist in Stamford, Connecticut.

James Coyne, PhD, is a clinical psychologist and professor of psychology in the Department of Family Medicine and Department of Psychiatry, University of Michigan Medical School.

David Dan, MSW, is coordinator of children's services for Community Behavioral Health in Philadelphia.

Victoria Dickerson, PhD, is the codirector of Bay Area Family Therapy Training Associates and coauthor of *If Problems Talked: Narrative Therapy in Action.*

Lawrence Diller, MD, is a behavioral pediatrician and family therapist practicing in Walnut Creek, California. He is the author of *Running on Ritalin: A Physician Reflects on Children, Society and Performance in a Pill.*

Barry L. Duncan, PsyD, is associate professor of family therapy at Nova Southeastern University. He is author or coauthor of more than 40 articles and chapters and eight books, including the forthcoming *The Heart and Soul of Change* and *Let's Face It—Men Are A____S!*

Bruce Ecker, MA, MFCC, is the co-originator of depth-oriented brief therapy and coauthor of *Depth Oriented Brief Therapy: How to Be Brief When You Were Trained to Be Deep, and Vice Versa* and *Spiritual Choices: The Problem* *of Recognizing Authentic Paths to Inner Transformation.* He is in independent clinical practice in Oakland, California, and teaches at John F. Kennedy University.

Joseph Eron, PsyD, is a psychologist, founder, and co-director of the Catskill Family Institute. He is the author of *Narrative Solutions in Brief Therapy.*

Leo Fay, PhD, is associate professor of sociology at Fairfield University and a marriage and family therapist. He is coauthor of *Evaluation and Treatment of Marital Conflict* and *Working with Relationship Triangles.*

H. Charles Fishman, MD, is a child psychiatrist and medical director of Community Behavioral Health, a Medicaid behavioral health managed-care company within the Philadelphia Department of Public Health. He is author of *Family Therapy Techniques,* with Salvador Minuchin, *Treating Troubled Adolescents* and *Intensive Structural Therapy.*

Michael Fox, MD, is an associate professor and directs the Child and Family Psychiatry Outpatient Clinic at the University of South Florida Psychiatric Center.

Linda S. Freedman, LCSW, is an ecosystems therapist in Chicago and Lincolnwood, Illinois. Since the publication of this case study, she has moved away from seeing the family as the subject toward work with the social system. She is working toward a PhD in social work at the University of Illinois and Hebrew University.

Judith Friedman, EdD, is director of training and supervisor in the Family and Couples Treatment Division of the Institute for Contemporary Psychotherapy in Manhattan.

Fred Gallo, PhD, is a psychologist in private practice in Hermitage, Pennsylvania. He is author of *Energy Psychology,* and teaches Thought Field Therapy and Energy Diagnostic and Treatment Methods.

Eliana Gil, PhD, is coordinator of the Abused Children's Treatment Program of the Inova Kellar Center in Rockville, Maryland, and president of the Association for Play Therapy.

Peter Goldenthal, PhD, is a board certified clinical and family psychologist and the author of *Contextual Family Therapy, Doing Contextual Therapy,* and *Beyond Sibling Rivalry.*

Thelma Jean Goodrich, PhD, is director of behavioral science in the residency training program in family medicine at the Columbia-Presbyterian Medical Center in New York City. She has authored two books and many articles on feminist issues in family therapy.

Alan S. Gurman, PhD, professor of psychiatry and chief psychologist at the University of Wisconsin Medical School, is a former editor of *The Journal of Marital and Family Therapy* and author/editor of such books as *The Clinical Handbook of Couples Therapy, Handbook of Family Therapy, Essential Psychotherapies,* and *Therapy and Practice of Brief Therapy.*

Kenneth Hardy, PhD, is a professor of family therapy at Syracuse University and an advisory editor to the *Family Therapy Networker.*

Mark A. Hubble, PhD, is a cofounder of the Institute for the Study of Therapeutic Change. He has coauthored several books, including *The Heart and Soul of Change.*

Laurel Hulley, MA, is the co-originator of depth-oriented brief therapy and coauthor of *Depth Oriented Brief Therapy: How to Be Brief When You Were Trained to Be Deep, and Vice Versa.*

Evan Imber-Black, PhD, is director of program development and senior faculty at the Ackerman Institute for the Family in New York. Her latest book is *The Secret Life of Families: Truth-Telling, Privacy and Reconciliation in a Tell All Society.*

Maya Kollman, MA, is one of five Master Trainers in Imago Therapy and in private practice in Pennington, New Jersey.

Jay Lappin, MSW, is the family therapy director for Centra, P.C., a private practice group in Philadelphia and southern New Jersey. He is a contributing editor to *Family Therapy Networker.*

Ella Lasky, PhD, is a faculty member and supervisor in the Family and Couples Division at the Institute for Contemporary Psychotherapy, and is in private practice in New York City.

Lawrence LeShan, PhD, is a research psychologist and author of *Beyond Technique: Bringing Psychotherapy into the 21st Century.*

Clifford Levin, PhD, is the director of research at the Mental Research Institute in Palo Alto, California.

Eve Lipchik, MSW, is cofounder and co-owner of ICF Consultants, Inc. She was a member of the original team that developed the solution-focused brief therapy approach, about which she has written extensively.

Elizabeth F. Loftus, PhD, is professor of psychology at the University of Washington and coauthor of *The Myth of Repressed Memory.*

Thomas Lund, PsyD, is a psychologist and codirector of the Catskill Family Institute. He is coauthor of *Narrative Solutions in Brief Therapy.*

Don-David Lusterman, PhD, FAFP, is in private practice in Baldwin, New York. His latest book is *Infidelity: A Survival Guide.*

Susan H. McDaniel, PhD, is professor of psychiatry and family medicine at the University of Rochester. She is coauthor of six books, including *Medical Family Therapy* and *The Shared Experience of Illness,* and coeditor of the journal *Families, Systems & Health.*

Julie Mencher, MSW, is a psychotherapist and clinical consultant in private practice in Northampton, Massachusetts. She also teaches gay and lesbian studies at the Smith College School for Social Work and is an affiliated scholar at the Stone Center.

Scott D. Miller, PhD, is a cofounder of the Institute for the Study of Therapeutic Change. He is the coauthor/editor of six books, including *The Heart and Soul of Change.*

Michael J. Murphy, EdD, is a forensic psychologist who consults to jails and prisons. He also writes a newspaper column, "All in a Family" and is the author of *Popsicle Fish: Tales of Fathering.*

Bill O'Hanlon, MS, has authored and coauthored 16 books. He was a developer of brief solution-oriented therapy, the founder of possibility and inclusive therapies, and a contributor to Ericksonian therapy and collaborative/constructivist approaches. He lives in Santa Fe, New Mexico.

Esther Perel, MA, is on the faculty of the Family Studies Unit, Department of Psychiatry at New York University Medical School, and in private practice in New York City.

Frank Pittman, MD, is a psychiatrist and family therapist in Atlanta and author of four books: *Turning Points, Private Lies, Man Enough,* and *Grow Up!* He writes "The Screening Room," a regular column of movie reviews in *Family Therapy Networker.*

Jerome Price, MA, is the director and founder of the Michigan Family Institute. He is also the author of *Power and Compassion: Working with Difficult Adolescents and Abused Parents.*

Cheryl Rampage, PhD, is a clinical psychologist and senior staff therapist at the Family Institute of Northwestern University. She is a coauthor of *Feminist Family Therapy: A Casebook.*

David E. Scharff, MD, is codirector of the International Institute of Object Relations Therapy. He is a clinical professor of psychiatry at Georgetown University and Uniformed Services University of the Health Sciences, coauthor of *Object Relations Couple Therapy* and *Object Relations Individual Therapy* as well as author of *The Sexual Relationship.*

Jill Savege Scharff, MD, is codirector of the International Institute of Object Relations Therapy, a clinical professor of psychiatry at Georgetown University, and coauthor of *Object Relations Couple Therapy* and *Object Relations Individual Therapy.* She practices family therapy and psychoanalysis in Chevy Chase, Maryland.

Henry Schissler, MS, is in private practice in Connecticut.

Lynne Schwartz, PhD, is an associate psychologist at Queens College Psychiatric Hospital.

Richard Schwartz, PhD, is on the faculty of the Family Institute of Northwestern University and is the developer of the Internal Family Systems Model. He is the author of *Internal Family Systems Therapy* and coauthor of five books, including *Family Therapy: Concepts and Methods.*

Wayne Scott, MA, LCSW, is a writer and family therapist in Portland, Oregon.

Nina Shandler, EdD, is a licensed psychologist who has worked in schools and taught at the University of Massachusetts.

Francine Shapiro, PhD, the originator of EMDR, is a senior research fellow at the Mental Research Institute in Palo Alto and executive director of the EMDR Institute in Pacific Grove, California. She has written two books about EMDR: *Eye Movement Desensitization and Reprocessing* and *EMDR.*

Leonard Sharber, MDiv, is the director of Circle Family Care in Chicago, Illinois.

Michael Shernoff, MSW, is in private practice in Manhattan and is on the faculty at Hunter College Graduate School of Social Work. His most recent book is *Gay Widowers: Life after the Death of a Partner.*

Carlos Sluzki, MD, is the director of Psychiatric and Behavioral Healthcare Services at Santa Barbara Cottage Hospital in Santa Barbara,

California. He is also clinical professor of psychiatry at the University of California-Los Angeles and editor of *American Journal of Orthopsychiatry.*

Ton C. Smets, PhD, is in private practice in the Midwest.

Anne Speckhard, PhD, is in private practice in Alexandria, Virginia.

Kiran Starosta is on the faculty of the Multicultural Clinical Center in Springfield, Virginia.

Martha B. Straus, PhD, is a clinical psychologist in private practice and lecturer in the department of psychiatry, Dartmouth Medical School. She is author of *Violence in the Lives of Adolescents* and *No-Talk Therapy for Children and Adolescents.*

Ron Taffel, PhD, is director of Family and Couples Treatment Services at the Institute for Contemporary Psychotherapy. He is the author of several books, including *Parenting by Heart.*

Stuart Tiegel, LCSW, is codirector of MedPsych Associates, Inc.

David Treadway, PhD, is a marriage and family therapist in the Boston area. He is the author of *Dead Reckoning: A Therapist Confronts His Own Grief* and *Before It's Too Late: Working with Substance Abuse in the Family.*

John VanDeusen, MSW, is a systems consultant and supervisor in Delaware.

David Waters, PhD, is professor of family medicine at the University of Virginia in Charlottesville. He is coauthor of *Competence, Courage and Change.*

Daniel J. Wiener, PhD, is associate professor in the Marriage and Family Therapy program at Central Connecticut State University, and in private practice in New York and Branford, Connecticut. He is the author of *Rehearsals for Growth: Theater Improvisation for Psychotherapists* and *Action Methods in Psychotherapy: A Practical Guide.*

Steven J. Wolin, PhD, is a clinical professor of psychiatry and director of family therapy training at George Washington University Medical School in Washington, D.C. He is coauthor of *The Resilient Self: How Survivors of Troubled Families Rise above Adversity.*

Contents

Introduction

Despite all of psychotherapy's theoretical and technical advances since the days of Freud, the case study, at its best, remains unsurpassed for capturing the experience of the therapeutic encounter. A good case study gives us something scholarly articles, research studies, and explorations of the sociocultural context of psychotherapy cannot readily convey—the ebb and flow of effective treatment and a feeling for the often subtle processes that enable people to change. No other form of clinical writing provides a better appreciation of the interpersonal chemistry of therapy or offers such immediate access to a therapist's moments of deliberate decision making, unexpected emotional responses and—for the fortunate clinician— flashes of illumination.

Writing a good case study is not easy. Too often, case studies can lapse into exercises in grandiosity, puffing up the most ordinary turns of a case with an aura of clinical omniscience. We have all read cases that seem to reflect some alternative universe in which therapy is free of the quandaries and questions that are most clinician's everyday companions. In such case studies, nothing is quite believable, especially the therapist whose humanity and clinical struggles are deemed too irrelevant to occupy center stage.

Over the past 17 years, the *Family Therapy Networker,* an award-winning magazine for mental health professionals that reaches 65,000 clinicians around the world, has published more than 100 case studies. Each case has been followed by commentaries offering alternative conceptions of the case, usually written by therapists with theoretical viewpoints that diverge from that of the clinician-author.

Our goal from the beginning has been to bring vivid writing, personal depth, theoretical coherence, and *believability* to this time-honored clinical genre. We have encouraged our writers—some might even say pestered them—to reveal not only their flashes of brilliance, but also their moments of surprise, indecisiveness, and even downright therapeutic fallibility. In short, we have asked them to describe as honestly as possible the unpredictable adventure of psychotherapy.

In this volume, we have collected 26 of the most memorable cases ever published in the *Networker.* You will find that our case study authors neither duck controversy nor offer facile formulas. And even if they try, there are always the formidable commentators at the case's end to hold the author's feet to the fire. To keep the conversation going, the author, whenever he or she wished to, was given the opportunity to have the last word.

The result of all this is the practice companion before you, *The Art of Psychotherapy: Case Studies from the Family Therapy Networker,* an eminently pragmatic book examining in vivid detail the full range of cases likely to come through any therapist's door. Seasoned practitioners will find this book a refreshing reality test, a detailed look at what their colleagues actually *do* in therapy, with plenty of forays into the areas of practice that bring up the perennial questions clinicians confront. For students and their teachers, the cases collected here can serve as a compelling orientation to handling common clinical problems. The study questions that conclude each case are designed to stimulate further discussion and sharpen the reader's appreciation of the issues the case has highlighted.

In selecting the cases for this collection, we were not guided by any theoretical or ideological agenda. While our only commitment was to offering case material that was original, clinically helpful, and timely, along the way we frequently chose cases that broke new ground. Nevertheless, as we worked on finding a way to organize this book, we quickly found that the contents separated out clearly into five discrete sections.

The cases in Chapter 1, "Couples Issues," demonstrate ways to handle the various crises of intimate relationships—with a particular emphasis on infidelity, the trap of being inducted into a couples struggles and the difficulty of reconciling the conflict between brevity and depth that clinicians face in this era of managed care.

Chapter 2, "Therapy with Children," offers plenty of clinical wisdom on one of the most neglected areas of practice, including approaches that help therapists avoid undermining parents, guidance in treating the stonewalling teenager and practical ideas about navigating through the ADHD/Ritalin controversy.

The cases in Chapter 3, "Psychotherapy and Modern Life," focus on how therapists' heightened awareness of the clinical impact of sociocultural issues such as gender, class, race and sexual orientation are reflected in everyday clinical decision-making. It offers some valuable advice on how to avoid unintentionally wrecking havoc on clients' lives in a culture in which therapists are sometimes regarded as secular priests.

Chapter 4, "The Tools of the Trade," critically assesses some of the most touted clinical innovations of recent years, including Eye Movement Desensitization and Reprocessing (EMDR) and Thought Field Therapy. Cases also describe ways to update and fine-tune older methods to make them more relevant and effective.

Finally, Chapter 5, "The Impossible Case," presents some particularly frustrating, albeit not uncommon, clinical dilemmas, and offers what should be required reading for therapists who have ever torn their hair out over a difficult case.

Even though *The Art of Psychotherapy*'s main purpose is to provide a useful guide to clinical practice, this is also a book filled with great stories. Each case can be read as a sort of suspense tale, a quest undertaken by both clients and therapists toward some elusive destination. For clients, the quest usually involves finding some way to change a pattern of behavior, transform a relationship or heal from pain. For therapists, the quest typically involves finding a way to guide people through some difficult-to-navigate territory in a way that opens up new possibilities. In most of the cases offered here, therapists and clients appear to have found a way to locate and mine these possibilities, but we have no wish to create the illusion of a series of happy-ever-after outcomes.

For some clients, resolutions endure and may even provide an emotional compass for the future. For others, while the answers they find in a therapist's office are temporarily satisfactory, those insights become part of a larger quest. We know that for the therapist readers of this book, some cases will be more enlightening and helpful than others. Our hope is that throughout this book you will continually recognize the core questions that are shaping your own journey as a therapist. And, when you finally put this book down, you will better understand how your questions are not just yours, but are part of the collective quest of this profession.

RICHARD SIMON

CHAPTER 1

Couples Issues

COUPLES THERAPY may well be the most demanding form of clinical work. Theoretically, it has lagged behind other therapeutic modalities. Until recently, there have been few encompassing models of couples therapy. But beyond that, there is the sheer volatility of engaging with couples in conflict. As one veteran therapist put it, "Most therapists have had problems in their own personal relationships, so this work hits you in the gut—it's where you live." Further complicating approaches with couples is growing awareness of the gender issues that pervade so many couples' problems and require therapists to rethink some of their most basic assumptions. Trying to grapple with the least systematized of the therapies, couples therapists are always looking for road maps for this difficult-to-navigate territory.

The following case studies highlight both the range of problems couples bring to the therapy room and the variety of approaches therapists use to make sense of the issues. This chapter opens with "What Textbooks Don't Tell You," therapist Kenneth Hardy's case of a volatile mixed-race couple struggling with violence, gender inequality, and racism. His work illustrates the messiness of real-life couples therapy, and the impossibility of imposing neat formulas on the interconnected issues couples present. "Becoming an Emotional Conduit," by Maya Kollman, describes how couples therapists can use themselves—their empathy, compassion, and skill—to help partners connect with one another. "Turning Down the Temperature" takes on the problems couples face after one of the partners has an affair, a crucial issue long ignored in the clinical literature. Therapist Leo Fay describes a highly structured therapy that defuses explosive emotions and stabilizes the couple so they can explore the consequences of the disclosure. In "Briefer and Deeper," therapists Bruce Ecker and Laurel Hulley adjust old-fashioned depth psychotherapy to the pressures for quick work, introducing Depth-Oriented Brief Therapy. Their case illustrates that working with unconscious "emotional truths" is not incompatible with the brief therapy framework required of most clinicians these days. Finally, bringing couples work fully into the late 1990s, in "Hot Chat," therapist Linda S. Freedman describes her difficulties working, under managed care's limitations, with a couple dealing with the aftermath of an Internet affair. This provocative case includes issues of violence, possible addiction, and childhood abuse with no clear resolution and brings the couples therapist face-to-face with the new, ambiguous world of virtual relationships.

CASE STUDY

WHAT TEXTBOOKS DON'T TELL YOU
ACKNOWLEDGING THE COMPLEXITIES OF REAL-LIFE THERAPY

Kenneth Hardy

A student once remarked to me with some disappointment that therapy is a lot messier than she had been led to believe from reading the professional literature. It may be that we therapists too often condense our case presentations to make them easier to follow, but in the process we may sanitize the untidy tangents that are part of real-life therapy. Rarely do clients I see come in with only one, discrete problem. I tell my students that there's no way we can narrow therapeutic success down to one intervention or a certain quality about us as therapists. Systems work is about staying with clients as they face up to the recurring problematic themes in their lives, and helping them wrestle with all the dimensions—individual, familial, and societal—that keep them chained to old patterns.

Georgia, a 39-year-old, dark-skinned Haitian teacher was referred to me by the psychologist at the high school where she taught French because she had been noticeably depressed and the principal was worried about her growing absenteeism. During our first session, she described a whole host of difficulties, including anxiety about her relationship with Bruce, her boyfriend of three years, an unemployed white man who sometimes used drugs and often became violent with her. I was concerned about her safety and saw many places where we could start to work, but before that could happen I knew I had to establish a trusting connection with her, and that wasn't easy.

From the moment Georgia met me in the waiting room, I sensed her hostility. Early in the interview, I asked a routine question, "Have you been in therapy before? What worked about that experience and what didn't?" I've found it a shorthand way of finding out how people like to be treated. After mentioning that her former therapist was a white man, Georgia told me, an African American man, "I'm glad he was white. The last thing I would have wanted was an African American therapist."

3

She then went on to tell me, in a loud, challenging voice, that she hated African Americans and, in particular, she hated African American men.

Georgia was setting herself up to be unlikeable—her strategy for keeping the world at a distance—and so I did the opposite, staying curious and interested in her. I asked her why she had trouble with African Americans. "They are lazy, loud, and rude," she told me. "They cry 'victim' and feel sorry for themselves with no cause." I didn't challenge her. I didn't say, "So why are you here with me today?"—but listened to her, and she became temporarily calmer. This became her pattern over the next few months of therapy: she would scream, curse, and slam out of my office. Along with her intense volatility, Georgia repeatedly canceled at the last minute or failed to show up. One day, I found her sitting in the waiting room distraught. She didn't have an appointment, but I carved out a half hour to see her and then scheduled her for the next day, but the very next week she showed up 20 minutes before her session was scheduled to end. I responded with consistent friendliness, saying how glad I was she had made it and "Let's take the 20 minutes we have together." Slowly, over months, as I maintained a nondefensive, curious, and kind attitude toward her, Georgia came to trust me. I remember the moment when she stopped seeing me as an object and started seeing me as a person. She had begun to open up about her relationship with her father, whom she loved very much but also felt a deep anger toward. I acknowledged the limitations of men, how sometimes we're not always thoughtful or mindful of the people we love. I didn't exclude myself from this critique, which I think surprised her. With tremendous caution, she said to me, "Maybe you're different from all the other black men."

The messiness of real-life therapy means that clinicians have to address many issues simultaneously. As I was working on building my relationship with Georgia, I was also helping her and Bruce stop the cycle of domestic violence. Although Bruce beat her on a regular basis, Georgia reported that she never became physically violent with him. When I asked her if she wanted to leave Bruce, she told me she didn't think she could because she loved him and wanted to marry him. But she was hounded by worry that he was cheating on her with white women. I addressed her safety from the first session in three ways. I spoke to her about a battered women's shelter where she might go if she needed to get away from Bruce, but she said that was unnecessary because he wasn't beating her every day. I suggested that she might want to take out an order of protection to keep him from beating her at all, and she said she felt like she could handle herself and didn't need to bother with this. I ended up getting her tacit agreement to call me or one of her friends when he was actively abusive or if she became afraid that the situation with Bruce was escalating into violence. Even though she was minimizing her own danger, my gentle persistence to create a plan for her safety, hopefully, communicated to her that I was concerned for her well-being and that I would help her if she felt herself getting into something she couldn't handle with Bruce.

From our first meeting, I suggested to Georgia that she might want to invite Bruce to come for a couples session, but she was against the idea. It soon emerged that she expected—and dreaded—that I would side with Bruce, because in her experience, men always stick together. I took it as a sign of her growing trust—about three months into the therapy work—when she announced that Bruce would come the next week. I was particularly relieved because it seemed from Georgia's reports of growing conflict at home that her therapy work with me was creating tension in her relationship with Bruce. As she began to feel better about herself and more able to stand up for herself, Bruce's attempts to control her were escalating. Georgia described not only physical abuse, but also more verbal abuse from Bruce.

Bruce came in the following week and challenged me right away, asking me if I worked with many interracial couples and what credentials I had. He said some of the strongest disapproval toward their relationship he had experienced had come from black people and was glad to hear that I had no problem with interracial relationships. When I asked about the violence in their relationship, he was full of the usual male denial I hear so often—Georgia had provoked him; it wasn't his fault, it was his substance abuse, because snorting coke turned him into a completely different person. He said he was in a recovery program and was finished being that person who was violent. In fact, from that session on, he never hit her again.

I was glad Bruce had put the issue of race on the table when he first came in, because I felt it was crucial to look at the way race was overlapping all the other issues in Georgia's life. But in real-life therapy, clients don't always agree with the therapist about what's relevant. During our second couples session, I told Georgia and Bruce, "I am

struggling here trying to understand how the dynamics in your relationship replicate the historical relationship between blacks and whites," I
said. "After all, it has not been uncommon for white people to physically dominate black people." Bruce said he could see that maybe this
was true, but Georgia dismissed the notion that she and Bruce were re-
playing a centuries-old drama of blacks being dominated by whites. "It
doesn't have a fucking thing to do with that," she told me. "Are you
telling me black people don't beat black people? Or white people don't
beat white people?" Having Georgia and Bruce agree with me was less
important to me than planting the idea in their minds that they weren't
a couple in a vacuum—racism was a force surrounding them both and
perhaps having an impact on their behavior toward each other.

I have some students who seem to expect that an open discussion of
race will turn a light bulb on in clients' heads, but, in fact, the difficulty
thinking about and talking about race is so deeply embedded in clients
of all races that I have stopped expecting to see any immediate effects
after broaching the subject. However, a few weeks later, the role race
played in their relationship started to make sense to both of them. I had
reflected back to them that the fact that Bruce was no longer hitting
Georgia was not enough: raising an eyebrow, his vocal inflection—the
behaviors that preceded Bruce's striking Georgia—were all ways in
which he manipulated and controlled her. I told them I saw this behavior as stemming from Bruce's feelings of entitlement as a man and also
from the difference in power between them because he was white and
she was black. Georgia had just accused him of always putting her
down in front of their friends or his family—all of whom were white. I
challenged him, "What if we had three other black people in the room
here, and Georgia convinced all of us she was right and you were
wrong, would it make a difference to you that we were all black?" I
asked. He said he had never thought about how it might have felt to
Georgia as a black woman to always look wrong and stupid in front of
white people. While Georgia had often cut me off when I raised the
issue of race as a relevant factor in their relationship, she nodded her
head in agreement. Bruce then admitted that he had fears that she was
going to leave him for a black man. Later the two discussed their
dreams for the future, and Bruce admitted that he couldn't see himself
marrying Georgia because of his parents' disapproval of his being with

a black woman. Georgia began to sob, then turned off her grief like a faucet, punched my wall, and left.

As a family therapist, I always look for ways the family history is being replicated now, but in real-life therapy, clients don't always want to tell us painful stories from the past. It wasn't until we had been working together for months that Georgia told me she had been raped as a teenager by one of her younger, African American half-brothers. Immediately, her antipathy toward African American men made a lot more sense to me. She described how neither her father nor her stepmother believed her, saying she had made up the story to get attention. She had tried to cut off from her father and pretend she didn't care, but she admitted to me that she felt terrible about not being close to him and being unable to act any way but angry around him. I encouraged her to reconnect with her father because it seemed to me that this was one of the most important relationships in her life, and achieving some sense of resolution about it would enhance her ability to connect emotionally with people she cared for. Georgia decided to visit him.

One of the turning points in her therapy was helping her prepare for this meeting. I told her, "I think you know what to expect—that your family and dad, in particular, haven't had a strong track record of listening to you and acknowledging you. I found out from working with you that if I don't get scared away by your strong language and yelling, there is a strong, passionate person there who has been hurt a lot." The more I reflected back to her the vulnerability that I was seeing in her, the more her defenses crumbled, and she started to sob. I told her I thought I was touching a chord in her that, with her rage, screaming and profanity, she had made very difficult for others to find. "What happened to you in your family before occurred because you were overpowered, and while you have scars, you are not the same person," I told her. "And even if he doesn't want to hear it, it's important for you to say what you have to say."

Once again, real-life therapy doesn't always deliver the tidy, happy outcomes we hope for. Georgia confronted her father and then, after losing her temper during the conversation, felt that she had failed. Although at first she felt desolate and defeated that he still would not acknowledge the rape, another emotion soon came out as we spoke: She was proud that she had stood up for herself and stopped being a victim in her family. It was subtle, but real-life therapy success tends not to have the obvious drama of cases showcased for public presentation.

When Georgia ended therapy, she hadn't decided to leave Bruce, but they weren't planning the wedding either. In real-life therapy, clients do some work and then leave before every loose end is tied up. Georgia was doing well at work—that had been her original presenting problem—Bruce was no longer hitting her and she felt better about herself. She was more thoughtful about her knee-jerk hatred of African Americans and less apt to fly into a rage. With Georgia, as with many clients, perhaps the most important thing therapy provided was help in her finding her voice—not the voice of fury and four-letter words that she came in with, but the voice of her sadness, her pain and the hard-to-speak truths about racism, abuse, betrayal, and hopelessness that so many of our clients keep hidden in their rage and depression.

CASE COMMENTARY
BY MICHELE BOGRAD

Ken Hardy's case study offers a realistic view of a gifted therapist slogging his way through the complex and often frustrating work of therapy. Not only does he reveal that single interventions rarely lead to transformations accompanied by cymbals and a heavenly chorus, he also reminds us that intimacy in and out of the therapy office is shaped by larger social forces that most family therapists typically ignore.

Hardy demonstrates that social variables like gender, race, and class are not abstractions, but deeply emotional presences in a couple's life and their experience in therapy. He models how to address these variables, revealing the insidious and previously unacknowledged impact of sexism and racism in the lives of Georgia and Bruce. We also learn that alliances based on sex and gender are neither simple nor straightforward. Hardy and Georgia are not joined by their blackness, nor are Hardy and Bruce by their maleness—contrary to expectations.

For me, the one moment in this case study that leaned toward the "can you believe it happened, but it's true" was Bruce's surprising cease-fire after years of chronic domestic violence. Hardy doesn't explain the why of it nor how he initially assessed the safety of the couple's work. From my perspective, conjoint work should not occur unless the man's violence is infrequent, not physically injurious, not psychologically intimidating and not fear-producing for his partner. Georgia's spontaneous invitation to Bruce notwithstanding, careful assessment should precede a conjoint meeting. Although some men desist from violence once it is made public, this is often not the case, and Hardy demonstrates that even when physical abuse ceases, verbal or psychological abuse doesn't automatically disappear.

It is easy to experience self-righteousness, impatience, anxiety, and anger when clients express their prejudices. I wanted to ask Hardy for pointers about how he remained caring and persistent when so much hostility was aimed in his direction. I wondered, whether, as a black man, he's had more experience as a target and, therefore, more practice at developing the strategies for forging ahead. His work demonstrates the loving tenacity coupled with the clearness of vision that is needed to help clients untangle the snarls of their lives and, in Hardy's words, find the voice of hard-to-speak truths. ■

STUDY QUESTIONS

1. How did the therapist handle his client's hostility? Do you think therapists should work with clients who express open hostility toward them? Why or why not?
2. What role do you think race differences played in this couple's relationship problems?
3. Why do you think the therapist was concerned about behaviors that weren't, themselves, violent, but that had often preceded violence in the relationship?
4. What do you think are some of the considerations a therapist should make before inviting an abusive partner or spouse to a therapy session?

CASE STUDY

BECOMING AN EMOTIONAL CONDUIT

Maya Kollman

When I first started out as a couples therapist, I tried my best to maintain a professional distance from the emotional vortex my clients so effortlessly seemed to generate. I thought of myself as a removed expert whose specialty was coming up with solutions to the messes troubled couples brought to me. Training with Harville Hendrix in Imago Therapy gave me a different perspective. I have come to see my role as a conduit of emotional connection between partners.

"Connection" is one of those muzzy terms like "spiritual" that everyone uses these days but that is hard to define. "Joining," "creating rapport," or "getting in tune" with another are all ways of describing it. As a therapist, I experience it as an intuitive sensing of client's emotional energy. It is what happens when, for example, a loving moment takes place in my office and my own heart feels expansive and open, filled with compassion for the people sharing that moment. A key to my work is to try to nurture and amplify moments like that with my clients. I still have to keep in mind my clinical theory and what I know about the nature of systems change. But being a conduit of connection, more than any mere technique, seems to be what helps couples find their own resolution to their problems. Even if partners decide to separate, when they do it from a place of connection, they can disengage with kindness and respect.

My own feeling of connection with clients is the first step to my becoming a conduit for their sense of connection to each other. Sue and Phil, a white, upper-middle-class couple in their late forties, came to see me because Phil was talking about leaving the marriage. As Sue gave me some background—how long they had been married, what they did for a living—I listened to her story without trying to analyze or jump to conclusions. I also opened myself up to her energy by noticing her body position and affect. I spontaneously shifted my body position to match hers. As she spoke, she leaned forward slightly, and when I also leaned forward slightly, she became more animated and open. When Phil talked, his voice was a monotone, and when I responded to him in a matching tone, he relaxed his shoulders slightly. Nonverbally, I was getting into rapport with each of them.

As I usually do, I verbally reflected back to each one what I was hearing. Instead of repeating word-for-word what I heard—which was usually a statement that blamed the other—I mirrored back their experience to them. For example, Sue said, in a mild voice, "We're struggling because Phil had an affair and I don't think he really wants to stay with me. It feels so bad because I don't think I can ever trust him again, but I want him so badly." I mirrored back, "You feel upset because you're not sure what's going to happen with you and Phil, and you hope it can be resolved. Did I get that right?" I asked. Sue nodded, blowing her nose. Irritated and defensive, Phil said, "I can't stand her clinging to me. She complains endlessly and I feel like screaming." I said back. "So you've been feeling really pressured. Did I get that?" In this way, they both felt heard by me and also became more thoughtful. Phil said, "Well, I *had* an affair, but it's over. I've been taking care of people all my life. I don't want to have to do it any more. I want my own life." Sue stopped crying and looked at him. It was the first time he had talked about leaving in terms of his own needs and not her shortcomings.

Soon, Sue and Phil began to put aside verbal jabs and express their inner experience of the relationship. Phil talked about feeling stuck and wanting a change, while Sue talked about her anxiety that Phil would leave. As Phil rolled his eyes and under his breath muttered, "Here we go," Sue, who had started crying, said, "And we've had this tragedy. Our 20-year-old son was killed almost a year ago. It was a car accident." Feeling for Sue's obvious anguish, I said to her, "So you're really struggling, because in addition to everything else, you've had this tragedy." Phil angrily broke the moment by saying, "I wish she would get over it. It's been almost a year! Why is she still upset?" I shifted into connection with him and said, "It makes perfect sense you want to move on. It's hard to stay with the sadness for a long time." I had to make sure I was balanced, being connected to both of them without invalidating either one's position. Just by doing that, I demonstrated to the couple that they could both feel the way they did without wiping the other one out.

The ultimate source of most of the wounds clients bring to us is a break in connection to others. Some may react the way Sue did, which was to try to make nice and not say what is true, hoping Phil would come back to her. Others react the way Phil did, which was to get angry, hostile, and reactive. Both reactions are ultimately disconnecting because neither allows real intimacy to emerge. Connection requires both safety and risk. The more I could stay in connection with the couple, mirroring them back to themselves and revealing who they were underneath their defenses, the more they could allow their authentic selves to be in the room. I had to be very aware of my own style of breaking connection when I get scared. I probably tend to be more like Sue than Phil, so I was especially mindful when Phil became angry, making sure I didn't automatically disconnect from him. When that did happen from time to time, I saw how Sue and Phil disconnected from each other. Particularly in the beginning of therapy, my role is to create a space that fosters authenticity and safety, because most clients cannot do that on their own.

At this point, my view of the case was that Phil and Sue had become so deeply entrenched in their opposing roles—she as the emoter, he as the stoic—that they couldn't grieve together for the death of their son. They were feeling stuck, and so I decided to take a break from talking about the affair and the death. "One of the ways I would like to begin to bridge this gulf is to get you to just notice each other," I said to them. "Just sit for a moment, look at each other, breathe, close your eyes and remember what it felt like to be in love. With eyes closed, think of a memory." I had them open their eyes and look at each other while I pictured myself as a container, holding them in the moment of connection. I then asked them to speak while in this state of connection. Sue said, "I am experiencing hopelessness and sadness, and I am remembering how good it was when the children were born." Looking at her, Phil said, "Well I feel hopeless, but it's interesting to look at you." It wasn't the most loving of exchanges, but both of them felt a kind of relief to be able to be honest with each other. Connection doesn't only mean you say wonderful, sweet things. It means being authentically who you are without annihilating the other.

Of course, couples who have long, bitter histories don't change with one exercise. After a minute or so in this tender state, Phil broke the connection by sniping at Sue, and she started to cry, he shut down, and they were right back where they had started. When couples are struggling, they often feel terribly alone, and one of the things I do as a conduit is help them to be together in the experience—even if it's a lousy experience. I said, "It sounds like it's not just that the pain of this uncertainty about your marriage is so crummy, but it's that you feel alone in it." They both nodded. I said, "Maybe you can use therapy to witness for each other what you are going through."

Over subsequent weeks, I became a witness to Phil and Sue's story—their increasing distance before the affair, their increasing alienation after the children moved out of the house. They described how it was to move into separate bedrooms, to stop eating dinner together, Sue's pain at discovering the affair, Phil's weariness with her constant crying and grief over their son, her bewilderment at his lack of emotion, as if he didn't care. But whenever they started to feel tender toward each other, the grief would well up and one or the other would panic and strike out.

When you work with a couple on very intense material, it can be overwhelming for them, so every once in a while I focus on their emotional connection instead of their presenting issues. I helped Phil and Sue practice the mirroring technique by having them talk about a safe, nonconflictual topic. One week, they each talked about what rocks meant to them, but it wasn't just chitchat. Phil remembered a trip they took as a family to the Rocky Mountains. Sue remembered a rock they had sat on by a lake when they were dating. They were able to have an experience of listening and speaking to each other without getting reactive. I had them describe how it was to look at each other and what they saw in each other's faces. "Notice who this person is," I suggested. Phil and Sue got to the point where they could have an amiable conversation and at one point, they even laughed. Those sessions helped them remember what it was like to enjoy each other's company, and I built on their connection by giving them homework assignments to do one fun thing together each week. I talked to them about their family traditions. They had routinely eaten dinner together, and before dinner—no matter what kind of mood they were in—they would put aside their difference, join hands and sit and think about their children. But when the son died, this had stopped. I asked if they would be willing to have one meal together in a week, knowing it might be painful.

The biggest roadblock for this couple continued to be how they managed their grief. When Sue tried to talk about their son, Phil became angry. During one pivotal session, Sue brought up the affair and Phil said he had done it out of his loneliness. He started talking about how he had felt that there was only one person who really cared about him, and that was his son. Then he described his last hour with his son, Brad, before the young man died. Brad had driven from his home three hours away to see Phil because he had learned about the affair and wanted to talk about it. He had told Phil he was worried about his mother, but that he loved Phil no matter what. On his way home from this visit, Brad was killed.

All my attention was on Phil as I allowed myself to be touched by his words. As he talked in his emotionless monotone about Brad's death, tears came to my eyes. Looking up, he was startled to see my tears, and suddenly he began to sob. While Sue's tears usually shut him down, mine reflected back to Phil his own pain. Sue was, for once, dry-eyed, a compassionate witness to the grief Phil had kept bottled up inside. As Sue instinctively put her hand on his head, Phil leaned into her.

It was a sweet moment, but that can be hard to tolerate, particularly when the couple is more used to dealing with discomfort and pain. They almost immediately devolved back into their old patterns. Sue started pushing Phil to say more about his grief, and he got angry at her for pushing him. Soon, they were polarized in their roles. Now, I drew on all the weeks of their practicing holding a loving connection. I said, "I want you, Phil, to notice what you feel this week after having opened up to Sue like you did. I want you to notice when you feel you might need to clamp back up and be tough, and call me if you start to feel the pain so intensely that you are really uncomfortable." Because I encourage clients to connect with me, I don't hesitate to make myself available by phone if they are in a crisis. I asked him to really look at Sue during the week and remember what she was like when he was crying—not hysterical, but strong and there for him. I told Sue that Phil might be particularly critical and invite her attack that week because he believed that if he was vulnerable, she would attack him. I asked her to try not to react even if he was provocative.

They made it through that week, and several more, holding their connection more and more consistently. Finally, one day, Sue said, "I know that even though it's hard for me to forgive you for the affair, our son did. I know you were a good father and he really loved you." For the first time, they cried together and shared their desolation. It was a major step toward healing.

Phil and Sue spent the next few months working on whether they wanted to stay together. Phil continued to talk about wanting to be on his own and Sue continued to lobby for saving the marriage. Finally, Sue told Phil, "Be whoever you choose to be, and it may work and it may not, but I am not making you bad. I am saying I have my limits. I can't live with you beyond those limits." As soon as she stopped being the one to carry the torch for saving the marriage, Phil stopped talking about leaving and started working on staying.

Becoming an emotional conduit for couples requires a keen under-standing of how fragile our awareness of connection really is. We are always in connection, but it's hard to maintain that awareness. I have to know how to be present with myself so I can be present with my clients. I have to overcome my own fears of intimacy in order to be open to intimacy with my clients. Having a strong theoretical founda-tion helps therapists feel grounded and relaxed so we can be present with our clients, but when researchers compared different therapy modalities to see which ones were most successful, they found that the particular technique and model didn't matter as much as the qualities of the therapist—the ability to be respectful, listen well, empathize—all of which are ways of talking about creating connection. It all boils down to artfully and gently being our authentic selves with each other.

CASE COMMENTARY
BY DON-DAVID LUSTERMAN

Maya Kollman's description of the case reveals her as being a wise and experienced therapist who has crafted her own way of helping couples connect. Carl Rogers's work comes to mind as I hear her de-scribe her intense effort to hear not only her clients' words, but also their silences. Through modeling and through direction, Kollman teaches Sue and Phil a new and more empathic way of talking to each other. I perceived her to be a sensitive therapist who looks into her ar-mamentarium of skills and knows which arrow to choose for which target. The suggestions that follow raise the possibility that there are still arrows in her quiver that might further serve this couple.

One overarching concern remains with me as I finished reading this case: the gender dynamic between Phil and Sue and the way he so readily silences her. The gender chasm across which this couple is speaking is typical of heterosexual couples. Very much in line with what we have learned about the culture of gender, Phil has been trained to accept the stoic role, while Sue tends to stay with her feelings. As Phil deals with the two major traumas in their relationship— the loss of their son and his affair—he continually tries to silence his wife. He rolls his eyes when she mentions their son's death, as if to say, "Enough, already!" When she tells Kollman about the affair, he corrects her by saying, "I *had* an affair. It's over," as if her feelings are no longer justified. Despite her intention to encourage mutuality and authenticity, Kollman may inadvertently participate in silencing Sue when she fails to intervene when Phil silences his wife. I understand that's Kollman's style as an emotional conduit, but it may have sent the couple the wrong message. I thought it might have been helpful for the therapist to discuss with the clients how gender differences can complicate their development as a couple. Where it might not have been possible for the two to hear each other, they might have been able to hear the therapist in a nondefensive way. Even if her overarching position is to be an emotional conduit, her strong empathy for both members of the couple is so evident that they might benefit from this psychoeducational intervention.

Kollman's focus on Phil and Sue's emotional connection is a positive step; however, I found myself worrying that it might also be masking some of Sue's distress at discovering her husband's affair. The discovery of infidelity is filled with trauma and loss. The discoverer has been lied to, often at great length, by the involved partner. It is important that the therapist validate these emotions. I wasn't sure if Kollman spent much time working with the couple on this part of their story. Many of my clients report that they felt their previous therapists had minimized their sense of betrayal at discovering a partner's affair. They say it often led them to try to bury their painful feelings and fears that it would never be safe to trust again. I wonder in this case if the therapist was planning on using her role as emotional conduit to help the couple make a full examination of what, in the marriage, made an affair a likely occurrence, and whether Kollman ever challenged Phil's readiness to silence Sue around her feelings about his infidelity.

The death of a child is an incalculable loss for any parent. Even though this couple seemed to be resolving to stay together, I predict that the ongoing loss and mourning will continue to haunt them, and hope that Kollman addressed the impact of the son's death on each of them. Phil needs to understand that he blocks their mourning and thus puts them both at risk. Many therapists have seen how couples can't hold together after the death of a child and end up separating. It might be worthwhile to help Sue and Phil come to a point where they can talk as much as they may both need to about this excruciating loss, and perhaps to develop some rituals to help them with their mourning. It might be something from their own tradition, or perhaps going to some favorite or meaningful place and burying some symbol of their mourning. Whatever it is, it would give this couple a chance to talk and share their loss, and help them to heal. ■

STUDY QUESTIONS

1. What do you think the difference is between being an *emotional conduit* and a *removed expert?* What might some of the challenges be for the therapist in each role?

2. Give examples of how Kollman forged a connection with the clients during the first session, and discuss what her techniques might have conveyed to the clients about her role.

3. Lusterman says that Kollman may have inadvertently participated in silencing Sue. What does he mean? Do you agree?

4. What do you think are the characteristics in a therapist to which the client responds most positively? What roles do training and theoretical orientation play in being a good therapist?

CASE STUDY

TURNING DOWN THE TEMPERATURE
HANDLING ONE OF MARRIAGE'S MOST EXPLOSIVE CRISES

Leo Fay

Every therapist knows that the disclosure of an extramarital affair can create an explosive crisis undermining the foundation of trust necessary to sustain a relationship. In the midst of that turbulence, our job is to help couples find a pathway to a new understanding of themselves and their marriage. But how is the therapist to maintain his or her bearings in such stormy cases? I have found a standard protocol, first developed at the Center for Family Learning, extremely helpful in providing a therapeutic structure for couples facing the crisis of infidelity. The protocol serves to keep the anxiety in the therapy room—both the couple's and my own—in check and makes sure that I don't get distracted from important issues either by the couple's emotional process or my own moral judgments.

Ed and Linda Green's marriage was in big trouble. Linda had just found out about Ed's nine-month affair with Nadine—an affair that ended when Nadine aborted a pregnancy. The couple had brought their problem to Ed's aunt, a physician whom both of them liked and admired, and she referred them to me. When they came for their first appointment, both Ed and Linda looked scared and told me I was the "last hope" for their marriage.

Before asking them anything about the affair, I began, as I always do, by taking a genogram. Calming down the system is my initial goal with couples caught up in the crisis of infidelity, and instead of making the crisis itself the first subject discussed, I try to relax the couple by asking them to give me factual information about their family histories.

Ed and Linda met in college and married in 1984, three years after Ed's graduation. They now had a 3-year-old daughter, Lauren. Ed, the oldest of four children and the only son, was a 32-year-old marketing manager for the local subsidiary of a large corporation. He lived in constant fear that the corporate headquarters a thousand miles away would sell the subsidiary and that he would lose his job. Both of Ed's parents were in their sixties, but while his mother was in good health and worked as a secretary, his father had a serious neuromuscular disease that made him an invalid and caused him to retire on disability eight years ago. Ed idealized his parents and was reluctant to say anything critical about them and this was an issue between Ed and Linda. When tears welled up in Ed's eyes as he told me that his father could die at any time, Linda interrupted to inform me that Ed's parents had always made him believe that "he's a piece of shit."

Linda, the youngest of four sisters, worked as a human resources manager for a mid-size manufacturing company. While she was in college, her father, to whom she had been close, had died of the same disease from which Ed's father was now suffering. Her mother had remarried, and no one in the family (except Linda's mother, presumably) liked her current husband. Linda said that her mother had had an affair during her father's years of illness.

When I finally asked Ed about his affair, he told me that Nadine and her husband had been friends and neighbors for four years. The mutual attraction between him and Nadine had begun the previous Thanksgiving, and by Christmas they were having sex regularly. Other than the attraction, Ed's only explanation for the affair was his wife's unwillingness to have sex as often as he wanted it. Linda had a different view—she believed that the criticism Ed received from his parents made him look to others to build him up. "I got tired of doing that, and Nadine picked up the slack," she said. Nevertheless, she did agree that her low sex drive since Lauren's birth had created a real problem in the marriage.

When I asked about the current status of Ed's relationship with Nadine, both Ed and Linda told me it was absolutely over. Ed had had no contact with Nadine since her abortion and he expressed great fear about seeing her. He was concerned that Nadine was responsible for some hang-up telephone calls he had recently received at work.

From my clinical viewpoint, this solved one potential problem. If the affair had still been going on, I would have explained that marital therapy was a waste of time and money. I would have asked Ed to agree to end it and, to see whether he was following through, I would have paid careful attention to his emotional state. In my clinical experience, if a person gives up an affair that has been serving some function or meeting some need, his or her sadness or anger about the loss will soon show up unless some fundamental changes take place in the marriage.

Another goal of the early stage of treatment in these cases is to encourage the nonaffair spouse to state clearly his or her conditions for continuing the relationship and, once this is stated, to pull back to a nonreactive position. Typically, the nonaffair spouse has not clearly indicated such a bottom line, hoping that things will change and the problem will just go away. Likewise, once the affair comes into the open, the nonaffair spouse typically pursues his or her partner with recriminations, questions, pleading, and so on. Linda, however, was very clear about her bottom line: any repetition of Ed's infidelity would mean the end of their marriage. She had difficulty, though, refraining from pursuing Ed with questions and recriminations, even though she recognized the importance of remaining nonreactive.

In the early stages of therapy, I helped Ed to express the impact of the loss of the affair so that his grief would not surface in some indirect way—depression, self-pity, resentment, or feelings that I, as the therapist, was on Linda's side. Although I was troubled to hear Ed deny any sense of loss, except for missing Nadine's admiration and praise, I reluctantly accepted his refusal to deal with the issue. When Linda complained that Ed was putting pressure on her for immediate forgiveness *and* for plenty of sex, I encouraged Ed not only to give up pressuring her, but to avoid subtly manipulating her by getting angry or emotionally distant. While Ed agreed to work on this, it was a real struggle and he tended to get somewhat depressed.

Ed and Linda's commitment to each other, and Ed's assurance that the affair was over, quickly calmed the emotional climate between them. My next goal was to tease out what led to the affair and to delineate each spouse's part in the process. I made it clear that I saw Ed's decision to have an affair as his responsibility and his alone, that if he was unhappy in his marriage, there were other options, like asking Linda to go for professional help. At the same time, I emphasized that the problems in the marriage were Ed and Linda's joint responsibility, and that they both had to look at their own parts in creating them. Both of these statements were pivotal in my approach. It is crucial to avoid misunderstandings about the concept of responsibility, and about where I stand on it.

Ed admitted that he tended to engage in what the three of us jokingly called the "F-A-L" pattern: fear, anger, leave. I find that labeling things this way lightens the atmosphere with humor, reassuring clients by normalizing their behavior and emphasizing the predictability of the behavior patterns that need to be changed. Ed, fearful of not being perfect, of failing, of feeling bad, would blame Linda for her lack of encouragement, support, and sex, and would withdraw into silence. Linda admitted that what she perceived as Ed's neediness frightened her. She would withdraw in the face of a problem or demand, feel resentful that it had been made, and then get critical of Ed. That became, of course, the "W-R-C pattern."

I pointed out the parallels between these patterns and the roles each had played in parental triangles in their respective families of origin. Ed had been the object of parental criticism and concern while growing up, and had always felt undervalued and unsupported. Linda had been her father's emotional support because her mother could not deal with his illness and weakness. The demands of this role had made her feel special, but very uncomfortable; she had learned to distance herself and put up a wall to avoid these demands, but she also valued her father's attention.

Once Ed and Linda were able to recognize these patterns, I assigned homework to help shift them. Because Linda complained about Ed's lack of attention except when he wanted sex, Ed agreed to take responsibility for talking about her day at dinnertime. He was not to make any sexual demands or even overtures. Because Ed claimed that Linda did not appreciate the things he did or care about what he needed, I coached Linda on giving Ed a few minutes alone when she came home (he got home from work first and took care of Lauren). She was also to take responsibility for their sex life—to initiate sex when she felt like she wanted it. These plans worked fairly well. Linda eventually recognized that she did indeed have a sex drive, which was not as low as she had thought, though not as high as Ed hoped it would be. Sex continued to be an issue between them, but their differences generated less hurt and resentment.

Ed and Linda agreed that their problems really began after Lauren's birth. Linda experienced a lowering of her interest in sex and guilt about her decision to return to work, while fatherhood intensified Ed's fear of failure and his need to be as perfect as he thought his own father had been. They had many disagreements over how to raise Lauren. For example, Ed thought they needed to "train" Lauren not to be bad (as he had been), while Linda read child-care books and normalized everything Lauren did. So, when Lauren had a tantrum, Ed often would lose his patience and yell at her, while Linda stepped in to defend her. As much as he resented his parents' criticism, Ed found himself repeating what they had done. Linda saw that, like her mother, she preferred not to vocalize problems and to act as if everything was okay, ignoring any indication to the contrary.

The more they understood their differences about childrearing, the more they began to moderate their behavior toward Lauren. I encouraged each of them to have his or her own relationship with Lauren and stressed that the other should not interfere with that. I also suggested that Ed develop a more personal (and therefore more balanced) relationship with his father, which meant spending time with him and talking—without blame—about some of the unresolved issues between them. When I asked Ed about his issues with his father, he cited his father's negativity and pessimism, which Ed believed he had inherited. My first suggestion was for Ed to spend some time alone with his father and talk to him about the problems that Ed was having with being hypercritical and gloomy. Eight months into the therapy, after Ed had begun some of this work, his father died. Although Ed certainly did not deny his grief (as he had about Nadine), he did minimize it, and I regretted not having pushed this part of the therapy harder.

Meanwhile, Ed and Linda's ability to face the fallout from the affair waxed and waned, depending on the level of stress in their lives. The tension between them increased, for example, whenever they thought Nadine was calling and hanging up, or asking mutual friends about them. It also increased when Ed's father died, and later at the time of the anniversary of Linda's discovery of the affair. I told them that such fluctuations are normal and explained the connections between stressful events and emotional reactions, while coaching them to use the relationship tools they now had—the ability to analyze interaction patterns, to discuss them, and to reverse predictable behavior.

When I asked Linda what she needed in order to start trusting Ed again, she said that it would help if Ed told her where he was going, who would be there, and what time he would be home. This reminded Ed of reporting to his mother when he was an adolescent, but nevertheless he faithfully honored Linda's request. He grudgingly grew to accept the fact that Linda still sometimes had doubts and worries when he went out—and that reestablishing trust would take time.

Once the crisis was past and their marriage was restabilized, it was appropriate for Linda to have her questions about the affair answered. Ed said that, painful as it might be to "rehash things," he was willing to answer any questions she had. But Linda insisted she was not curious about anything, even after I emphasized that having questions is normal, and that, at this stage of treatment it is productive to deal with them. Her reluctance to voice her questions certainly fit with her style of not verbalizing problems and avoiding directly facing tough issues. Even when I periodically went back to it in later sessions, her answer was always the same.

From the very beginning of therapy, Ed blamed himself for the affair and expressed deep remorse that, at times, bordered on self-hatred. Ironically, such extreme emotionality can keep an affair alive by maintaining the focus on the remorse rather than on the issues that still need to be dealt with between the couple. A *realistic* view and acknowledgment of one's responsibility, and the expression of *appropriate* remorse is necessary to put the affair triangle behind the couple.

Meanwhile, Linda had a tendency to help perpetuate the dysfunctional marital triangle by expressing "hatred" for Nadine and wondering how a woman could have an affair with her friend's husband. This, of course, kept Nadine in her and Ed's lives mentally and emotionally. The best way to get Nadine out, I explained without much success, is to see her as a *person,* shaped by her own life history, with understandable assets and limitations just like everyone else. It is very rare that people can hear this from a therapist, because it sounds like the therapist is protecting the third party, and so it is very rare that people fully disentangle themselves from an affair triangle.

The spouse who has had an affair invariably has a parallel, or symmetrical, trust issue with the nonaffair spouse that has previously stayed underground. It was a challenge to the marital system to frame Ed's problem with their sex life as his difficulty trusting that Linda really cared about him and his needs. But at that point, Ed and Linda, at

Linda's urging, decided to terminate therapy. It had been 13 months since they first came to see me.

In my experience, Ed and Linda's case was typical of couples still maintaining their commitment in the face of the crisis of infidelity. They had weathered a very difficult time, but chose to terminate therapy before they had completed what I considered to be the "whole program." It is naive to regard couples therapy as something that fixes all the problems in a relationship. I appreciated how exhausted Ed and Linda were from dealing with the trauma of the affair and respected their decision to terminate. When a couple like Ed and Linda successfully manage a crisis in their lives together, they are more likely to return if they wish to make further changes. I would not be surprised to see Ed and Linda again in my office one day.

CASE COMMENTARY 1
BY FRANK PITTMAN

Fay shows great sensitivity to the pitfalls of treating the crisis of infidelity, while he expertly avoids most of the dangers. Less sensitive therapists often believe certain myths about infidelity that can cripple the therapy and destroy the marriage. Some even accept the idea that infidelity is normal, expectable behavior, not really worth mentioning, while jealousy and guilt are the real pathology, indicating sick dependency and control.

Some therapists don't take strong stands against affairs, dishonesty, or the continuation of any relationship with the affairee who intruded the marriage. Many believe affairs are caused by imperfect marriages, and that the cuckold, who wasn't even there, must share the responsibility for it. Some therapists assume affairs are about sex, and ignore the psychopathic, suicidal, or passive-aggressive underpinnings of the decision to betray the marriage. Other therapists see infidelity as proof of character flaws too serious and unchangeable to treat, so they try to extract angry cuckolds from their damaged marriages.

Fay does none of these things and is willing to deal with infidelity openly, rather than doing what so many skittish therapists do—bypass it, fail to ask about it, and pride themselves on helping people get all the way through a divorce without ever revealing anything that might help them understand one another. When a therapist finds infidelity frightening, and will even conspire to keep it secret, then infidelity is clearly unforgivable and intimacy between us flawed mortals impossible.

Fay does get perilously close to a blaming-the-victim position when he tells us, "The spouse who has had an affair invariably has a parallel, or symmetrical, trust issue with the nonaffair spouse that has previously stayed underground." I've worked with a lot of infidelity cases and I haven't noticed that. In fact, I haven't noticed that marriages in which affairs occur are closer or more distant, happier or unhappier, more nor less conflictual than others.

Many women have affairs as they give up on their marriages, discount their husbands, and look for a painless route out. But most men have affairs after assuring themselves their marriages are solid, while they struggle with issues of their masculinity, and mourn their fathers or the lack of closeness with them. When a man is unfaithful, the problem is more likely to be in his relationship with his father than with his wife. This was certainly the case here with Ed, as Fay understood.

Fay avoided the danger of this crisis, but I don't think he fully exploited its opportunities. He tells us that "the disclosure of an extramarital affair can create an explosive crisis undermining the foundation of trust necessary to sustain a relationship." Actually, it is not the *disclosure* that undermines the trust, but the affair itself. The disclosure is the first step in creating the *intimacy,* or knowing of one another that will replace the trust that has been screwed away.

Fay keeps the emotional level so low, in the therapy and in the marriage, that the couple does not use this crisis to achieve greater intimacy. The couple, at the end of the year of therapy, is still sad and distant. Ed has no real feelings about Nadine, which is not uncommon in affairs—affairees are likely to be fleeting fantasy figures rather than real people in an infidel's life. But he has no real feelings about Linda either, just about the sex he needs to make him feel like a man. Ed is a painfully needy man, but his only way of connecting with anyone else is sexual, and Linda (like her mother) pulls back from male desperation. Ed has not learned from his crisis or from his therapy to communicate his needs effectively.

The therapeutic maneuver that might solve this problem would be to have Ed reveal all the emotional and physical details of the affair to Linda, letting him think and talk about how he experienced this turning point in his life, and letting Linda come to know and understand this husband she distrusts and distances.

There will be further crises, which may or may not involve further infidelity. Eventually, Ed will have to come to grips with his relationship with his father, which was overshadowed here by Fay's concern with the infidelity. Fay achieves his goal of keeping "the anxiety in check," but he does not teach these sad and lonely people very much about intimacy. He leaves Ed still depressed, mourning (not Nadine, but his father), ashamed, alone and still unaware of what he feels and unable to reach out to his wife.

Crises of infidelity require our sympathy with people who have faced a turning point in their lives and hurt themselves and their loved ones by making a wrong turn. But we have to be aware that people may betray their marriages not because the marriage is flawed (all marriages are), but because they have reached a point of desperation in which they can't continue the life they have been living, and are not willing to commit suicide yet. The inevitable uproar, guilt, anxiety, and anger may do little to relieve the underlying desperation. Therapy, while cleaning up the mess of the affair, should not fail to address the desperation.

CASE COMMENTARY 2
BY THELMA JEAN GOODRICH

Kurt Vonnegut maintains that when one spouse says to the other, "I'm unhappy being married to you," the statement behind the statement is, "You're not enough people for me." Yes, that old familiar feeling: "I need more attention than what I'm getting from (only) you—more company, more stimulation. I just need more." In the case of Ed and Linda, both seem to think that Linda is not enough for Ed and he needs at least two people. So if he must pare down to one, that one will somehow have to do the work of two.

Fay quite rightly observes that therapists and clients need a clear framework for dealing with the aftermath of an affair. In many ways, his protocol is an excellent guide through this process. There are, however, three modifications that I would make.

First, I would assess the distribution of power behind wife and husband. As they come together to renegotiate the terms of their marriage, do Ed and Linda come as equals—with equal money, equal ability to know and state their desires, an equal stake in the marriage? Usually, compared with her husband, the wife has less money she regards as her own and feels less entitled to set forth terms for the relationship. Typically, she has a greater stake in the survival of the marriage because divorce imposes a greater financial, social, and parental burden on her than on him. How does an affair affect the balance of power? Sometimes, the status of the wife may get raised, at least temporarily, by her husband's disclosure of an affair. It appears, however, that this is not the case with Linda. She goes to great lengths to excuse Ed, blaming his affair on (1) her own failures as a sexual partner, (2) her inadequacy as an ego booster, and (3) Nadine.

A further indication of her low status is evident in the apparent assumption that only Ed has a decision to make about whether or not the marriage would continue. Linda is the receiver of Ed's decision, not someone who must wrestle with a decision of her own. Ed's choice of her over Nadine seemed to settle the matter for Linda.

I would work with Ed and Linda to make explicit what aspects of their relationship are unequal, what part such inequalities had in producing the conditions for the affair, and what effect they will have on intimacy, sex, problem solving and the children, even if no further affair occurs. Usually, the picture of their relationship that emerges in this process contrasts so sharply with their idealized view of themselves that a couple is motivated to correct the imbalance.

The second area I would focus on would be to help Linda locate her hurt and anger. It is crucial for her to talk about these feelings and for Ed to hear them in order for both of them to remove her from the category of object—the "explanation" for the affair, the "failure" against whom Ed acted, the unresponsive wife to whom Ed was sending a message. Instead, both Linda and Ed need to see her as someone who has her own story and is the center of her own experience. Even to invite her to ask questions about Ed and Nadine, as Fay suggests, supports the view that Linda's shortcomings caused the affair.

Third, the area of sex needs further discussion. If Linda is to work on intensifying her sex drive, a fair-minded compromise would require Ed to work simultaneously on moderating his, not just on refraining from initiation, which is easily read by any wife as exactly that, refraining. Meanwhile the pressure remains, in our culture, the husband's level of desire is taken as set-point, buttressed by his entitlement to satisfaction. Thus, it falls to the wife to match his drive, pretend to match it, or suffer a penalty. Even in therapy, the wife's deviation from her husband's drive is typically seen as the problem to solve. Fay's idea of putting Linda in charge of initiating sexual contact does not challenge this construction of the rights and privileges of husbands. Without an understanding of that, Linda's self-proclaimed increase in sexual desire is impossible to interpret, even by her.

To address the politics of sex, which is central to the presenting problem Ed and Linda bring to therapy, I would pose a series of questions designed to make commonly implicit assumptions about marriage explicit. As a couple struggles with answers, they are able to examine how an imbalance of power in the sexual relationship creates tensions and binds there just as it does in other aspects of the relationship. I would ask such questions as:

"Linda, if I ask you how sex is for you with Ed, how would I know if you were answering me with a good wife voice, a scared voice, or your own voice?"

"Ed, how do you tell whether Linda is having sex with you as a kindness to you, out of fear of losing you, or out of her own desire? Do you care which it is?"

"Linda, what other transaction in your marriage feels to you most nearly like the transactions about sex? How would changes in either one affect the other one?"

"Ed, what if Linda didn't want sex at times, but thought she should have sex anyway out of duty or fear? What do you think she should do? What if you found out that she was fearful of your anger or of your straying if she said 'no' and you wanted her to feel safe instead, what would you do? What would you gain?"

"Linda, what if Ed only wanted you to have sex when you really wanted to, how would that affect your desire?"

As a preventative to the you're-not-enough-people-for-me dead end, Vonnegut once told a young couple who had been married only two weeks, "Get as many people in your life as you can, both of you." His advice could help Ed and Linda, who seem to regard the marital contract as a promise to fill each other's every emotional and sexual need, an expectation that shows itself in Linda and Ed's shared belief that Linda's slacking off from attending to Ed prompted his affair. Both ignore the fact that Linda felt unattended to as well. Future resentments and troubles loom if their basic conception of the marital contract remains unchallenged.

As they renegotiate their marriage, Ed and Linda may need help in recognizing that some needs will never be met anywhere, that lots of needs can be and should be met by people other than one's spouse, that such relationships need not be sexualized, that sexual fidelity, in fact, does usually make for left-over desire. Regarding the latter, as Fay tells Ed, various options exist other than an affair. A friend of mine used to say to her persistent 4-year-old, "Why do you always have to treat hunger as a problem to solve? Can't you just *be* hungry for a little while?"

AUTHOR'S RESPONSE
BY LEO FAY

I appreciate the free supervision from two fine therapist-thinkers. I was especially grateful for Goodrich's point about power and its

connections with sex, and for Pittman's focus on the affair as an opportunity for teaching about intimacy.

While I agree with Goodrich that gender is sometimes the major
determinant of power distribution in both marriage and therapy,
power should not be equated with gender roles. While women often
have fewer financial resources and more parenting responsibilities,
as Goodrich points out, men typically have fewer emotional resources and greater emotional neediness. Gender is one variable
among many affecting power, and family therapy still awaits a clear
understanding of those variables. Nevertheless, Goodrich is absolutely right in tying power and sexual complaints together. Her
process questions are terrific examples of the sort of clinical research
questions therapists dealing with couples need to ask more often.

There is a real conundrum in Pittman's observation that in
keeping "the emotional level so low, in the therapy and in the marriage, . . . the couple does not use this crisis to achieve greater intimacy." My own experience is that, in just about every marital
crisis, the emotional level is so high that thinking—and therefore
change—is impossible. Lowering the emotional level is a prerequisite for achieving the focus on self, the reestablishment of trust and
detriangling that are essential to reconstruct the marriage.

Timing, and the personal style of the therapist, are the real issues
here. The problem at one extreme is that the therapist who is anxious about a couple's lack of intimacy may move too quickly to work
on it directly. This may produce a fairly rapid and intense closeness,
followed by an equally rapid and intense recycling of their problems
that can blow the marriage out of the water. At the other extreme is
the therapist who waits too long to focus on emotional issues with
the result that the couple goes away with symptom relief but without any change in their level of marital intimacy.

I have always understood that couples like Ed and Linda leave
therapy before they face issues of intimacy (both emotional and
physical), because they are exhausted and relieved that they have
gotten through the crisis of infidelity without divorcing. Sometimes
I've gotten psychodynamic and thought that their leaving early had
to do with their fear of intimacy. Pittman's comments suggest to me,

however, that it might have to do with the *therapist's* fear of intimacy. Of course, as an ex-Jesuit, Irish Catholic from Boston, I've never had any trouble with that. ■

STUDY QUESTIONS

1. What do you think about the therapist's view that seeing a couple in therapy when one is still engaged in an affair is a waste of time and money? Should ending the affair be a prerequisite for coming to therapy?

2. What roles do remorse and taking responsibility play in the therapy work when couples are dealing with the aftermath of an affair?

3. Do you think that the therapist in this case places equal responsibility for the affair on both partners?

4. Do you agree with Pittman that it might be important for couples to discuss the gritty details of the affair in order to be able to move on?

5. Why does Goodrich ask about the financial equality of the relationship? What difference might power inequalities make to a couple dealing with an affair?

CASE STUDY

BRIEFER AND DEEPER
ADDRESSING THE UNCONSCIOUS IN SHORT-TERM TREATMENT

Bruce Ecker and Laurel Hulley

While everybody grumbles these days about the pressure to limit therapy to as few sessions as possible, it may be that clinicians' professional
satisfaction is threatened less by managed care's demand to be *brief*
than by the failure of brief therapies to be *deep.* The case that follows
demonstrates that clinical depth and short-term treatment are not irrec-
oncilable, and that it is possible to quickly ameliorate symptoms while
also tapping the unconscious basis of the presenting problem.

Linda and Phil were in their late twenties and had lived together for
several years. Each was a recovered alcoholic who in childhood suffered much emotional and physical abuse. They had come for therapy
previously and in 10 sessions had dispelled other issues, and now, after
a hiatus, scheduled a session because of a volatile, ongoing conflict that
was seriously jeopardizing their hopes for marriage.

Phil, clearly aggrieved, sat down and described "a big issue in this
relationship." He had been hoping it would just "go away," but it kept
flaring up and had again erupted the night before. He had wanted to
spend the evening with Linda and make love. In preparation he took a
shower, but then found Linda talking with a friend on the phone. When
she hung up nearly an hour later, he was "livid." "You're always doing
what *you* want!" he complained bitterly. "The relationship is always following *your* schedule!" A scathing verbal battle followed.

When the therapist asked them to walk through the events of that
evening, it became obvious to all that Phil had never given Linda any indication of how he wanted the evening to go, and that this was, in fact,
a pattern for him. The therapist, thinking this was a key symptom with
deeper themes, said to Phil, "Let's see what's making it important to
not be up front about what you want."

Unlike therapies that would try to improve Phil's communication, the
approach taken here, depth-oriented brief therapy (DOBT), is based on

the theory of *symptom coherence*—the view that the client produces the symptom because it seems truly necessary within some unconscious, compelling theme and purpose. This passionate but unrecognized area of personal meaning is what we thing of as "the emotional truth of the symptom." In DOBT, the goal is to generate swift therapeutic effects by helping the client become experientially aware of this emotional truth.

The therapist prompted Phil, "Imagine you're back in the situation right before taking the shower—[pause]—and imagine you *do* say a few words that let Linda know how you'd like the evening to go. Just imagine that. Feel what that's like. [Long pause] And just notice—what makes this something to avoid doing?"

After some moments of silence Phil, now animated, reported, "If her answer is 'no,' it comes with this," and made a forceful shoving-away gesture. He said he always feels extremely hurt and rejected by that shove, adding resentfully, "I don't want to set myself up for that." The therapist asked, "So you generally are not telling Linda what you want, in order to avoid getting shoved away like that?"

"Damn right," said Phil, bristling with indignation.

The therapist asked Phil to make a direct statement to Linda "from this part of you that expects the shove-away." As Phil groped for, found, and voiced the words expressing this emotional truth, he got in touch with his own feelings more and more fully. With help from the therapist, he finally said to Linda: "I'm not going to tell you what I want, even though then we wind up doing only what you want, which I really hate, but even more important to me is not getting that shove-away that hurts the most." As Phil's statement shows, the emotional truth of a symptom is an active stance, a powerful *position* the client holds and carries out without knowing it.

Linda reacted strongly to Phil's characterization of her. "Bullshit! That 'shove' is totally how he takes it! There's no way for me to say 'no' so that he wouldn't hear it that way!"

Phil again insisted that she always put a stiff and unnecessary "kick" into her "no."

Does she or doesn't she? If the "kick" is purely Phil's construct, Linda would be entirely comfortable saying a relaxed "no." On the other had, if she did habitually add a kick, eliminating it would thwart her unconscious purpose for adding it and create some conscious distress. To find out, the therapist invited Linda to carry out the same experiential technique used with Phil (we call it *symptom deprivation*). "Picture a recent time you needed to say a definite 'no' to him, and let me know when you've got it. [Pause] Good—now, would you just look at Phil and replay that moment of saying 'no' as if it's happening now, by saying the 'no' clearly, and with absolutely no special edge in it. I'm not saying this is how you should always behave. I just want to see what happens when you say 'no' in a clear but relaxed way, with no edge at all."

As soon as Linda said "no" neutrally, her eyes became teary and her chin quivered. She began describing a childhood and young adulthood laced with emotional and physical violations, a world in which she could never trust anyone to respect her "no." She looked at Phil in anguish and said, "It's true. I don't assume a 'no' from me will be respected by you or by anybody. How *could* I?"

The therapist asked what, specifically, she experienced while saying "no" to Phil without adding force. After reflecting silently for a moment, she said, "It made me feel really unease, like now I'm wide open."

THERAPIST: "And so, how do you say 'no?' "
LINDA: [Pause. Gazing at her lap, low voice] "I do put a push-away in it just to make sure."

To deepen her connection with the unconscious emotional truth now emerging—a position very different from the conscious view she had asserted just minutes earlier—the therapist asked her to repeat her last words directly to Phil. She did this.

THERAPIST: "Stay with that—how it *feels* that you have to put that force behind it—and imagine you're about to say 'no' to Phil about something and there's no sign at all that Phil would ignore or violate your wishes. [Pause] And see if that makes any difference."
LINDA: [Pause] "Actually—no."
THERAPIST: "So would you try out saying to Phil, 'Even if you haven't actually done anything that violates me . . .' and finish it yourself." (The *sentence completion* technique is often a simple way to elicit and establish clients' conscious awareness of their previously unconscious themes.)

LINDA: "Even if you haven't done anything that violates me . . . it doesn't matter what you do! I *have* to know I'm going to keep myself safe."

THERAPIST: "So try saying the whole thing to Phil, and see if it feels true: 'Even in a situation where you might not actually deserve it, I *have* to know I'll keep myself safe, so I'm going to put that push-away in it when I say no.'" (This *trial sentence* simply puts together her own pieces of emotional truth with no interpretation added. Having her voice her full position to Phil keeps the work experiential, which is essential for genuine integration.)

She said the sentence and confirmed it was "very real" for her. A look of grief came over her face and she explained through tears, "It's so sad to look all the way back and see that I've been so badly treated that I can't trust I'll be respected when I say 'no.' It feels so sad to see that." The therapist, recognizing that she was beginning the genuine grieving so vital to healing this old wound, quietly commented, "What an important sadness to feel."

Linda's self-protective shove-away, and her emotional purpose behind it, had been completely unconscious. Yet, it was brought to light in just a few minutes through these simple, noninterpretive, experiential methods designed for accomplishing exactly that. Phil's unconscious position of protecting himself from rejection by not telling Linda what he wanted also emerged very quickly, although, initially, his angry protest of victimization and her righteous denials were the only pieces of the problem's ecology of which either of them was aware.

The experiential nature of the work is crucial—cognitive insight alone is completely inadequate and nonproductive. Because the therapist works experientially, clients do not need high levels of conceptual insight or verbal skill, making this approach applicable with diverse populations. Linda and Phil discovered their own unconscious emotional truths not through introspective thinking, but by bumping into them and feeling them directly.

Phil seemed visibly affected by what Linda had just revealed, and in a voice noticeably warmer and more relaxed, he said it was a "big relief" because it was now clear that the push-away wasn't about him. He paused, then said, "Actually, this problem feels like it's gone."

As therapeutically golden as this moment seems, the therapist must not be naive about its staying power. The clients' new awareness of emotional truths may quickly revert to unconsciousness unless focused steps of integration follow immediately. In DOBT, the goal of integration is for the client to experience the problem, whenever it occurs, consciously feeling and knowing the specific theme and purpose that make the symptom necessary and worth having, despite the pain or hardship it beings. People are able to change only those positions they know they have.

To solidify integration, a between-session task is necessary. On an index card, the therapist wrote Linda's words of emotional truth: "I expect that a 'no' from me won't be respected by you or by anybody. How could I? I feel I *have* to put a push-away in it, to make damn sure I'm safe." Her task was to read this each morning and night. This is a simple but highly effective technique to maintain her new awareness of having this position in relation to Phil.

The therapist gave Linda a second task, saying, "You've gotten in touch today with a very important part of yourself that's dedicated to being safe from any more violations. I recommend you not try to just override that part of yourself; don't try to stop yourself from doing that protective push-away. But whenever you or Phil notices you are doing it, that's your signal, right then and there, to know and feel that, 'Right now, I don't trust he'll take seriously this no and I'd better put a push-away in it to make sure he does.' You might read the card right then to make it very clear for yourself." In this task, the client uses the symptom's occurrence as a signal to reexperience and reinhabit the symptom-generating position discovered in the session.

Phil's task was to read daily an index card with his own words of emotional truth on it: "Getting shoved away hurts so much that I'm determined to avoid it. So I'm not going to tell Linda what I want, even though then we do only what she wants—which I resent—but it's worth it to keep from feeling hurt by that shove-away."

These position statements on index cards should not be confused with paradoxical prescriptions—DOBT's therapeutic strategy of dispelling symptoms by accessing their unconscious emotional truth is fundamentally different. The symptom, which the client took as evidence of defectiveness, irrationality, or lack of control, becomes recognized as a powerful part of a coherent purpose he or she is carrying out. This beings a new sense of genuine agency where there seemed to be none.

At the next session, Linda and Phil each reported that fighting over "doing only what she wants" wasn't happening anymore. The therapist asked them, "How was it for you to stay in touch with what we put on your cards?" Linda said, "At first, when I'd look at the card, it would just bring me right back into that sadness I felt last time. After a couple of days, I didn't have to look at it anymore, it got so obvious how I've been carrying around so much mistrust and reacting to Phil." Phil, referring to his task of knowingly staying safe by not revealing his wishes to Linda, reported, "I didn't do it: I *did* tell her what I wanted a couple of times. I was ready for the shove, but it didn't come, even when she said 'no.' Even if I had gotten the shove, I really don't think it would've hurt my feelings, because now I know what it's about."

As occurs in the majority of cases, focusing solely on integrating a symptom-producing position had triggered a spontaneous revision of it. When the client no longer has any position in which the symptom seems necessary, he or she stops producing it. Phil and Linda changed their symptomatic behaviors (his nonasking, her shove-away) without any attempt by the therapist to eliminate those behaviors or "correct" any "distorted" cognitions. Phil's "big issue in this relationship" did not arise again. The couple ultimately married.

DOBT is not a function-of-the-symptom model; its coherence model of symptom production fully accounts for both functional and functionless symptoms. Neither is it a secondary-gain model, because coherence constitutes primary gain. The central assumption of symptom coherence is that the client unconsciously expects not having the symptom to being an even worse suffering than the familiar suffering with the symptom. We have found this to be the source of a vast array of symptoms, including anxiety and panic, depression, attachment problems, attention difficulties, low self-esteem, procrastination, and a wide range of couples and family problems.

There is no fundamental antithesis between deep and brief psychotherapy, if we organize therapy around the dual convictions that symptom production is always coherent—a functioning, rather than a dysfunction of the client—and that the unconscious emotional realities necessitating symptoms are directly accessible and changeable in every session. Depth-oriented brief therapy is one way in which we clinicians can adjust to the pervasive demand for time effectiveness and still fully engage the passionate themes and purposes most important in people's lives.

Case Commentary
BY LOIS BRAVERMAN

It is always satisfying to find a clinical moment so succinctly described and a couple's dilemma so artfully resolved. Ecker and Hulley's success at economically tapping into the deeper emotional issues beneath the symptom with their experiential exercise demonstrates what is best about their brand of brief therapy and the power of their conviction that the symptom is truly necessary, given the client's emotional history.

While I was intrigued overall by the approach in this case, I was troubled with how Phil's emotional material was handled. Although both Phil and Linda were identified early in the case as suffering from childhood emotional and physical abuse, only Linda's symptom was tied to her past history. Phil's "emotional truth" was not considered in the context of his family-of-origin experience, and was viewed instead as a more generic fear of rejection. I can't help but wonder whether this difference in how deeply each partner's emotional truth was explored was not in some way shaped by gender expectations. Was the therapist so pleased that, given his maleness, Phil was able to express his insight, that he did not press him to probe further into his inner life? Too often, the deeper connections between the past and the present are easier to develop with female clients, as was the case here with Linda, than with their male partners. But what are the long-term implications of this insight imbalance for couples? When Phil and Linda, now in their twenties, are in midlife, will she feel she did too much of the relational work of the marriage? Will her emotional truths always have more depth than his? Will she be seen by him and herself as having more of a problem than he does?

Just because therapy is brief does not mean that the therapist can avoid issues of gender. Phil's difficulty in asking for what he wants is multilayered, and not questioning him about those other layers seems problematic. For example, I would have asked Phil how men in his family made their wishes known to other family members. Was it a sign of weakness for a man to ask for something directly? Should men even *have to* ask directly for what they want, or did he learn that women should be able to intuit their subtle cues? Without exploring these questions, Phil is left with a fairly simplistic notion of his dilemma—I have problems with rejection and so I avoid asking for what I want. A more complex reading of this issue might be: I have difficulty with asking for what I want not only because I fear rejection, but also because it is not congruent with my idea of how men should act. In addition, he might also have difficulty asking for what he wants because when he called attention to himself and his needs as a child, it often led to abuse.

Establishing a connection at the emotional level between clients' behavior and their need for self-protection, as Ecker and Hulley do, is a powerful intervention. Joining those insights to an understanding of gender expectations observed in one's family of origin can add to the effectiveness of couples work, diffusing further the projected identifications that lead to blame and conflict. In the future, I hope the authors will integrate a sensitivity to unequal gender expectations in their depth-oriented brief therapy model.

AUTHORS' RESPONSE
BY BRUCE ECKER AND LAUREL HULLEY

It is quite a leap to conclude "gender insensitivity" from a session in which one partner's symptomatic material was tied to past history and the other's was not. While Braverman seems to assume that therapists should always explore the gender socialization of each partner, or at least that both should be worked with in the same way regarding their childhood history, we share neither assumption.

We have often found with couples and families that one person's unconscious position is a more potent key to swift change than anyone else's position in the system. There is no reason to artificially require symmetry of depth. (Although we do believe that it is important to attend to whether any asymmetry of depth is being used countertherapeutically by anyone.)

In DOBT, our rule of thumb is to go into unconscious emotional truth, including historical material, as deeply as necessary for achieving a lasting resolution of the presenting problem, and no deeper. It is, after all, intended to be a time-effective therapy. Braverman overlooks the fact that by having Phil access and own just the depth of material described, he made a fundamental shift and began asking for what he wanted. Is that not enough therapeutic effectiveness? Whose agenda of needs is really served by insisting on a thorough archaeological dig?

Phil's symptom is nowhere described or regarded by us as a generic fear of rejection. Actually, it is Braverman who disregards its particular context of being a response to Linda. In DOBT, there are no generic symptoms as such, only the precise, empirically discovered, unique constructions held by individuals. The rejecting "shove" Phil was always avoiding turned out to be real. Once Linda experienced her position of regularly resorting to that shove-away, it was then only natural for the session to go more deeply into that rather than into Phil's self-protection from a shove he correctly expected to receive again and again. And since he was dealing with real jabs of rejection, it would have been therapist-constructed pathology to view his current guardedness as being what Braverman calls a "projected identification." As mentioned, Linda and Phil had prior and subsequent sessions focused on other problems. We can assure Braverman that Phil was not excused from deeper emotional work and that Linda was not cast as the problem partner.

We respect Braverman's perceptiveness and concern for gender issues in therapy, but we are uneasy with the stance of any therapist who would use the power differential between client and therapist to impose a focus on his or her own cherished themes. As important a dimension as gender is, it is not a universal key to effective therapy. More fundamental, in our view, is the therapist's willingness to meet the client's construction of emotional meaning entirely on its own terms, without interpreting it. ∎

STUDY QUESTIONS

1. How do the emotional "truths" of these clients' childhood experiences express themselves in their adult relationship with one another?

2. How did these therapists help the clients integrate their newfound emotional truths into their relationship? What do you think their homework assignment taught these clients?

3. Why does Braverman believe the therapists' work with this couple was shaped by their gender expectations? Do you agree? Why or why not?

4. Do you agree with the authors' response to Braverman? What might you have done differently with this couple?

CASE STUDY

HOT CHAT
VIRTUAL AFFAIRS CAN BECOME VERY REAL EMOTIONALLY

Linda S. Freedman

The Internet has entered the consulting room in ways that few therapists could possibly have anticipated. Today, Internet chat lines allow individuals to express themselves intimately with strangers and to engage in relationships (and fantasies) bounded only by the computer screen and modem. Universal access to chat rooms has expanded our interpersonal world, and many people who are having difficulties with their family and friends are drawn to their computers for companionship.

This case study is about an extramarital affair that exemplifies how people struggling with their marriages can seek out on-line relationships to see what else is out there. When they become intimate, these *virtual affairs* can become very real emotionally, stressing a marriage every bit as much as a flesh-and-blood infidelity.

I believed Jerry when he told me he was so furious that he wanted to kill someone. I had seen Jerry and his wife, Beth, briefly about a year before. At that time, their HMO authorized only six sessions, in a *see 'em and fix 'em* kind of therapy that leaves many goals unmet. Now he had come back to tell me that he was enraged at his wife, Beth, because he was convinced that she had at least one on-line lover. He had found a computer printout of a picture of a naked man and knew that Beth was having explicitly sexual conversations in computer chat rooms. Jerry said that Beth's computer habit and on-line friendships were threatening their marriage. She stayed up all night and spent her days on-line, as well. According to Jerry, their two children played in the streets as Beth pecked at the keyboard, talking to her new Internet friends.

When they had initially come to see me, Beth was the identified patient—depressed and dissatisfied with her husband, offering a litany of individual complaints, including her weight, her PMS, and her job. Her only interest and area of pride seemed to be her growing aptitude for computers. Beth had been married to Jerry for 15 years, and came into therapy, she said, because they had grown apart emotionally and sexually. She felt Jerry spent too much time with his boss, a surrogate father to him. Beth felt trapped and isolated by marriage and motherhood, and wanted more attention from Jerry. Their worst conflicts were about Beth's spending—both agreed that Beth had driven them into bankruptcy—and Jerry's lack of attention.

While Jerry had helped support her when she was a teenager, and had served as both father and lover to her, Beth now resented his possessiveness. When they were teenagers he hadn't let her go out with her friends, and this pattern continued into adulthood—she could go out with him and his boss, but not with women from work. He had made the rules when they were young and hadn't changed them in 15 years.

I focused the brief therapy on changing the marital relationship to help relieve Beth's depression. Together we identified generational patterns that underlay Jerry's possessiveness. We also addressed Jerry's own abandonment fears and Beth's spending. We discussed Jerry and Beth's making lifestyle changes so that they could spend more time together. Soon they were spending romantic evenings together and having sex again. Jerry was bringing home flowers. In this honeymoon atmosphere, Jerry was eager to leave therapy, but Beth wanted to continue. After their insurance ran out, she and I met several times. Beth talked about issues with her overbearing mother and with being a parent herself. When Beth ended therapy because she felt she couldn't afford it, she was a little concerned that Jerry had become inattentive again, but she didn't feel shut out. I didn't hear from either of them again until Jerry called, enraged.

In his session with me, Jerry told me that his wife had found new friends and a lover on the Internet. Afterward, I called Beth and set up an appointment. She came in alone and said that Jerry had become increasingly distant and that, starved for friendship, she had fallen in love with a man on-line and even traveled to see him, although she had lost interest after she met him. She had remained true to Jerry, she said, and had not had sex with the boyfriend. She agreed to begin marital therapy again. In the next session, they agreed that Beth would "stop the on-line stuff for a while" and work on their marriage. But they missed their next appointment.

Three months later, Jerry called to see me again. This time, Beth had left Jerry and her kids and told him she wanted a divorce. He gave me a letter from Beth, who was living with her sister. She wrote that she was afraid of Jerry because he had threatened one of her on-line boyfriends. Although she realized she should break her chat room habit, she wasn't ready to go back to Jerry. She said her on-line friends were just that, friends, and she asked me to call her.

When I told Jerry that Beth claimed that her computer relationships were just good friends, he laughed and said that he had caught her at the computer with her clothes off, face flushed. He said that he knew about 'Net sex because he had tried it himself, with Beth in the room, to see what the great attraction was, but he found it embarrassing. He wanted me to help him get his wife back, and get her out of the chat rooms. He had lost weight and cut back the time he spent with his boss to prove his sincerity.

I agreed to call Beth. On the phone, Beth told me that Jerry had threatened to kill her and she wanted to see me alone. We set up an appointment and didn't tell Jerry when it would be. She showed up, confused about her feelings for Jerry. She missed him and wanted to come home, but she also liked her new freedom. She dreaded the possibility that he would make her give up her on-line friendships. She said that she knew these relationships had gone too far, but explained, "It's like being in high school! Twenty-three best friends talking all night long. To Jerry I was some kind of possession, and now that he's lost me, he's freaking out."

Jerry and Beth came for three sessions. Jerry worked on his anger and need to control his wife. Beth pointed out how he bullied her when he got jealous of her friends. Jerry agreed to be patient while Beth's love for him grew gradually, but said he wouldn't tolerate her being sexually involved with anyone else. Beth refused to stay out of the chat rooms altogether, however; she said she needed adult conversation and doubted Jerry would ever be able to replace what she got on-line. After the third session, they abruptly dropped out of therapy and their last two checks bounced. They had moved and left no forwarding address; their phone number was disconnected.

I still wonder if I missed the clues that might have led me to treat this case differently. Beth did have early childhood experiences with pornography, and had some shame associated with it. Perhaps she did obsess about sex privately and was ashamed to tell me she had a sex addition. If we have learned nothing else about addictions, we know that shame is the operative emotion. It is the therapist's task to neutralize it, and I failed.

What we're seeing on-line is a natural extension of life beyond the boundaries of home and family. Adults who can, will set healthy boundaries and balance their private lives with their virtual relationships. I am sure we will see many future cases in which that desire for a healthy boundary is superseded by a compulsive desire for attachment, both emotional and sexual. Virtual reality is no longer a game. Its impact is real and we, as consultants and experts on human relationships, may increasingly be asked to help our clients cope with their virtual lives.

CASE COMMENTARY 1
BY DAVID C. TREADWAY

The Internet invites us to transcend the limitations of race, gender, age, even our names and personalities, to enter a world where we are free to become whomever we want to be. One of my clients, a 42-year-old schoolteacher, surfs the net as "Sarah." He explained, "I'm just looking for the kind of intimate friendship and openness with other women that my wife has with her girlfriends. That's all." Another client, Annie, a shy, plump 13-year-old, said to me, "Don't take me wrong, but you're old. It's so great to be able to just be yourself without worrying whether you have a zit or people are going to think you're too fat. I get to be me. At school, I'm a loser, but now I have friends from all over the country."

I thought of "Sarah" and his poignant, but contradictory, yearnings for openness and connection and Annie's youthful exuberance when I read Beth and Jerry's story. Beth seems to be lost between being an innocent young girl just looking for friends and a confused woman mistaking hot chat and masturbation for freedom and intimacy. Clearly feeling very threatened, Jerry tried to solve his marital crisis by taming the technological beast, becoming a modern-day Luddite.

The main difficulty in Jerry and Beth's story isn't the Internet, but their painful struggle to open their marriage and break free of their teenage father-daughter dynamic. Although that dynamic worked at one time, it clearly broke down long before Beth was captivated by the cyberworld. Given the description of Jerry's dominating, controlling behavior, which included not allowing Beth any friends of her own, I think it's safe to assume that this marriage would have imploded sooner or later. The struggle over Beth's use of the Internet was the match, not the munitions factory.

It's always easy to offer an armchair critique of someone else's work. (I shudder at the thought of some of my cases being reviewed on these pages.) However, I do want to address a few of the key dilemmas in this case. The first difficulty was the handling of the original managed card, six-session limitation and the "honeymoon" that resulted. The therapist seemed to make considerable progress with them, and yet I'm always suspicious when a hierarchically unequal couple snaps back into romance. Spacing out sessions, teaching the couple how to manage conflict, restraining them from too much change and working extra hard to hold Jerry in the therapy could have made a difference. They needed time, and practice, to learn how to manage the inevitable tensions that would result from the healthy developmental changes they were experiencing. The way they drifted out of therapy was a major warning sign that their progress was too fast. While it's always difficult for us to know when to pursue a case, more often than not, going the extra mile (e.g., calling Jerry and asking for a closure session) is well worth the work.

Once Jerry called the therapist and accused his wife of having and affair, the therapeutic challenge was to sustain Beth's emerging independence, while avoiding a destructive adolescent rebellion, and simultaneously support Jerry enough so that he could make room for Beth's increased autonomy. It's important to note that Beth did not act out the cyberrelationship in the flesh and was still appropriately committed to the marriage. I would have encouraged them not to rush back to working on the relationship until they had confronted in therapy their feelings about what happened. It was premature to make rules about Beth's time on the Internet because that just reinforced the old pattern of Jerry's being in control and Beth's being submissive.

The case really veered out of control once Jerry was threatening violence and Beth left home. The trade-off that they tried to negotiate—

that Jerry promised good behavior if Beth did what he wanted—was part of an escalating abuse cycle in this couple and a dangerous moment. I believe it would have been more helpful for the couple to remain separated at this point, rather than trying to again negotiate a compromised solution to their conflict. Beth was clearly not willing to return to her old one-down position and Jerry should not have been rewarded for his threatening behavior. A separation might have provided enough safety for them to have the time to fully explore themselves and their marriage.

I don't think the most serious problem in this case was Beth's hidden sex addition. The Internet did, however, allow her to explore her sexuality in relative safety and thus enabled a dramatic acceleration of her pulling away from her marriage. It's unlikely that Beth would have so easily found hot chat on the soccer field or in the car pool. Yet, suddenly intense sexual experiences were readily available in the privacy of her own home. Clearly, both Beth and Jerry were overwhelmed by the suddenness of this change in her and in their relationship. The complexity of Beth's compulsions and Jerry's fears needed a lot of time to be addressed safely and without coercion.

The most difficult issue in the case, however, was not the sex play on the Internet, but the dominant/submissive structure in the couple and the emergence of the abuse, once Beth began a shift toward more independence. The true villain in the case was the extreme limitations we are all working with under managed care. I thought the therapist did and excellent job under very difficult circumstances.

Facilitating change in couples like Beth and Jerry can be like patching a gaping hole in the bottom of a boat being tossed about in a force-ten gale while the water is gushing in. Sometimes our best effort isn't good enough. Sometimes the boat just doesn't make it.

CASE COMMENTARY 2
BY EMILY M. BROWN

Anonymous sex is commonly regarded as sleazy, shameful, and dirty. Cybersex has a different aura—one of titillating respectability. There's a veneer, a surface polish, to cybersex that goes with all things computer these days, especially the Internet. Cybersex is a high brow form of anonymous sex.

The motivations for cybersex and extramarital affairs are much the same: avoiding conflict or intimacy with one's spouse, using sex as anesthesia or filler, or finding the fantasy partner who will bring you back to life. (Cybersex, however, is usually less effective than a real affair if your intent is to get your spouse to kick you out the door.) With both affairs and cybersex, there's a yearning for something different. However, a real affair involves some degree of emotional risk.

The case of Beth and Jerry is classic. Beth's on-line affair is similar to the typical affair in which the spouses engage in ritualized fights and can't identify or talk about what hurts or has them scared. In the face of Jerry's inattention, Beth acted out her dissatisfaction. She tried overspending first, which got them to therapy briefly, but the positive results didn't last long. She yelled, Jerry controlled, and the dead space between them developed into a monster. Beth's next attempt to get attention was the chat room and on-line sex.

If Beth and Jerry had remained in their father-daughter dynamic, their marriage might have continued to plod along. But marriage is not static. It's likely that Jerry's role in fathering Beth since she was 15 helped her grow out of her need for the kind of father a young child needs. As Beth reached "adolescence," the dynamic between them changed, but Jerry's possessiveness continued to be extreme. Adolescents with possessive and controlling parents rebel. Beth did just that with her spending and chat room habit.

Beth wanted change, but is appears that Jerry saw no need to change. He seemed to take it for granted that the control he had in the marriage would, and should, continue. Also, he was getting some of his emotional needs met with his boss. Why would he want to change anything? After all, with a little therapy, Beth would get back in line.

If I were the therapist, I would frame the situation as a couple's problem from the beginning, not just Beth's problem. I would assert, "Jerry, it seems to me that Beth is trying to get your attention with her spending, since she hasn't been able to find a better way that works. And Beth, Jerry seems to be trying to keep everything under control all by himself, and he's having a difficult time doing so, especially with your spending."

Neither Beth nor Jerry is emotionally self-aware, both are tremendously dependent on each other, they lack communications skills and seem frightened of real intimacy. I assume each has deep ego wounds from childhood. Moreover, I have concerns about whether Jerry is potentially violent. My priorities for the work would be:

- To address the current crisis, which is, at its heart, about whether the marriage will resume its old pattern or whether substantive change will need to occur. This is a huge issue that needs more than the flowers and sex that managed care allows.
- To teach Jerry and Beth how to pay attention to their emotions and how to effectively give them a voice.
- To prevent potential violence.

Addressing the crisis starts with encouraging each to talk while I listen and acknowledge both. I would translate between them and frame their issues as reciprocal. I would explore the feelings underlying their complaints, and in so doing, shift the work to a deeper level. What is each one most afraid of? What does each one need to feel safe enough to talk honestly?

In the presence of both, I would ask about family history. How did Beth learn to stuff her disappointment and her anger? What was the nature of the abandonment that Jerry experienced that he counters with such control? What were the ego wounds to each? Was there abuse? What ghosts of the past are alive in Beth and Jerry's relationship?

I would be gently persistent in asking, "What are you feeling at this moment?" adding a touch of humor to take the edge off my persistence, so that I didn't push Jerry over the edge into feeling powerless. I believe that staying with emotions is the most effective way to work, as opposed to laying on a "fix." In exploring emotions, I would be on the alert for instances in which Beth and Jerry have similar feelings—maybe loneliness or fear. I would highlight these commonalities to help them connect emotionally.

Jerry's fanatic need for control strikes me as covering a brittle personality: low self-esteem, little awareness of his own emotions and motivations, terror of feeling powerless, and a resulting difficultly in controlling his anger. Not everyone with these characteristics is abusive, but everyone who is abusive has these characteristics. Once we had enough rapport for honest answers, I would ask if they had gotten physical. If not, my antennae would still be up, because an ego wound to a brittle personality can precipitate violence.

I would ask Jerry to monitor himself to identify what scares him or makes him feel powerless, and to identify how he reacts to those feelings. What behavior of Beth's could trigger his rage? Beth is not responsible for Jerry's behavior, but being provocative (as opposed to expressing her needs and feelings) could be dangerous.

As Beth spoke more about her needs, Jerry's sense of control would be threatened. This would be difficult for them. The temptation would be to flee therapy and go back to the old ways. Or Jerry might explode in response to Beth's increased demands, if he hadn't learned ways to cope with feeling powerless. So a brief anger group for men would be a useful adjunct to the couple's work. Not wanting to make him the problem spouse, I would refer Beth to a brief therapy group for women focusing on self-esteem.

Jerry's rage at Beth's on-line affair is normal. However, his difficulties with anger mean that he could easily lose control. I would take Jerry's threats seriously, checking out how much is talk and how close he is to losing it. If safety was assured, I would bring them together to talk about whether the marriage is going to continue or whether a trial separation might be in order. My guess is that Beth has not grown up enough to successfully leave home. However, if she stays in the marriage and continues with the chat room, the risk would be great that Jerry's anger would become physical. It would be essential to structure supports and ways to distance, so as to prevent violence.

Just as with affairs, cybersex is a symptom and not the problem. Good, old-fashioned therapy that focuses on awareness of emotions, on taking responsibility for choices and on giving one's self a voice—in person, not on the Internet—is what is needed. ∎

STUDY QUESTIONS

1. How did this couple use triangulation to express their marital unhappiness?

2. What do you believe the therapeutic challenge was in this case, and how does or doesn't your view differ from Treadway's or Brown's?

3. Do you think Beth's virtual affairs should have been treated as no different from a flesh-and-blood affair? Why or why not?

4. What happened to the therapy when the clinician framed the problem as a couples issue rather than Beth's problem or Jerry's problem? Do you think it was helpful? Why or why not?

5. When there is the threat or existence of violence in a couple's relationship, what is the therapist's responsibility with regard to reporting it? What would you have done in this case?

CHAPTER 2

Working with Children

Even though most family therapists generally believe young children should be present during sessions, many still don't know how to engage them in the process. Too many family therapists still believe that the only way to resolve problems with children is to bolster the family hierarchy. This is regrettable, because the active participation of children can enrich the therapeutic process, establish deeper emotional connection, and help families learn more effective and harmonious approaches to problem solving. At the same time, there is always the danger of the therapist's becoming overinvolved with children in a family in a way that can disempower parents.

The following cases illustrate both the clinical challenges of working with children and their families in a range of settings and the cultural pressures that can make raising children in the 1990s such an arduous process. In "Leaving the Mothering to Mother," Nina Shandler demonstrates the pitfalls of taking over the parental function with a child whose mother seems unresponsive to the school's requests for more parenting. "Treating AD/HD" looks at one of psychotherapy's most controversial issues and shows how prescribing Ritalin can be a family intervention as well as a way of relieving symptoms. In "The Boy Who Loved Catwoman," H. Charles Fishman presents a puzzling case that exemplifies the difficulties in our postmodern age of defining the nature of a family's problems, and the need for heightened sensitivity to gender issues. "Adrian's Choice" highlights not only complex family dynamics of adoption, but how the therapist must always be sensitive to issues of cultural diversity. In "Joining the Family," David E. Scharff and Jill Savege Scharff emphasize the issue of the self of the therapist and understanding their own emotional resonance with their clients as they work with the parents of a troubled child. In "Nunna Yer Beeswax," Martha B. Straus shows how to engage a sullen, silent teenager with "no-talk therapy," and how to make silence work for, rather than against, the therapy.

CASE STUDY

LEAVING THE MOTHERING TO MOTHER
HELPING A PARENT BECOME ACCOUNTABLE

Nina Shandler

As a psychologist in an elementary school, I am involved in the day-to-day lives of children, not as someone set apart from their normal routines, but as a person who works, plays, and talks with them every day and is part of their daily trials and triumphs. With a job so all-encompassing, the risk of overinvolvement runs high. This is the story of how Ron, a 7-year-old second grader, built a bridge between home and school, teaching me to be his advocate and insisting that his mother be his parent.

As is often the case in school, I had heard a lot about Ron before I met him. Teachers, teachers' aides, the school nurse, the guidance counselor, even the principal had stopped me to talk about him. They told me how, in the lunch line, on the playground, at circle time, even at work tables, other schoolchildren moved away from Ron because he smelled. These children didn't understand why he stank, but they knew they didn't want to be near him. Wherever Ron went, he was alone.

Ron peed and defecated in his pants consistently—but unpredictably—every day. The school nurse and his teachers helped clean him up, but the problem was getting worse. All of them reported that his mother, Pam, was no help. Pam, a single mother who worked in a restaurant and had two older children, refused to acknowledge that Ron soiled his pants even occasionally, much less daily. She insisted his teachers were concocting imaginary accidents because they hated her son and had a snobbish disdain for the poor. When the school nurse suggested that Pam take him to the doctor, Pam refused, saying the nurse wanted only to humiliate Ron.

By early October, I had been called in. My goal was clear: Before Ron's teachers could teach him successfully, before he could be accepted by his peers, he had to be toilet trained. I would have to take on a task normally reserved for parents. Before I had even met the boy, I later realized, my role was blurred.

I decided to attack on four fronts simultaneously: To rule out medical factors, I arranged for the visiting school physician to see Ron as soon as possible. To educate Ron about toilet training, I designed role modeling and rehearsing sessions. To build his motivation, I set up a reward system for him. But knowing how to deal with the function of Ron's problem within his family was the most complex part of the intervention. I hypothesized that Ron's accidents were a way of rebelling against school and were, somehow, part of a self-defeating alliance with his mother. After all, what more potent metaphor for defiance of school and its authority than to literally shit all over it? If Ron's accidents were an expression of his family loyalty, only an intervention that would enable him to demonstrate a disdain for school by controlling his bowels would be successful. So, I decided to design an intervention; I would trick him into being toilet trained.

I walked into Ron's classroom, braced to meet a steely, well-armored predelinquent, and was immediately disarmed. There stood a fragile little person with angelic eyes and a choir-boy face. I asked him if he'd like to play with me. He nodded. Looking at me with sadness and solemnity, he reached out for my hand. Immediately, he touched the placed in me that was as much mother as psychologist.

Hand in hand, Ron and I walked into the playroom—a small space, filled with toys—where I planned to use a doll to model toileting skills. I offered Ron a doll, which he took carefully, with the cautious, quiet excitement of a child who has few toys. He sat down and cuddled the make-believe baby. In a short time, at my suggestion, we pretended to cook lunch and feed the doll. Then I exclaimed, "This baby is old enough to be toilet trained. We need to train him."

We brought the doll to an imaginary bathroom, sat it on the toilet, waited for the baby to defecate, took it off the toilet, showed it how to wipe itself, and then praised and hugged the doll. Ron participated in every stage with quiet fascination.

"This baby might have accidents for a long time. Let's teach him what to do if he has an accident," I said. This time, I pretended the baby didn't make it to the toilet, and that we needed to teach the doll how to clean himself and change his own clothes. Ron played the game with intense concentration, mimicking my forgiveness and encouragement. "It's okay, small person," I told the doll. "Everyone makes mistakes. You did a good job cleaning up." To complete the educational phase of my strategy, I had to move from using the doll as a model to having Ron practice himself. I said to Ron as nonchalantly as I could, "You have accidents too, sometimes. Maybe if you have accidents, you can clean up just like the baby." I chose my words carefully, thinking that Ron's baby status was precious to him and not wanting to deprive him of a special place in his family. But I did want him to give up soiling his pants and to find a functional place among his peers. He looked at me intently.

I suggested we practice. With the doll in hand, we walked to the bathroom in the nurse's office. Ron pretended the doll went to the toilet successfully. Then, he pretended the doll had an accident and cleaned up. Next, Ron pretended he used the toilet successfully. Last, Ron pretended he had an accident and cleaned himself up.

When we returned to the playroom, I began the motivational part of my plan. I quickly explained a simple reward system to Ron: If he got through a whole school day without anybody knowing he had an accident, I would play with him at the end of the day.

Thus far, all was simple, smooth, straightforward. Now, I turned to the complicated paradox that would enable Ron to maintain his rebellion against school, remain loyal to his mom, and stop having bowel movements in his pants. "It's okay if you have an accident," I said. "Maybe you can't help having accidents. You can even have accidents and fool your teachers. You can even fool me."

Ron burst into a mischievous smile, as if buying into the therapeutic conspiracy. I whispered, "All you have to do is clean yourself up good, then no one will know, and we can play."

In the first week, Ron soiled his pants only once. He crept quietly off to the nurse's office, cleaned himself up, and returned to his class. The same pattern was repeated during the second and third weeks. In the fourth week, Ron did not soil himself at all. After three accident-free weeks, I joined his teachers in a premature sense of relief.

During this period, the school medical staff had remained involved with Ron. The school physician found no evidence of a physical problem. Still, the school nurse saw him often. When Ron wanted a break, he'd go to the health room, use the toilet, and visit with the nurse. She became nervous about his attachment. Even though she had seldom helped Ron go to the toilet or clean himself, she wanted to protect herself against the possibility of misunderstanding or a charge of child abuse. The nurse asked the principal to inform Ron's mother, Pam, who was unaware of our toilet-training program. The principal wrote an enthusiastic letter to Pam, expressing appreciation for her mothering and congratulating Ron for controlling his accidents. I saw the necessity of the letter, but I felt a deep sense of uneasiness; it contradicted my message to Ron. I had never suggested he succeed at school; I had suggested he trick all his teachers. I gave him permission to have an accident and make us think he hadn't, or to not have an accident and make us think he had. Was Ron's success really dependent on his maintaining his own conspiracy against school? What would happen? Despite my fears, the letter was sent.

A few days later, Ron had his first accident in three weeks. The next week, he soiled twice. The third week, he soiled every day. We were back where we had started. It looked to me like Ron was proving his allegiance to his family by resuming his old habits.

Not knowing what to do, I reverted to straightforward toilet training and traditional play therapy. I started taking Ron to the toilet twice a day. I celebrated his successes—clapping and cheering and giving great hugs—and reprimanded his failures. I saw him twice weekly for play therapy. I saw him twice weekly for play therapy. He created games where he was in charge, master of his life and body. He was a loving father giving elaborate gifts, a trainer subduing wild animals, a prince commanding adoring subjects, a trapeze artist walking the high wire. In real life, he remained unwilling or unable to control his bowel movements. I wondered about the meaning of the metaphors—was he totally in control or totally in need of control? By late November, the schools' supply of extra clothing had been depleted. I wrote and called Pam daily, asking her to return the clothes the school had lent Ron, but she didn't respond. So, I did the things any good mother would do—I bought him cute, little-boy outfits at secondhand stores. He changed into them after soiling himself, wore them home, and never brought them back. I began washing his soiled clothes at school. My mothering had no effect. Ron continued to soil himself daily.

Then one January afternoon, Ron put me in my place. During one of our scheduled sessions, he had a bowel movement in the toilet. Ten minutes later, he returned to class and wet his pants. I reacted with a strange mixture of admiration and frustration. I led him to my office in silence, with uncharacteristic seriousness. "I don't know what to do next," I said. "Very few people can do what you did today—have a bowel movement, walk back to class, and then pee. That takes incredible control. You have all the power. I want to help you, but I don't know how. Ron, tell me what to do." Tears flowed from his eyes. "Get my Mommy to come to school," he sobbed.

I studied his sincere, pitiful face—I was looking at truth. He didn't need a well-intentioned, overly involved, manipulative psychologist to toilet train him. He needed his mother. Ron was clearly torn by his loyalty to his family and to me. Ron was saying, "My mom is supposed to do this. If it's going to happen at school, my mom should be here." I looked at Ron and promised, "I will get your mother to come to school." I didn't know how I'd keep my promise, but I knew I'd find a way.

Early the next morning before school, I drove straight to Pam's house and knocked on the door. I waited, knowing my visit would be viewed as an intrusion. I suspected she would see me as an authority out to destroy her, to report her negligence, to question her love, to take her child, to decimate her family. For Pam, I was the embodiment of social control.

Ron opened the door, dressed only in a T-shirt. He hugged me and yelled enthusiastically, "Mommy, it's Nina!" He ran off to the bathroom to fetch her. "Fuck her," came the spontaneous response. "What's she dong here? She doesn't belong here. Why doesn't she keep the hell out of our business?" Ron protested, "Come on, Mom. Talk to Nina."

I planted myself on a dilapidated couch and waited. I was not about to be moved. There were clothes strewn about the room and I smelled the unmistakable stench of urine. A cat ran over a pile of laundry, hid in a corner, and peered at me from the shadows. At once I understood yet another source of Ron's acrid stench.

Pam came out of the bathroom. Shyly, not unlike her timid cat, she peeked around the corner of the room, tears streaming from her face. Ron clung to her leg. Reaching up, he wiped her tears with his small hand. "It's all right, Mommy," he said. "It's Nina. She's nice." Involuntarily, pity welled up in me—truly pity, not empathy. Seeing her hunched over before me, I found myself saying, "Please sit down," before I realized I had invited her to sit down in her own home. She lifted her head and glared at me, a flash of rage in her eyes, but she sat.

"I know it's a shock to have me come here without notice, but I really had to talk with you," I said. "I need your help with Ron. He's having accidents every day." Her sobbing became audible. Ron kissed her repeatedly on the cheek. "I see how much he loves you, how much he needs you, I can tell how much you love him," I said. As her sobbing calmed, I got to the point. "Will you toilet train him?" Pam exploded again. "He is toilet trained, you ass. You're all the same. You lie about him because you want to make a fool of him. I'm taking him out of that goddamn school right now. I'm going to teach him at home. I'm his mother. I have rights. I know who you are. You're the bitch who tries to embarrass him by sending clothes home. You think you're his mother. Well, I have news for you, lady—I'm his mother."

"You are his mother and you do have rights," I said. Seizing on an opportunity to keep my promise to get Pam to come to school, I continued, "Home schooling might be possible. I don't know the rules. You'll have to talk to the principal." Pam's body straightened; she stood up. "Okay, bitch, let's go. I'm going to meet that bastard. Ron, get in the car."

I got to school a few minutes ahead of Pam and warned the principal that Pam would walk in angry. He asked me what he should say to her. I made a few suggestions, and he agreed. "Good plan. I'll play the heavy here."

With Ron in tow, in full view of the principal, secretaries, and children, Pam arrived and began to yell at me.

"You fucking bitch! You fucking asshole, keep your fucking paws off my son," she shouted as I led her, still raging, into the principal's office. "I'm taking Ron out of school," she screamed, flush with anger, full of adrenalin. "I'll home-school him."

The principal invited Pam to sit down. Then, in a low and authoritative voice, he laid down the law.

"Every parent is welcome to apply to the school district for permission to home-school," he told her. "I approve several requests a year. However, you must outline a specific course of study for all academic areas, you must supply a list of materials to be used, and you must have your child taught by an adult with a bachelor's degree from an accredited college or university. I doubt you can meet those criteria.

"Even if you could, you would not be allowed to take your child out of school today," he went on. "You would have to submit your application to the superintendent, and approval takes time. In the meantime, Ron must come to school or the truant officer will be notified."

The principal paused and stared at Pam, waiting for a response. She crumbled. Her head hung limply; she said nothing.

"Your son is in second grade," the principal went on. "He's too old to soil his pants. Nina is working hard to toilet train him. You don't even return the clean clothes she brings in for him. Now I'm insisting you send two clean changes of clothing a day. Any day Ron comes to school without two sets of clothes, including underwear, we'll call you at work and expect you to come for him. If you don't, we'll consider it a medical emergency and bring him to your work.

"I expect you to meet with Nina regularly. If you don't, I fully plan to contact the Department of Social Services and file for the protection of your child." Pam began to gag. She stood up with her hands over her mouth and begged for a toilet. I led her to the nearest bathroom and she vomited.

When we came back to the principal's office, I extracted promises from her in front of Ron to meet with me every week, and to send two clean sets of clothes to school. She kissed Ron, and we both watched as he skipped off to his classroom. Then, she slowly made her way to the exit at the end of the hall, making no attempt to avoid me as I walked beside her. "You're Ron's mother," I said. "He needs your help." She nodded, looked me in the eyes, and said, "And you're not his mother."

For the remainder of the school year, I remained Pam's vigilant enemy. When Ron came to school in thin cotton pants, with no socks, on a snowy day with a windchill factor below zero, the principal and I filed a neglect complaint with the Department of Social Services. When she did not come to our weekly meetings, I went to her home. When she failed to send clean clothes, I brought Ron to the restaurant where she worked. She had declared herself Ron's mother, and I was insisting that she act the role. She had exposed the ineffectiveness of my surrogate mothering, and taught me to advocate for Ron in another, more effective way.

By the time the school year was finished, Pam was sending clothes regularly, and Ron was toilet trained.

That summer, Ron and his family moved to a nearby town. Later in the next school year, I contacted his new school and learned he had no further problems with toilet training. I never saw him again except once, the summer after our school year together ended. I was riding on a bus with my daughter when Ron and Pam got on. Ron paid no attention to me. He ran up to my daughter and sat down next to her. He reminded her she had read to him in a buddy program at school. Pam motioned for Ron to sit next to her, but he protested, "I want to sit with my friend."

Pam looked at me self-consciously and said, "Aren't you gong to say hello to Nina?"

"Oh. Hi, Nina," he said, and went back to his conversation with my daughter. Pam smiled at me.

I shrugged, and said, "Kids."

At that moment, we were both just mothers.

CASE COMMENTARY 1
BY LEE COMBRINCK-GRAHAM

Thank you, Nina Shandler, for presenting a cautionary tale about the dangers of playing with other people's children. While most children in individual play therapy do not express their inevitable confusion about what is going on, Shandler was fortunate to have as a client someone as articulate as Ron. He underlines the problem at the core of this case with unmistakable clarity when he says, "Get my mommy to come to school."

In retrospect, of course, it is easy to see that the actions ultimately taken by school personnel should have been taken at the outset of this case. The question is, why did it take so long? What preconceptions kept them from holding Pam accountable for Ron's personal care?

At first, I was stunned by Shandler's elaborate hypothesizing and treatment planning before she even had met Ron. Certainly rapid assessment and intervention are important, but, all too often, I hear about school psychologists making treatment plans without ever meeting a child. Just because Freud did it with Little Hans doesn't mean it's good practice.

Therapists who have had training in individual child therapy often develop a habit of using indirect play interactions instead of more direct conversation. After all, the tradition of play therapy is built on the premise that children cannot express themselves in words. But, in my experience, this indirection often is unnecessary. In fact, play therapy may be most useful in helping both adults and children practice what has already been talked about.

Shandler clearly illustrates one pitfall in working with small children—thinking *for,* rather than *with* them. Even with children as young as three and four, I have found that discussing the problem and clarifying what adults are concerned about helps the child to participate more fully in the treatment plan, as Shandler found out when she finally asked Ron what to do.

Increasingly, school personnel feel saddled with responsibility for children who come to school hungry, dirty, or improperly clothed. The school personnel's response in this case is not atypical. They initially tried to involve Ron's mother, and when she balked at cooperating, they then assumed total responsibility for solving the problem. As Shandler vividly describes, Ron and his mother then proceeded to show the futility of an approach not based on an explicit agreement between parent and school. Certainly there are situations in which parents who do not have the means to provide adequate clothing for their children may accept assistance from the school. But when the school undertakes these efforts in the face of obvious parental indifference or neglect, they cross a line, further alienating already sensitive parents and confusing already vulnerable children.

So what can be done? Ron's mother presents a familiar challenge and articulates her position more clearly than many parents. "I am unavailable," she says. "This is not a problem. If this is a problem for you, it is of your own making. You are trying to embarrass my son and humiliate me."

In the end, Shandler and her colleagues discover a last-resort approach that works. The child can be sent home or to the parent's place of work to be cleaned up. The mother can be called to come in and clean her child and to teach him how to be clean. Ron's mother can be directed to provide the school with what is necessary to care for the child in school (e.g., clean clothes). When all else fails, child protective services can be involved. While this approach may be tough, it is not mean, and, ultimately, it is respectful, because it holds the parents accountable for their children's healthy development rather than assuming that they can't or won't be responsible. In those rare instances when parents either can't or won't be responsible, child protective services should step in and the school must avoid putting itself in the position of protecting parents from this outcome.

Nina Shandler says that this case taught her to be an advocate rather than a substitute parent. It is a fine lesson, beautifully illustrated. Anyone who works with children should keep it in mind.

CASE COMMENTARY 2
BY BRUCE BUCHANAN

Nina Shandler describes a scenario that takes place daily in public schools: A child misbehaves, the flow of teaching is disrupted, school staff feel increasingly beleaguered, and parent(s) are called in for a meeting about their child that results in a confrontation about faulty parenting. The family mirrors the attack by insisting that the school is doing a lousy job and that all is well at home. In the ensuing stalemate, the school assumes a rigid hierarchical position, threatening the parents with the child's expulsion, special class placement or being reported themselves for abuse and/or neglect. If that doesn't work and there are insufficient grounds for such drastic measures, an expert, such as a school psychologist, counselor, or socialworker, is called in to fix the problem through individual work with the child. Often, at this stage, the child will be evaluated and labeled emotionally disturbed or ADHD. Finally, if the child's difficulties persist, the sequence once again begins, with renewed attempts at family involvement, albeit with potent memories of an already scarred relationship.

I wish that Shandler's final realization—that she and Pam were both just mothers—had been the guiding principle in her work from the get-go. The primary goal, then, would have centered on building a working relationship with Pam, and other interventions in Ron's treatment would have flowed from that. Unfortunately the connection with Pam was too little and too late, and ended up shrouded in coercion and threats. Even though Ron improved, nothing changed in Pam's perception of the school as hostile to her and her child.

Early on, Shandler recognizes her overinvolvement with Ron and the enraged reaction that this was likely to trigger in Pam. The question some readers may have is, "With all her awareness, what prevented her from conducting a more collaborative, family-school-based therapy?" In fact, Shandler's approach in this case says a lot about the conflicting roles and expectations experienced by many therapists working in school settings.

Schools see their mandate as attending to the needs of the entire student body. Deviance from the norm, in this case, Ron's encopresis, becomes an obvious problem. The initial solution—to alert Pam—was experienced as accusatory, and Pam defensively denied responsibility and counterattacked. The school decided it couldn't work with her and called in its specialist to bypass Pam and to cure Ron. The adversarial relationship between the school and Pam was then played out through Shandler's interventions. Paralleling that power-unbalanced relationship between the school and Pam is the position of the psychologist within the school. Shandler's job title is school psychologist, not family therapist, and it is unlikely that she would have the power to challenge the focus on fixing Ron without being viewed as uncooperative, or incompetent, by the principal, teachers, and nurse.

The political context of public education, particularly in schools that deal with poor families, exacerbates these imbalances. Private schools and wealthier public school districts allow parents to be consumers of a product in a competitive market economy. They are empowered to challenge existing beliefs within the school, and family-school discussions have relatively equal amounts of give and take. But for poor families, schools are part of a larger service economy. Parents—especially single parents—are in a perpetual one-down position. If they do not accept what's provided to them and their children, they are labeled "resistant" and "hostile."

So what might have been done differently in this case? The family-school rift was clear from the start: "All reported that his mother was no help," and "She [Pam] insisted his teachers were concocting imaginary accidents because they hated her son and had a snobbish disdain for the poor." I would assume that both statements were true and would proceed accordingly. The school's and Pam's divergent realities each need to be valued and respected. Shandler certainly succeeded with the school by wholeheartedly accepting its definition of the problem. But, in so doing, she excluded Pam from the equation.

So how does one go about developing a relationship with someone like Pam, who probably has had a troubled history with schools? First of all, to ease her suspiciousness, someone has to listen nondefensively to her charges of classism and discrimination and to accept that as at least a partial explanation for what is going on. I would telephone Pam fully prepared for a verbal barrage—after all, in her mind, I am not a representative of the school, I *am* the school. I would need every ounce of clinical detachment in my repertoire to not react defensively. After listening quietly while Pam vents, I might say something like, "Pam, the bottom line is that you have absolutely no reason to trust me. I am a complete stranger to you except that you know that I work for the school. You've made it clear that, as far as you're concerned, the school is down on you and Ron. You might be right. We both know that not all kids and mothers are treated equally by teachers and principals. But now we have a problem we need to tackle. The school has asked me to figure out a way that Ron can be in class without messing his pants. I understand that you don't believe that he's doing that, but we still have a problem. If he is soiling himself, we need to figure out how to help him so that he doesn't get teased by the other kids. If he isn't and the school is lying, we need to figure out who and why so that Ron can start being treated fairly. What I am asking for is that you give me an opportunity to prove that I really am interested in seeing Ron do well in school. If I'm fake, you'll pick it up pretty quickly and I would expect that you would let me know that in no uncertain terms. Ron has a big problem—he's either messing himself, being mistreated, or maybe something neither of us has considered. We owe it to him to figure it out."

This kind of approach, of course, is only effective if the clinician believes it. It won't work if I view this merely as a strategy to get Pam into treatment. My goal is to offer the promise of an honest relationship and differentiate myself enough from the school so that the parent will give me the opportunity to work collaboratively and neutrally. If I am successful, Pam will be open to another phone call, or better yet, a meeting, scheduled at a time and place that recognizes the difficulty Pam has as a working, single parent in fitting into the ordinary school schedule.

I would encourage Shandler to examine two aspects of her work. First, she should discard the concept of the "the function of the symptom" as she works with more families. This is the family therapist's version of the *DSM-III,* and it places the therapist in a one-up position with clients (i.e., "I know this about you—you somehow need your child to act out so that you don't have to deal with your marital problems"). Frankly, I don't know whether symptoms have functions. What I do know is that when a family gets blamed, the opportunity for a healthy relationship is decreased.

Second, Shandler should be willing to throw away any definitions of the problem that a client is not accepting. With Ron, the problem was framed as "toilet training," which Pam rejected as a legitimate problem. She accurately viewed it as an attack on her parenting. I would never mention toilet training. Beyond the ongoing necessity of forging a positive relationship, the next most important issue is to develop a *shared* definition of the problem. Without it, you have a chaotic therapy of differing agendas.

Had Pam been included as a key part of Ron's treatment throughout, the school probably would not have had to play the heavy by being agents of social control. Pam would have been empowered and would not have had to automatically defend herself or Ron in knee-jerk fashion. And if she did, Shandler would be able to invoke the strength of her therapeutic bond with Pam as a motive for sorting through the conflict. I am reminded of the words of a former trainee in her work with a diagnosed paranoid schizophrenic mother, when she failed to show up for sessions following some minor gripes about the therapy: "Barbara, what's this about? I thought we had a relationship." That one sentence, following months of difficult, but deeply committed work, was enough for her client to reevaluate her stance, despite severe psychopathology, and to exercise her all-too-new choice of testing and persevering with a relationship over time.

I am not minimizing the severity of Ron's circumstances. Pam still might have been reported for neglect. However, as her trust in Shandler increased, she might have allowed Shandler greater access to other helpful people in her life, including neighbors, extended family, and friends. Once the circle of support grows, there is often not as much need for external policing. Clients become less isolated, and are able to accept offers of assistance and to even ask for it without fear of being judged.

Finally, for all this to occur in public education, schools need to commit themselves to become more family-friendly and to encourage parental involvement in a multitude of activities—not just when a child is doing poorly. We also need systemically trained professionals in the schools, including teachers, administrators, and human service providers. Increasingly, schools are utilizing family therapists as consultants to work with children and families as connected parts of a larger system, but we are just at the beginning—similar to where family therapy was in the mental-health system 30 years ago. Yet, only when schools engage in what Howard Weiss refers to as "climate building"—a long-term restructuring that includes families—will the destructive gap between children's two most important socializing contacts begin to narrow.

AUTHOR'S RESPONSE
BY NINA SHANDLER

In their commentaries, Lee Combrinck-Graham and Bruce Buchanan offer some valuable insights. Combrinck-Graham reminds us that children are capable of conversation and worthy of respect.

Buchanan's treatise on how schools should work with families sounds uncannily like my own admonitions to my interns, graduate students, and colleagues. While I find no need to take exception to details of their analysis or argue points that can be seen from multiple perspectives, I do find the tone of their comments distressingly typical of attitudes toward school professionals.

Those of us who work on the front lines involved in the day-to-day lives of children—who forsake traditional weekly sessions and discard standard therapeutic roles—are too often treated as part of the problem rather than respected as capable professionals. Combrinck-Graham and Buchanan appear to be looking for a neat and tidy illustration of watertight psychological theory and practice. This case is not meant to be neat or tidy. It is not an example of perfect practice or an illustration of flawless theory. It is about the messy business of real life where sincere mistakes often lead to genuine successes. It is one person's honest telling of a study about three human beings— a psychologist, a child, and a parent—who all shared a difficult predicament and all learned to be more competent. ■

STUDY QUESTIONS

1. Do you think the therapist overstepped her role in this case? Why or why not?

2. Do you agree with Combrinck-Graham that the therapist could have been more direct with the client, rather than using play therapy to make her point?

3. How might the therapist have brought the mother into the process as a collaborator earlier in the therapy? Do you agree with Buchanan that this should have been the therapist's goal from the outset? Why or why not?

TREATING ADHD
UNDERSTANDING ATTENTIONAL DEFICITS CAN SHARPEN OUR
TREATMENT STRATEGIES

Susan Bogas

Seven-year-old Nick was both the class clown and a loner. To other first graders, he seemed more than a little odd because of his awkward attempts to gain attention and acceptance. They teased him mercilessly. Though his teacher supervised him closely to get him to do his work, he continually disrupted the class by calling out, making animal noises to get laughs, and leaving his seat without permission. He was often in trouble for shoving other children or calling them names.

One day, egged on by other boys (he claimed), Nick chased some children around the playground and touched their genitals. A few days later he exposed his penis. Because of these incidents, plus his highly disruptive and distracted behavior, the school ordered a battery of psychological tests. There was talk of placing him in a classroom for emotionally disturbed children.

Bill, Nick's father, brought the boy to see me. He felt the school had developed a negative view of Nick and that things were only going to get worse if something wasn't done. An entomologist working for the state, Bill had separated from Nick's mother, Rose, several years ago. Until the past year, Nick had been living with his mother. However, after the boy was late for school 23 times, the Division of Youth and Family Services transferred him to his father's custody. Nevertheless, Rose maintained regular contact with Nick, who frequently witnessed prolonged arguments between his parents. A loving but somewhat young father, Bill knew little about setting up routines and creating consistency for the child.

Needing no introduction, Nick, a waiflike child with a home haircut and clothes too small for him, walked confidently into my office for the first session and picked up a rock from a shelf before I could introduce myself to his father. "Nick refuses to follow my directions," said Bill.

"Everything is a battle. Every morning I have to stand over him and tell him repeatedly to get dressed, wash his face, eat breakfast." Homework and bedtime routines required the same constant supervision. Left to his own devices, Nick would play with any object within reach, name all the insects he knew, or make up addition and subtraction problems.

"Nick wants what he wants when he wants it. When he gets a 'no,' first he questions it, then he argues, then he cries and has a tantrum," explained Bill wearily. "He is relentless in his demands. I dread going into a store with him. He wants everything he sees. Sometimes something he likes gets 'stuck' in his head and he pressures me for days to buy it."

Bill described Nick as always "on-the-go," either mentally or physically. On a recent car trip, for instance, Nick entertained himself by teasing his father, putting his feet on Bill's head, pulling the headrest off the passenger's seat, and waving and making faces at truck drivers, trying to get them to honk their horns. Bill also described Nick as a child with a great sense of humor and a love for making puns and other plays on words. He also told me that Nick, who had memorized the names of many species of insects, butterflies, and sea life, was a very motivated learner. During the session Nick sat and drew a "tree with roots," thoroughly engaged. He paid exquisite attention to the detailed root structure and even included a cardinal sitting on the grass.

Inattentive, distractible, impulsive (behaviorally and emotionally) and overactive, Nick matches the profile of a child with Attention-Deficit/Hyperactivity Disorder (ADHD). He has better control over himself in structured than unstructured situations, but needs constant monitoring. He has great difficulty following through on tasks that aren't of particular interest to him and tends to resist daily routines and anything that's obligatory. But while it's one thing to diagnose a child with ADHD, the question remains: What do we know about offering these children the best possible treatment?

Despite almost 25 years of intense study and research, confusion and skepticism still surround the ADHD diagnosis. Neurological researchers are making significant progress in linking sites within the brain and ADHD symptoms, as well as identifying differences between normal and ADHD brains. Nevertheless, there is no conclusive evidence regarding the biological underpinnings of ADHD and its exact etiology, so there's no core concept of what the condition is. There is also no empirical way of evaluating an individual for ADHD. Brain-imaging techniques are economically impractical for routine assessment. Commonly, ADHD is diagnosed by using a combination of detailed history; pencil-and-paper assessments given by a specially trained pediatrician, neurologist, or learning specialist; and parent/ teacher checklists. To make the diagnosis even more difficult, learning disabilities frequently coexist with ADHD: oppositional and conduct disorders; obsessive-compulsive disorder; Tourette's disorder; and thyroid problems. Depression, anxiety, and self-esteem issues are also often associated conditions. Furthermore, ADHD symptoms interact with the character, temperament, intelligence, physiology, and other traits of the individual and family, while other contextual factors come into play as well.

Unfortunately, the complexity and controversy surrounding ADHD encourage practitioners to bypass the whole issue of an appropriate model in favor of a more pragmatic route: treating the symptoms. This approach particularly appeals to many family therapists who may be uncomfortable treating a dysfunction that probably has a biological base and would require them to use medication and focus on the individual child, rather than on the family interactional patterns.

A structural family therapist might see Nick as a child triangulated between two parents in a serious conflict and embedded in a chaotic family system with a weak executive system, weak structures, and poor interpersonal boundaries. The hypothesis about Nick's behavior would be that he is acting out the family pain, including his recent separation from his mother. His parents' dysfunction, individually and as a system, would be targeted as the primary source of the problem. The therapist would avoid focusing solely on the child and would conceptualize Nick's problems as contextually based, and treatment would emphasize family intervention. In contrast, within a biopsychosocial framework of ADHD, the issue of Bill and Rose's parenting would be considered separate from the problematic patterns that arise from Nick's biology. Within this perspective, individual assessment of Nick would be critical and medication would become a crucial consideration.

Based on knowledge of brain functioning, pediatrician Mel Levine says that attentional difficulties have to do with weaknesses in the regulatory controls involved with *mental energy, input* (the processing of information), and *output* (producing a product). Children with mental energy weaknesses—too high, too low, inconsistent—have difficulty staying awake or alert and getting started on tasks. Children with input (processing) problems are inattentive and distractible. They tune in and out, take in information too shallowly or too deeply, too passively or too actively. Consequently they have difficulty sustaining a focus. Children who are weak in regulating output (intentional behavior) are impulsive and/or hyperactive. They fail to plan, strategize, and anticipate the consequences of their actions. They are weak in inhibiting irrelevant stimuli (including their own impulses), working within a time frame and self-monitoring.

A circular relationship exists between mental energy, processing, and production, says Levine. Low mental energy leads to inadequate processing of information, which results in the weak formulation of a goal carried through in a careless, impulsive manner and resulting in a poor product. The child who functions this way experiences low satisfaction and consequently low motivation for further purposeful activity. This is a vicious cycle for many ADHD children.

With this framework in mind, I told Bill and Rose that many of Nick's symptoms suggested that he had ADHD and that, if this was correct, medication could provide a foundation for helping Nick achieve better control in various areas. They agreed to a medication trial.

Nick's pediatrician put him on Ritalin and the effects were immediately and dramatically visible. His level of control increased in every area. He listened without interrupting, he was less distractible, more focused, and far less disruptive. At home, Bill still had to deal with plenty of resistance to routines and directions, but in a new, more positive school environment, Nick settled down to work and was much less distracted and not at all disruptive. He made progress academically and socially, two areas in which he was significantly delayed.

Once the medication took effect, I began to focus more on the precise nature of Nick's symptoms. At times, Nick could attend without distraction—as when drawing. But much of the time he had great difficulty staying on task. The question was, what was causing the behavior at any given time? Did Nick go off track because he tuned in and out (a problem with mental fatigue), because he had difficulty deciding what was important (a processing weakness), or because he failed to control competing stimuli that were more exciting (an output weakness)? Did he become hyper because he liked the intensity (a processing weakness) or because he was experiencing boredom and mental fatigue, and becoming revved up made him more awake and alert? Or was there a contextually based reason for the behavior—for instance, that his parents had a fight and he was upset?

To address these questions, I concentrated on increasing the structure and consistency in Nick's life. I helped Bill develop a schedule and regular routines at home, using small units of time—say 10 to 15 minutes—for homework and then a short break for distracted activity. Bill set and maintained a regular dinner time and bedtime, something Nick had never had. I encouraged Bill to tie whatever constructive activity or behavior Nick was doing at the time to a privilege or reward soon to follow—for instance, accomplishing his morning routine in 20 minutes earned 10 minutes of TV before school. These rewards for productive behavior encouraged Nick to mobilize his energy and effort for nonexciting activities. This helped him learn to delay gratification and strengthened both processing and production skills.

To increase structure, Bill had to learn to set limits effectively. I explained to him that when Nick refused to accept "no" and had a tantrum, he couldn't see other ways of dealing with the situation or the consequences of his actions. In short, in this emotionally impulsive state, Nick had no capacity for reason. So Bill needed to learn to handle Nick calmly and without anger, delivering expectations and consequences with a clear, firm, "I mean business" attitude. I used the metaphor that Nick needed at these times to be "boxed in," and Bill learned to give Nick two choices: to cease demanding or to go to his room for a time out. While Bill had difficulty delivering directions with clarity and absoluteness, he quickly saw that fewer choices and no equivocation on his part helped Nick to think ahead, anticipate the consequences of his actions, and avoid inappropriate emotional and behavioral reactions.

These interventions focused on Nick's behavior, or output, targeting weaknesses through reinforcements designed to modify behavior. While essential, this is only part of the treatment strategy—it does not affect a child's cognitive controls and internal resources for problem solving, developing persistence, overcoming frustration and boredom, or deriving satisfaction from taking on challenges.

To work with Nick's processing of information, I focused on his distractibility. I coached Bill to have Nick "hold that thought" when he got distracted. Bill praised and rewarded Nick whenever he managed to wait, hold several thoughts at the same time or concentrate on one topic. Then the two would enjoy a good laugh as Nick, who had waited, was now allowed to reveal his pun. Gradually, Nick began to recognize when he was off track. Bill also used this method to coach Nick to do his homework more independently.

After seven months of treatment, Nick began second grade in a new school with a supportive, well-organized teacher. He did extremely well academically, gaining 39 points on the standardized achievement test given. There was no longer any talk of special education. Both Bill and Rose are now handling the ongoing challenges presented by Nick with more consistency and competence. Without a doubt, medication provided the foundation for Nick's dramatic progress, and structural family therapy interventions, as well as individual cognitive behavioral changes, reinforced that progress.

It is vital for therapists working with children with ADHD and their families to understand that the range of cognitive, behavioral, emotional, and social problems these children display may be related to weaknesses in cognitive controls. When this expanded perspective is incorporated into the family therapist's repertoire, the therapist will think in terms of strategies for helping the child, as well as helping the parents to help the child. As the treatment targets specific biologically based weaknesses, the family therapist will begin to be able to distinguish the family's response to the child's attentional weaknesses from any dysfunction that exists separate and apart from the child's behavioral problems.

CASE COMMENTARY 1
BY LAWRENCE DILLER

The explosion in the diagnosis of ADHD and the use of Ritalin is a uniquely American phenomenon. The United States uses 90% of the world's stimulants in the form of Ritalin. Since 1990, there has been an unprecedented 700% rise in the production and use of the drug in this country. Between 2 and 3 million children, primarily boys between the ages of 5 and 12, are taking Ritalin.

A host of medical and social factors have been involved in this increase. The diagnostic criteria have broadened with the current *Diagnostic and Statistical Manual,* leading psychiatrist Peter Kramer to coin the terms "diagnostic bracket creep" and the medicalization of coping behavior." Demands on children's performance in school and at day care have increased, while social and economic supports offered to families with children, teachers, and schools have decreased. In some instances, ADHD has become a much sought-after diagnosis offering opportunities for special education services and disability rights. The media have exaggerated the benefits of Ritalin, while ignoring evidence that it has no positive long-term effects for children who take it. Finally, the propaganda of biological psychiatry has lent greater acceptability to the use of psychotropic medication for everyone, and Ritalin, in particular, for children.

Many children today receive Ritalin for nonspecific behavioral and performance symptoms that do not meet even the broadened criteria of ADHD. Essentially a variant of amphetamine, Ritalin works in small doses to increase vigilance and endurance and decrease activity in everyone—child, adult, ADHD or not—and can be useful in the short-term. But now one hears recommendations for lifelong use of Ritalin, reflecting the observation that the problems of ADHD do not end in adolescence, as one thought, for many of the children with ADHD behavior. Counseling and special education services have been relegated to adjunct status to treatment with Ritalin.

With all this in mind, it is refreshing to review a relatively well-managed case of ADHD. It is clear Bogas got to know this child and family before recommending a medication intervention. She describes Ritalin as a "foundation" for helping Nick. I agree that the use of Ritalin can make the other modalities of treatment more effective. Reframing Nick's behavior within the ADHD metaphor appeared helpful in developing a more structured and consistent environment for Nick. She spent considerable time supporting and developing Bill's parenting efforts. She recognized the need for Bill to communicate to Nick what I've come to call the "Emphatic No!"

in a methodical and controlled fashion. Spending some individual time with such a disturbed and out-of-control child as Nick was also probably useful.

Most of my criticisms are quibbles. I am not a diagnostic junky, but I felt that Oppositional Defiant Disorder (ODD) could describe Nick's behavior as well as ADHD. It is ODD rather than ADHD behaviors that usually lead to referrals and treatment with Ritalin. Nick's feelings about his parents' breakup, his mom's erratic behavior or the trouble he was getting into at school and at home could certainly have made his biologically based temperament worse. I'm surprised that Bogas did not note this aspect of Nick's problems as a cause for some of his poor and unusual behavior. That Ritalin improved Nick's behavior doesn't preclude anger and unhappiness from being part of his problem.

I am not familiar with Mel Levine, but his theories sound as plausible as those of Russell Barkeley, who talks about frontal lobe disinhibition. Still, I'm not sure how helpful these conceptualizations are on a clinical level. The most effective psychosocial treatments all include creating highly structured environments at home and at school without overwhelming stimuli. Immediate and tangible behavioral reinforcements are also important. Bogas criticizes some traditional family therapy models for overlooking biological factors. She invokes a biopsychosocial model of ADHD to emphasize Nick's biology where I feel both Nick's temperament and the responses to it are equally important. Nowhere does she bring up the possibility of learning problems that can present as behavioral problems and are associated with them. Nick may have qualified for special education services at his school or modifications in his regular classroom. A complete ADHD evaluation includes screening for learning problems and creating an individualized educational plan, if necessary.

Although Bogas sounds almost casual about referring Nick for medication, this is usually not a routine experience for most children and their families. Despite Ritalin's popularity, many parents have a natural reluctance to place their children on psychotropic medication. A thorough explanation of the pros and cons of medication should have been offered to Nick and his parents, including a discussion of the process for determining the right dosage and frequency, which may take a few weeks. I was surprised to learn that Bill and Rose agreed to use medication with Nick, considering they had been fighting over everything else until then.

I am impressed that even though the Ritalin seemed to work miracles in this case, the therapist continued to work with Nick's father (but what about his mother?) on parenting, which I find the most useful intervention, in combination with drug treatment. I've had less success with cognitive behavioral approaches used directly with the child, such as those the therapist attempts with Nick.

Nick now seems to be on the right track, with a multimodal approach to treatment. I do not object to the use of Ritalin to help children cope; it is the use of Ritalin alone, as the sole answer to a range of performance and behavioral problems in children, that riles me. I wish more cases were handled like this one.

CASE COMMENTARY 2
BY PETER GOLDENTHAL

My approach to working with Nick would differ from that described by the author in two major ways: how I would conduct my assessment and my expectations regarding medication. Bogas may be correct in concluding that Nick's problems are due to Attention-Deficit/Hyperactivity Disorder (ADHD), but my reading of the case leads me to be concerned about several diagnostic issues. Unless Nick's mother and teachers also reported similar observations, I would question Bill's description of his son's refusal to follow directions, get dressed, wash or eat breakfast, and his "always being on the go," since Bill's lack of knowledge about setting up routines or creating consistency could naturally lead to Nick's oppositional behavior. Like the structural family therapists the author mentions, I would find it difficult not to see Nick as "a child triangulated between two parents in a serious conflict and embedded in a chaotic family system."

I would also have questions about the reason for Nick's removal from his mother's home. In my experience, child protective agencies have neither the time nor the will to remove a child from a custodial parent because of truancy or tardiness, but only when they believe a child to be in imminent danger. What is undeniable is that Nick's touching other children sexually and exposing himself suggest impulsivity; neither is behavior I routinely see in young children with ADHD, unless they have also been exposed to experiences that precociously stimulated their sexual interest. Without leaping to conclusions, I would be concerned about the possibility that Nick had been molested or that he had witnessed a disturbing sexual experience of some sort.

Several other features of this case leap out as quite different from the typical ADHD cases I have seen. It is very rare for a child with ADHD to be a "motivated learner." Although an inattentive child may become wrapped up in a highly stimulating activity like a video game, it is highly unusual for such a child to have the persistence to memorize the names of butterflies, insects, and sea life. If his parents told me that these were his only interests, and especially if he had no or very poor relationships with his peers, I would think about the possibility that Nick might be showing symptoms of Asperger's disorder or an atypical, pervasive developmental disorder. Both of these disorders are characterized by restricted interests and equally restricted social interactions in the absence of either language delay or mental retardation, and both are associated with impulsivity, overactivity, and distractibility.

I do not share the author's opinion that "there is no empirical way of evaluating an individual for ADHD." In my experience, psychological tests, if correctly selected, administered, and scored, can—in combination with a developmental evaluation, a good developmental and family history, and objective reports of a child's behavior at home and in school—provide a solid empirical basis for diagnosis. Computer-based assessment procedures also provide useful information about how a child responds to a boring task over time and how his attention span, freedom from distractibility and impulsivity compare to other children of his age.

Unlike the author, I do not use a medication trial to confirm a diagnosis of ADHD. First of all, the only way to be sure that what appears to be a drug response is not due to a child's, parent's, or teacher's expectation about the effectiveness of the drug is through a doubled-blind drug trial, which is difficult to arrange and monitor. Second, stimulant medications such as Ritalin often produce heightened attention (just as caffeine produces heightened alertness) in people of all ages who do not have ADHD. Third, Ritalin can cause tics (and even more severe reactions) in susceptible children. For this reason, I would want the history, behavioral measures and results from the developmental evaluation and computerized assessment, in addition to the psychological testing the author mentions before referring any child for medication.

I was surprised at how quickly and dramatically Nick responded to the Ritalin. I do not recall ever seeing an otherwise medically healthy child's capacity to listen and focus increase so markedly or his disruptiveness decrease so totally in response to medication alone. Especially when working with children from chaotic and highly conflicted family situations, it is typical to see a modest response to medication at best, one that facilitates the real work that must be done with the child and the child's family. In this case it appears that once the medication was started, most of the changes in Nick's behavior and relationships occurred immediately, leaving only some fine-tuning to the therapist. While I do not share the author's experience regarding medication effects, I have found behavioral interventions like those the author used—increasing structure and consistency in Nick's life, helping Bill to develop a routine, to set limits, to remain calm even when Nick was upset—to be extraordinarily practical and helpful.

Finally, I am not at all surprised by Nick's response to a more positive school environment. I have seen symptoms drop away like leaves in November after a child moves from a classroom with too much stimulation, inconsistent expectations, and punitive discipline to one where structure, calm, kindness, consideration, and praise for making an effort were the watchwords. I commend the author for her attention to the issue: She may have helped Nick as much by facilitating this change as by any other intervention.

Author's Response
BY SUSAN BOGAS

It is interesting that each of the respondents raised issues about my diagnosing Nick as having ADHD. Diller framed his concerns more generally, while Goldenthal focused specifically on my treatment of Nick. I am aware that ADHD has become the diagnosis du jour, a label that many clinicians feel is being used as a catchall pathology for every child with a behavior or school problem, and one they believe immediately requires medication. But I wonder whether there is also, in reaction to this phenomenon, a negative backlash against using the perfectly legitimate diagnosis of ADHD when it does match the child's symptoms. What many clinicians want to know is how they can tell whether what they are looking at is really ADHD, since, like stress and anxiety, ADHD offers a vague, nonspecific set of symptoms.

I believe clinicians need to be at once skeptical of the ADHD category (which, rather than one disorder, may comprise several different problems) also be familiar with the gestalt of various ADHD patterns in children. As Mel Levine and others are teaching us, although there is no one profile of ADHD, there are certainly hallmarks, many of which might even seem paradoxical. The one truth about ADHD children is that they are consistent in their inconsistency. They focus when an activity is a passion and are inattentive any time the activity seems to be work, not play. They are extremely oppositional and defiant under some circumstances, and sweet-natured and cooperative in others. They are overactive in some situations, and then sluggish and slow to react in others. The uniqueness of ADHD patterns lies in the contradictions and the extremes, and the difficulties of coping with everyday life manifested in these children.

Once the ADHD metaphor is determined appropriate through use of checklists, evaluations, and a thorough history, I favor going ahead and treating for the ADHD and any other learning problems that might also exist. Knowing that ADHD symptoms can negatively impact on every level of the child's functioning, I initially

tend to suspend judgment about what may be personality, temperament, or coexisting conditions (with a few exceptions) and focus on
the ADHD. Then, as treatment proceeds, I look to see which problems resolve, which ones are controlled by medication, and which
ones persist no matter what we do.

With Nick, I observed that much of what looked like a serious
level of disturbance began to shift as he received medication for his
distractibility and impulsivity, and as he received more structure,
limits and nurturing from his father (his mother was always nurturing but completely lacking in structure and limit-setting). While
Nick reverted to being destructive and impulsive when taken off Ritalin, his extremely disruptive, defiant behavior all but disappeared
when he was on it. I credit both the medication and the more stable
home environment with his positive changes. ■

STUDY QUESTIONS

1. Therapists are often divided when it comes to recommending medications for clients. Some, like Bogas, believe it can be a helpful adjunct to therapy; others, like
   Diller, believe we overmedicate clients. What do you
   think about using medication with therapy? What are
   some of the benefits and some of the dangers?

2. What might have been some of the reasons that focusing
   on family structure and limit-setting helped Nick's behavior and concentration improve?

3. What are Goldenthal's reasons for saying it's problematic
   to use a medication trial to confirm a diagnosis?

4. After reading this case and the commentaries, do you
   think Nick was suffering from ADHD? Why or why not?

CONSULTATION CORNER

THE BOY WHO LOVED CATWOMAN

Deciding Who Has the Problem in a Case that Challenges Gender Norms

EDITED BY H. CHARLES FISHMAN

As therapists, we are taught to respect diversity and to question societal prejudices against people who make lifestyle choices that challenge mainstream norms. At the same time, we are looked to as guides, skilled in helping clients understand and adapt to the realities of the world in which they live. The following case of a 10-year old boy struggling with his gender identity offers a provocative example of the dilemmas clinicians sometimes face as they try to understand both their clients' needs and their own personal and professional values.

H.C.F.

Doris, age 36, and her 10-year-old son, Davey, were referred to treatment by the child-study team at Davey's school, which has been involved with them since Davey started school four years ago because of Davey's temper tantrums, violent acting out in school and frequent destruction of property. Doris is reluctant to admit that her son has a conduct problem and denies that he ever destroyed property. She insists that Davey's behavior is normal, and that the child-study team and school officials are overreacting to the situation.

Davey's violence is often in response to taunting and abuse by other schoolchildren because of his effeminate manner and his fascination with women's clothing, long fingernails, and makeup. Davey frequently affects a feminine posture and tone of voice while playing with the other children; he also prefers to assume the role of a female during playtime activities. Doris is concerned about Davey's obsession with impersonating female characters in the movies, especially

(Continued)

(Continued)

Michelle Pfeiffer's portrayal of Catwoman. On more than one occasion, Davey, an articulate and friendly child, has acted out his impersonations during therapy sessions.

Doris described an incident in which Davey did a "ballerina leap" across the soccer field instead of running like the other boys on the team. He was ridiculed and called "girlie" by his teammates. In sessions, Doris and Davey often describe episodes in which Davey is harassed for imitating a girl. While Doris thinks that Davey has a normal curiosity about the opposite sex, she says she is very upset about his interest in imitating women and wants to have Davey tested. Davey especially likes to impersonate seductive women, pursing his lips and fluttering his eyelashes, while speaking in a woman's voice. He also strikes seductive poses and struts around the room in the exaggerated style of a female fashion model. Doris is ambivalent about her son's sexual identity: On several occasions, she has let Davey wear makeup and women's clothes, telling him he may do this only at home, and that he must not tell anyone about it. Doris refers to Davey as being pretty, which seems to please him. More than once, Davey has stated that he would prefer to be a woman. He reports feeling happier when he is with female peers or when he is allowed to act out as a woman.

Doris divorced Davey's father when Davey was an infant. Doris and Davey have lived with Doris's mother, Susan, in a one-bedroom apartment for the past year because of an injury Doris got on her last job. Doris wants to save enough money to move out of her mother's house so she and Davey can have a less stressful home environment.

Susan has been divorced three times and has a cut-off relationship with her son. She treats Doris like a child and the two women are in constant conflict. They admit that they frequently bring Davey into the middle of their battles, and are aware of the burden this imposes on Davey, who often assumes the role of husband and father to his mother and grandmother.

Since he started therapy, Davey's acting out at school and in social situations has improved somewhat, and Doris finally has started imposing some consequences for his behavior, as well as establishing

(Continued)

(Continued)

more age-appropriate boundaries between herself and Davey. Until now, their relationship had been extremely enmeshed; Doris devoted herself totally to Davey, forsaking a life of her own. Six months ago, Doris got a job as a health aide to a homebound individual, but within weeks, Davey's behavior deteriorated to a level that warranted his being suspended from school on several occasions.

Davey spent most of the remainder of the school year in isolation from his peers. The teacher and the child-study team placed him in a structure they refer to as a carousel—a desk surrounded by three large panels on each side so that Davey would be totally obscured from view by his classmates. During the lunch period, Davey was forced to eat alone, with his back to the room, and was not permitted to go outside to play. School personnel justified this action, stating that Davey distracted the other students and destroyed property.

According to school officials, this isolation was an attempt to maintain some order in the classroom. However, after the therapist attended several conferences with the child-study team, the teacher, the principal, and Doris, it became obvious that Davey's condition was exacerbated by the excessive punishment and prolonged periods of isolation, and Davey was allowed to return to the regular lunch table as well as to his seat in the classroom. Two weeks prior to the summer recess, Davey began a trial of Ritalin, which has considerably modified his hyperactive, aggressive behavior.

In their last session, Davey discussed his feelings about his father and expressed a desire to meet with him. A year ago, Doris and Davey saw Davey's father while they were shopping. Davey's father berated him because of his "sissified appearance," renouncing any parental claim to or responsibility for him. Now Davey is afraid that his father will reject him again. The therapist suggested that the father's parents be invited to the session in order to explore the possibility of a reunion between Davey and his father.

Doris is very concerned about Davey's return to school—school officials want to send Davey to an out-of-district school for emotionally disturbed children. Doris is convinced that such a move would

(Continued)

(Continued)

destroy Davey. She believes that Davey's compliance with Ritalin dosages will help him with his behavioral problems, and she wants him to stay at his current school.

Our approach has been to help Doris assert herself in her parental role; she had relinquished her authority, not only to her mother, but especially to her son, with obvious deleterious effects. We have tried to help Doris explore the consequences of the inconsistency in her relationship with Davey, particularly with respect to discipline and to clear boundaries.

Trying to convince Doris and Susan to examine how their relationship affects their son and grandson has been almost impossible. To the extent that Davey remains split between the two of them, it is unlikely that he will feel comfortable enough to give up the control that keeps him feeling secure in the family. Asking Doris to change her perception of her son has been extremely difficult. We have tried to focus Doris on developing a life for herself to relieve Davey of his responsibility for her. Currently, Davey is in a relationship with a man from the Big Brothers organization. It is our hope that this individual will prove to be a strong, male role model for Davey.

How might the therapist proceed in helping this family in light of the complexities involved in this case?

COMMENTARY 1

A Strategic Family Approach

BY LYNNE SCHWARTZ AND JAMES COYNE

The difficulties of this case are made all the more difficult by the breakdown of the collaborations needed to figure out what the problem is. Given the rigidity and defiance of both the family and the school personnel, one of our first moves would be to undertake a bit of shuttle diplomacy to find some common ground and get some small concessions to each other's point of view. For instance, we would work to get the school to acknowledge to Doris that Davey has indeed been harassed and that further isolating him in the carousel was inappropriate. Building on Doris's concerns about Davey's being harassed, we would coach the therapist to ask her to discourage Davey from wearing nail polish to school, hopefully diminishing provocations from his classmates. Getting a commitment to a small change of this kind, the therapist could then go to Davey's teacher, acknowledge that he is a challenging child, point out the mother's cooperation and work to identify ways in which the school, and particularly the teacher, could cut down on the harassment that Davey has suffered. Rather than simply discouraging classmates from picking on Davey, the teacher might try to develop some simple ways for him to be successful or at least tolerated by his classmates. This could mean involving Davey with classmates who have not tormented him or getting Davey interested in some project that does not call for sex-typed behavior, male or female, such as art, music, or a science project. This might have the added advantage of taking some of the emphasis off gender issues. In contrast, we don't think pushing Davey to play baseball or football is going to achieve these aims.

The goal of these small steps is to focus everyone on breaking the pattern of provocation, rejection, and acting out. Initially, this is best done one-on-one, rather than in group meetings in which everyone is required to talk to each other. Davey is likely to give a less confusing account of himself if he is not overwhelmed by having to deal with both his mother and his teacher at the same time. Similarly, Doris is going to be more forthcoming if she does not have to defend Davey against the teacher, and the father is more likely to show up and talk more freely if he gets a private hearing with the therapist, rather than a confrontation with his ex-wife.

Beyond these initial moves, the therapist needs to get a better sense of what is going on. There is a lot of information that is not given in the write-up, perhaps because the therapist simply has not obtained it yet. For instance, what is Davey like at home or in the neighborhood? The write-up states that the mother is reluctant to admit that Davey is aggressive at home, but maybe he simply isn't. It is reported that six months ago, there was an improvement in Davey's behavior, followed by a deterioration when his mother went to work. We are curious about what brought about the improvement and the extent to which the deterioration was a matter of how the mother's starting work was handled. Much is made of the negative encounter Doris and Davey had with the father at the mall. Was it negative just because the mother was there? Does the father really resolutely reject any relationship with the boy? Did Ritalin actually produce such a dramatic change in Davey's behavior? If so, where was this evident? Or was it just a matter of his getting out of school for the summer? More details are needed to provide answers to these questions.

It sounds as if the therapist has actually had some success in this case. For a while, at least, the mother asserted herself as a parent and was more consistent in setting limits. Yet, at other times, the therapist seems to have become locked in unproductive struggles, trying to convince the mother and the grandmother of the damaging effects of their relationship on Davey, or trying to get Doris to move out of her mother's house before she is ready. The case needs a more sustained focus, grounded in the details of key interactions and relationships.

The issue of Davey's gender-role confusion is probably the most delicate aspect of this case, and again we are missing key details. Some issues are more clear-cut than others. Effeminate behavior is going to provoke the wrath of other 10-year-old boys on the playground, and blatant cross-gender behavior is likely to lead to Davey's being ostracized. Nevertheless, there are ways of broadening the opportunities for Davey to feel accepted. The therapist needs to bear in mind that being male does not have to equal rough-and-tumble and rough-and-tumble does not have to equal male. Davey's ballerina leaps may be upsetting on a soccer field, but they can be appropriate in a dance class. Why not let Davey dress up in an akido outfit with some other boys and girls his age and put his gracefulness to new uses? The therapist can help him develop some competencies where sex-typed behavior is irrelevant or at least less apparent.

It is absolutely essential for the therapist to be familiar with the literature concerning gender-identity problems and be prepared to offer, in an authoritative manner, both what is known and what remains unknown about the long-term outcome in cases like this. We do not know the strength of Davey's commitment to cross-gender interests and behavior, and whether these are transient or likely to persist in some form. At this point, his behavior is probably presexual and not erotic, representing an interest rather than a sexual orientation. We note that his mother comments on his "normal curiosity about the opposite sex," but we are not sure what to make of this. Possible long-term outcomes for Davey include heterosexuality with or without some effeminate behavior; homosexuality, also with or without some effeminate behavior; and transsexualism, as an adult wanting to be a woman and seeking a sex change. But we think it would be a mistake to become too focused on long-term outcomes at this stage. The emphasis ought to be on Davey's current alienation and distress and how he and others are contributing to it. At times, the therapist will have to step in and keep others from getting too focused on resolving the gender-identity issue to the neglect of the other needs of an "articulate and friendly child"—getting comfortable and integrated with his peers, for example. Like other 10-year-olds, he has general tasks like becoming self-reliant and more in control of himself, but also specific tasks like learning how to deal with teasing and bullies. The mother needs to be made aware of anything she might be doing that promotes conflict between Davey and others concerning gender roles. If it has not been done already, Davey needs to be told about anatomical differences between boys and girls and the physical obstacles that prevent him from being a girl. Maybe the mother could be coached to help him with these matters. Davey has choices, too, and he needs to know that walking and gesturing in an effeminate manner provoke some people. He could use help finding friends who are less bothered by effeminate behavior. Teachers may need to be reminded of how they can create opportunities for Davey to feel more comfortable and less alienated, but also that their responsibility is to foster tolerance.

We propose that the working goal in this case should be enlisting Davey and others to help him be more comfortable in as many situations as possible. Gender identity is only a piece of this, but cross-gender behavior is interfering with his education and his social relationships. At this point, he might be better able to get a fresh start in another school, but we are skeptical about it needing to be a school for emotionally disturbed children. We also think an effort has to be made to ensure that there is a good match between Davey and the new setting and that any transfer not be seen as punitive. It might help if Doris and Davey or Doris and the grandmother were less "enmeshed," if Doris got a life of her own or at least an apartment, or if the father was less alienated. Yet, we do not want to wait for such things to happen and we would be cautious about pursuing these goals if it meant the focus was no longer on Davey's needs.

COMMENTARY 2

A Feminist Family Therapy Approach

BY CHERYL RAMPAGE

It is part of this culture's pervasive gender bias that a girl's supposedly masculine behavior is tolerated, and sometimes even lauded, while a boy's feminine behavior is almost universally regarded as disturbing and unacceptable. Given this, the case of Doris and Davey would challenge the gender values of any therapist. Here is a boy who is not just unmacho, but who seems to delight in being stereotypically hyperfeminine. Davey not only likes playing with girls, he enjoys trying on the accoutrements of seductively sexual, adult female characteristics. He goes considerably out of his way to draw attention to his differentness from his peers.

What struck me as odd in reading this case is that, although the therapist provides several dramatic examples of the extent to which Davey mimics the extremes of feminine behavior, nothing in the treatment description directly addresses the issue. While I understand the relevance of focusing on the issues of organization and hierarchy in the family, it seems to me that *not* directly dealing with Davey's effeminate behavior must reflect the therapist's confusion over the meaning of such behavior or the propriety of attempting to modify it.

A 10-year-old boy who crossdresses and *only* wants to take on female roles in play is not being androgynous, he is rejecting a male identity. There is no chance that this behavior will lead to anything but unremitting rejection and persecution from his peer group, both female and male. Most children, at Davey's age, rigidly conform to traditional gender roles, and they can be brutal to someone who doesn't fit. Clearly, from the therapist's description of the school's draconian efforts to isolate Davey, some of the adults in Davey's life also reject his behavior.

So, the issue for me is, what are the therapist and Davey's family doing to help him modify his presentation of self? First, his family should make clear to him that they are content that he is a boy, and would like to help him become more comfortable with that fact. I would be inclined to externalize the problem, describing the family as collectively being caught in a dilemma (I might even be tempted to call it "the spell of the Catwoman"), and I would define my task as helping them identify ways of resisting this spell. I would encourage the mother and grandmother to find ways to encourage Davey's expression of appropriate maleness. By this I do *not* mean that they should buy Davey a G.I. Joe® and a pack of Camels,® but that they should watch for opportunities to support and reinforce his engagement in gender-neutral play, discourage his crossdressing and seductive play at home, and voice their preferences for his comporting himself as a boy.

There are many reasons why Doris may not have given Davey clear messages about his cross-gender play. The most straightforward is that she fears that Davey will experience any restrictions she imposes as further echoes of the rejection he has already received from peers, teachers, and even his own father. I would reframe Doris's restrictions on Davey's cross-gender behavior as loving guidance, instead of rejection. Indeed, a key to gaining Doris's cooperation may be the creation of a new set of responses to Davey other than passive acceptance and outright rejection.

Of course, it is possible that Doris may actually be more comfortable with Davey's apparent rejection of maleness because of her own ambivalence toward or fearfulness of men. Highly effeminate behavior in latency-age boys is sometimes associated with sexual abuse, either of the child or the parent. If the strategy outlined above fails, then this hypothesis should be investigated by the therapist. If either Doris or Davey has a history of sexual abuse, it should be directly addressed, probably individual therapy.

I should say, by the way, that I think there is a reasonable chance that Davey is transsexual, one of those cosmic mistakes who end up feeling trapped in the body of the wrong gender. There are treatment programs for such people, and drastic interventions. Perhaps someday Davey will want to avail himself of such a program. But like it or not, Davey is stuck being a male for at least another decade. Davey needs help learning to get comfortable with his gender identity. If conversation with Davey reveals that he does have a serious desire not only to be feminine, but to actually be female, then I would be straightforward with him about the possibility of such a transformation, including that he is many years away from that solution, and encourage him to consider the alternative of finding ways to be comfortable with himself. Perhaps his Big Brother could be helpful in providing Davey with a model, as well as for providing encouragement and support.

In this era of rapidly changing notions about appropriate gender behavior, all of us are struggling to find our place, somewhere between outmoded sexual stereotype and genderlessness. I tend to see Davey's problem as a special case of that struggle. Like many males today, he is rejecting the constraints of traditional masculinity, and for this brave act, I think he needs support. Unfortunately, he is in danger of escaping one prison only to find himself locked into another. The cause of Davey's need to fully express himself as human will not be served by substituting feminine stereotypes for masculine. Someone needs to help Davey and his family discover ways of being human that transcend the clichés of machismo and temptress and that allow him to be authentically and comfortably what he is: a 10-year-old boy. ■

STUDY QUESTIONS

1. Discuss what you think the most relevant focus of the therapy might have been (e.g., helping Davey become more "normal" in his gender presentation, or helping his teachers and parents become more tolerant of his effeminate presentation).

2. Do you think homophobia plays a role in this case? Why or why not?

3. How did the therapist's own values emerge in this case, and how do you think therapists should handle their own values in therapy?

CASE STUDY

ADRIAN'S CHOICE
HELPING A YOUNG ADOPTEE DECIDE WHERE HE BELONGS

Ton C. Smets

It was a busy August afternoon when the phone rang. I was not taking new referrals in my pediatric practice, but my secretary urged me to consider the request. A pleasant, down-to-earth woman from the county Human Services department was on the line, asking me to see Adrian, the 13-year-old adopted child of a local Mennonite farming family.

Until recently, she told me, Adrian's history had been unremarkable. He had come to this Mennonite family in rural Indiana as a foster child at the age of four and was legally adopted by them four years later at the age of eight. He seemed to have adapted well to life among the Mennonites—a devout, cohesive community of evangelical Protestant farmers who live simple lives, similar to those of the Amish, but far less restrictive.

Then one evening in July, the family's barn had burned to the ground. All of the summer's hay was lost, but farmhands managed to save the 25 milk cows, the livelihood of Adrian's family, and move them to a neighbor's barn. Ten days later, that barn burned, too, and with it, all of the cows. A few days later, Adrian's father discovered the boy running out of the family kitchen as thick smoke poured from the windows and doors.

Under the questioning of the local fire chief, Adrian confessed to setting all three blazes. Adrian's case was referred to the social worker by the juvenile court. At first, her reaction was to look for another placement for the boy, but much to her surprise, after consulting with community elders, Adrian's parents decided to keep Adrian. The Mennonite community set to work rebuilding the barns, claims were filed with insurance companies, and the family agreed with the social worker's recommendation to have Adrian enter therapy.

In early September, Adrian, his parents, and their three biological children came to my office for the first time. In their simple, modest clothes, they could have stepped out of a Norman Rockwell painting.

The father wore no tie. The mother wore a long print dress buttoned to the neck and a small black cap tied over her hair, which was put up in a bun. Adrian's clothing, too, was old-fashioned, and his hair was cut short, in 1950s style. At 13, he had the small-framed, childlike body of a boy of 10.

The father was the spokesperson. The mother would not speak unless I insisted that she answer questions, and then she simply echoed what her husband said. Their 14-year-old daughter, who had left school after eighth grade to work with her mother on the farm, also barely spoke a word. Her two younger brothers, ages 9 and 7, were a marked contrast. Initially shy, they quickly warmed up and seemed at ease with drawing attention to themselves.

The family described themselves as typical Mennonites and reported no unusual conflicts brewing below the surface. Their lives were focused on God, work, and community. Adrian, they said, was a pleasant, cooperative child who went to a Mennonite community school, worked on the farm, and played with friends. I was struck by the fact that they seemed to have no hostility toward him. And the only fear I noted came from the daughter, who had asked to sleep downstairs so that she could escape more easily in case of another fire.

I told them that I had never worked with a Mennonite family before and that I did not want to violate any of their principles. I asked if they felt forced by the county to bring to a therapist what they might have thought was better left to God. But the father, who seemed to have a quiet interest in psychology, reassured me. Unlike the Amish, Mennonites pick and choose among the blessings of modern life—they use tractors and electricity, for instance, but not television—and the family's attitude was a mixture of curiosity about psychotherapy and a certainty about their own beliefs. The father said he felt I would be able to help all of them understand why the fires had happened, and thus help prevent them from happening again. He seemed more sophisticated than I had expected, and remarkably secure.

All through the fall, I met with Adrian alone. He loved coming to see me, just as he also seemed to love his contacts with the police and with the lawyer representing him in negotiations over the insurance claims. He was fascinated with what he called "the world," and at the same time critical of it. Why did I, unlike Mennonite men, wear a tie? Did my children, unlike Mennonite children, watch television? Had I been to the local amusement park? What was it like? His questions ranged from clothes and habits to religious beliefs and morals; he wanted to know where I stood.

When I asked about the fires, he told me readily that he had set them to "get back at Dad" for refusing to allow him to drive a tractor or do other important farm chores that Mennonite boys learn as they come of age. He wanted to convince his father, he said, that he needed more responsibility. I asked if he really believed his actions would result in more responsible chores. Could he not see the paradox? He shrugged. When I talked about the danger to which he had exposed other people, and the loss of the animals' lives, he cried and told me repeatedly that he expected only property to be damaged.

In October, I met alone with Adrian's father. He was a sensitive man, quick to cry. Gentle and eloquent, he loved to talk and speculate about Adrian. By all outside appearances, he loved the boy. He seemed interested in my progress with Adrian, but never pressured me or his son for details. He did not question his parenting, and seemed confident that if he learned of different ways to deal with his children, he would simply change. He was the involved and yet noninterfering parent that any teenager's therapist would want.

He told me he felt Adrian was not yet tall enough or strong enough to drive a tractor. And he added that Adrian also showed the poor attention and concentration that I recognized as a characteristic of attention deficit disorder. Adrian's problems, he said, carried over into the classroom at the small Mennonite school the boy attended, where they seemed to be well handled by the Mennonite teachers.

I asked him whether there were other pieces of farm equipment, less dangerous than the tractor, that Adrian could be taught to operate, and he agreed to look into it. His meetings with me seemed to open up communication between him and Adrian, and they had long talks in the evening, after chores, in the barn.

About three months after the start of therapy, Adrian and I stopped talking about the fires, and he began, step by step, to tell me his story. At about the age of eight, he told me, he would often walk out in the farm field—up to the fence, but no farther—and think about running away. At first, he would not say where he wanted to go. Later, he spoke of wanting to see "the world." Finally, Adrian allowed himself to nod confirmingly when I asked him if he wanted to find his biological mother.

I did not think it would be a good idea for Adrian to actually reconnect with his mother. I have seldom seen a case where adolescents who contacted blood relatives were better off. Usually, such teenagers are motivated by a wish to be reparented, and that rarely, of course, works out.

But I welcomed his search to understand his past and to know more about his birth family. I have noticed that as adopted children come of age, they wrestle fiercely with questions of identity arising not from conflicts in their present families, but from their pasts: Who are they? Where did they come from? As puberty approaches, they long for closure on these questions; they long to know where they belong. In Adrian's case, these issues were drawn in extraordinarily sharp relief because his adoptive family was devout, stable, and Mennonite. Adrian's birth mother and father, I had discovered, were none of those things.

It was in November, after a protracted struggle with the county Department of Human Services, that the records of Adrian's adoption were mailed to me. The life reflected in those pages could not have contrasted more vividly with the quiet, stable farm life in which Adrian was now embedded. The file was thick with social service reports. His mother, Joanne, was 18 when Adrian was born, one of 6 children from a chaotic local family well known to the police and local social workers for family violence, alcoholism, abuse, and neglect. Joanne had dropped out of school in seventh grade and left home at 15. In the 6 years after Adrian's birth, she moved 15 times, often living with relatives and friends, often being evicted for drinking and violence. When she went to the bars, she usually took her little son with her.

Adrian's father, Karl, also 18, saw Adrian only once. Then he left the state, fleeing several burglary charges. To this day, his whereabouts are unknown.

In the spring of his fourth year, Adrian was hospitalized, and Joanne, who was pregnant, did not visit him for 8 days. The hospital found that Adrian had decaying teeth and other health problems associated with neglect. His family doctor had already seen him 14 times for poor health and had earlier reported Joanne for suspected neglect. Another report was made, and Adrian was placed in foster care with the Mennonite family.

Adrian saw his mother only once after this, when he was eight and the county Department of Human Services was urging her to terminate her parental rights. She was pregnant with her third child; another child, born after Adrian, had also been taken from her for severe neglect. After the visit, Adrian told the social workers he did not mind seeing his mother, but he wanted to stay with his foster parents at the Mennonite farm.

A few weeks later, Joanne was convicted of shoplifting. Her third child was born in prison. Shortly before her release, she signed papers relinquishing her parental rights to the two older children. She took her newborn baby out of the state and was never heard from again.

One social service report particularly drew my attention. Late one summer night when Adrian was two, Joanne returned home after a day of drinking with friends. The electricity was either defective or turned off, and Joanne and a girlfriend, both apparently drunk, lit the curtains to provide light. The house burned down, and Joanne was convicted of arson. I closed the file and thought that at some time soon, it would help Adrian to know more about his family and its history.

Not long before Thanksgiving, I told Adrian I wanted to help him remember his family. His memories were sketchy: he remembered visiting his mother at age eight, but couldn't remember ever having lived with her. He had some visual images of coming to live with his adoptive parents, but these, too, were vague and incomplete.

Equally vague was his understanding of the facts of conception and birth. He understood that he was born from his mother and that babies came out of women's "bellies," but he seemed completely surprised that he had a father other than his adoptive father.

After asking his Mennonite parents for permission, which they easily gave, I discussed sexuality and procreation with him. He obviously enjoyed learning, and it was delightful to watch him place human sexuality in the context of the wonders of animal sexual behavior that he saw on the farm.

Just before Christmas, with this foundation laid, I gave Adrian a careful picture of his first years of life. I tried to present enough facts to help him understand how his mother's problems had made her incapable of taking care of him. For two sessions, with my encouragement, he asked questions: Where was his father? Did he have siblings? Would his father ever come and see him? I told him what I knew: Yes, he had siblings.

And no, nobody knew exactly where they were, or where his biological mother and father were.

I was prepared for withdrawal, hostility, and perhaps some depression and acting out. But Adrian's mood and attitude surprised me. It was Christmastime and he was very upbeat; between questions, he shared his excitement about the holiday. In one of our most moving sessions, he asked me if he could sing and then, in a pure, high voice, he sang 30 minutes worth of simple Christmas carols from his church's holiday program.

After the new year, Adrian seemed to change gears again, and a third stage in therapy emerged. He occasionally thought of setting a fire again, he said, but insisted he wasn't "serious." The fires, he said, were being openly discussed in the Mennonite community because the families were negotiating an insurance settlement, and he had come into town to give depositions. His thoughts, he said, were a reaction to the questions that other Mennonite boys were asking him.

At first, I thought his comments revealed a fear that therapy was about to be terminated. But when I asked him about this, he responded rather noncommittally. It turned out that he had more to tell me. In the spring before the fires, he said, he'd made a phone call, misdialed, and reached a stranger. Several days later, he said, "I made the same mistake again," and this time had a short conversation with the man on the other end of the line. The next weekend he "misdialed" several times, and talked enough with the family to discover that the man had a wife and two daughters. The calls ended abruptly when the man threatened to call the police and complain of harassment.

With considerable prompting from me, Adrian admitted he had daydreamed about living with this "worldly" family. He had fleetingly thought about calling them again.

It was in early spring, in this state of ambivalence about "the world," that Adrian told me that many of his Mennonite peers were "getting the call" to adult baptism. Adult baptism—a coming-of-age ceremony with similarities to confirmation or Bar Mitzvah—is one of the most religious rituals in a Mennonite boy's life. Mennonites are not baptized as babies, because they do not believe in original sin and the need to wash it away. Baptism, to the Mennonites, is a responsible pledge to lead a Christian life, made by an adult with the ability to distinguish good from evil.

Adrian told me that he had not felt the call, but he thought it would be "just a matter of time." I told him that I thought he might experience a struggle with the commitment, because he was not born of Mennonites, and there were drives in his life suggesting he might want to leave or experience "the world." But Adrian dismissed my suggestions. His worries, he said, were not about him, but about me.

Quite unexpectedly, he asked me if I would bring my family to visit the Mennonite church and his family home. After talking it over with my wife and children, I accepted the invitation. Within a week, Adrian's father called, expressing how happy they were with the plan, and we set a date that was two months away, the first weekend we could match our schedules.

From that moment on, Adrian aggressively launched a mission to convert me to the Mennonite faith. He cried easily at the thought that I would "burn in Hell" if I did not convert. It seemed to me that in order to answer his call, Adrian needed me and my family to become Mennonite.

I told him I understood his need, that getting to know me—the only "worldly person" he knew intimately—may have been both a joy and a pain. I told him I understood that it might confuse him to care for a person whose lifestyle was not condoned by the community in which he lived. But I would not become a Mennonite, and neither would my family. We would come to visit as a courtesy, to learn more and to expand our own horizons. If Adrian was to answer his call, I said, he needed to do that by himself.

In April, I arranged, through his parents, for Adrian to have meetings with his pastor explaining his dilemma. The parents seemed comfortable dealing with the issue; they assured me that Mennonite children often had some temporary trouble reconciling the church's teachings on belonging with their respect and affection for non-Mennonites. After meeting with his pastor, Adrian seemed less obsessed with the issue and also less interested in our family visit. A week prior to the agreed-upon weekend, his father called me and told me Adrian had second thoughts, that he did not want to deal with the many questions his peers might ask. We decided not to go.

Adrian continued his discussions with church elders, and soon afterward, he told them he had felt the call, and began gradually working toward his baptism. In June, not long before the start of another harvest, we terminated therapy. Adrian was doing well, both at school and at home. He and his father had learned to negotiate and talk more openly with each other; Adrian had learned to operate some complicated farm equipment, although his father still did not feel he was ready for the tractor. The barns had been rebuilt and insurance companies had made a financial settlement. The charges against Adrian in the juvenile court had been dismissed.

I firmly believe that things turned out so well because of his family's unshakable commitment to him. They loved him and they had given him time, privacy, and the help of a third party to explore all of his family ties. He was lucky to have such a loving and stable context in which to move through his coming-of-age.

Adoptive parents, especially those who adopt older children, often must brace themselves against the inevitable challenges and rejections that adoptive children express as they come of age. In such times, children need firm support and reassurance, and parents need to understand that the crisis is not about them. Many adoptive parents suffer from a profound insecurity that makes this difficult.

But the Mennonites are not self-doubting people. Whatever the limits inherent in their way of life, they find security in their community and their religion, which emphasizes absolute love and nonviolence, and in the rigidity of their familiar hierarchy and order. Held in this loving and stable context, Adrian had grappled with his choice.

In the beginning, the "world" outside his domain was as unknown and fascinating as it was undesirable. It was the undiscovered reality at the other end of the field where he wished to run as an 8-year-old; it was the mysterious "telephone family" that he wanted to adopt.

Through knowing me, he learned that "the world" was not a purely chaotic and sinful place, nor was it purely positive. And although I was of "the world," I let him know that I was very impressed with his family. This lovely boy, despite the deficits of his early childhood and perhaps some neurological problems related to his mother's drinking, had found a secure, accepting, and loving environment in which he could grow.

I may never know what caused this loving and soft-hearted child to set fires that killed animals and endangered people. It may have been etched in his unconscious from the day his mother burned down the house. Perhaps it was an extreme version of testing: he burned the home and livelihood of his adoptive family and they kept him anyway.

He may have doubted whether he belonged with his adoptive family, but they had no such doubts. Through their actions, his Mennonite family had told him: "You belong to us; you are part of us. We made a decision to give you a home, and whatever difficulties you have—even if you burn down our barn—we're going to stick with you."

Adrian had walked to the fence, and learned more of what lay beyond it. Held in his family's unshakable love, he had decided to stay.

CASE COMMENTARY 1
BY ESTHER PEREL

This case describes the moving and inspiring treatment of a troubled boy. Approaching the case as a family therapist, however, I would have begun by inquiring about each family member's understanding of why Adrian has to express his distress in such an extreme fashion, and whether there were any warning signals preceding his fire-setting. Knowing the family's response to these signals would give me a sense of their awareness of internal tensions, as well as their resources for handling them.

Smets sensitively addresses the dynamics of adoption—Adrian's testing of the adoptive family and their need to let him doubt and spurn them while standing by him and not taking his rejection personally. I would also want to know whether the parents had any ambivalence about keeping Adrian, despite their expression of commitment to him. After all, he had burned down the barn and destroyed a major part of the family's livelihood. Their lack of open anger may be an indication of the difficulties in expressing hostility in this family (and in their culture) and Smets's acceptance of this lack of response may have prevented the development of a broader repertoire of emotional interaction within the family.

Smets is keenly aware of the cultural/religious gulf separating him from Mennonite society. He carefully defers to the father in matters such as sexuality that could infringe on his sense of cultural integrity and hierarchy. At the same time, Smets fails to more directly involve the father in helping Adrian cope with his emerging manhood. As a therapist, I would have tried to facilitate a man-to-man conversation between father and son on matters such as sexuality, aggression, and group identification. It is important to bear in mind that Adrian's transition into adolescence is also a transition for the whole family.

We know that Adrian wants to get back at his father and wants to be granted more privileges, but his unexplored agenda with his mother and siblings, particularly his teenaged sister, gives an incomplete picture of the family as well as leaving many of its strengths unexplored. In the light of his early traumatic relationship with his mother, Adrian may need special mothering, yet his adoptive mother is a background figure in this case who functions primarily as an echo of the father. It is unclear whether this exclusion of the mother is a clinical oversight or a misguided act of cultural sensitivity.

In placing himself so centrally, Smets took it upon himself to be the sole representative of the larger world and the principal cultural broker who knows Adrian's secret wishes and aspirations. The result is that rather than the family's being helped to deal with Adrian's interests, conflicts, and fascinations with the world, an important part of parenting is relegated to an outsider.

The traditional world of the Mennonite community is organized around a religiously prescribed and ritualized code of life. While Adrian's intense focus on the individual freedom, leisure, technology, and adolescent relationships of the world beyond the fence may be traceable to his origins as outsider, it may be, as is often the case in families removed from the cultural mainstream, that he is carrying the rest of the family's unspoken yearnings to know what lies beyond the boundaries. I would explore with the family what elements of the modern world are allowed into the family and how Adrian's curiosity and longings must be openly acknowledged within his family. The role of the therapist is to bring this threatening tension to the fore and to facilitate conversations about the two worlds within the family. Part of this involves the parents' sharing with their children how they have handled their own feelings and doubts about group identification.

Smets implies that Adrian's baptism somehow permanently resolves the family's and cultural conflicts so vividly presented in this case. However, I would prepare the family to see the fire-setting episode as a part of Adrian's ongoing existential dilemma, and warn them that it is the nature of cultural ambivalence to potentially resurface in the future. I would explore the possibility of enlisting a sanctioned ambassador or cultural broker, like a Mennonite Big Brother who had had contact with the larger world, to help Adrian develop a clearer window on what lies beyond the insular Mennonite community.

Traditional groups like the Mennonites, who are so visibly distinctive and whose culture prescribes separateness, experience an especially intense conflict with the values of modern society. Respecting the boundaries of life within such groups, especially for young people, involves an inherent sense of missing out on the gratifications the mainstream society so actively promotes. But ongoing self-denial is the cost for maintaining a cohesive traditional culture in this secular society, and Adrian's struggles with this legacy may only be beginning.

CASE COMMENTARY 2
BY MICHAEL FOX AND STUART TIEGEL

Most of family therapy's founders discouraged the arbitrary distinctions between individual, couple, and family therapy. Jay Haley often said we should stop talking about family therapy and focus on identifying the vital components of psychotherapy. According to Milton Erickson, the goal of psychotherapy, however practiced, is helping patients extend their limits. Carl Whitaker saw psychotherapy as an encounter between a professional and patients seeking to grow, which ultimately leads to both growing. Resisting all orthodoxies, this case is an excellent illustration of clinical work that transcends simplistic categories, enabling the people involved to push past their limits and experience genuine growth.

It is also an example of what we could call excellently managed care. Smets succeeds in producing massive change in a dangerous and potentially lethal situation in approximately eight months. He has a clear overall strategy in mind, respecting both the values of the family and its community as he moves through each phase of treatment. In addition to psychosocial issues, biological factors, such as the possibility of attention deficit disorder, are also considered and, we are confident, biological interventions would have been framed within an understanding of family dynamics if they had been deemed appropriate.

The case highlights the considerable strengths of the people involved. Clearly Adrian fits Steve Wolin's definition of a "resilient" child—he seems to have the innate ability to attract and use competent adults who can provide what he needs developmentally. Another key to this case is the strength of Adrian's adoptive family and their commitment to him, even if it means delegating authority to someone like Smets from "the world." For his part, Smets showed the essentials of a culturally competent therapist by being both respectful of his own culture and keenly aware of the family and cultural context of his patient. The bond of mutual respect that develops between Adrian, his family, and Smets is vital, and grows out of the reciprocated sensitivity to cultural and religious differences. In the absence of covert or overt attempts to control him, Adrian is given the opportunity to pursue the information he needs to choose his own path.

Adrian's struggle between the pull of "the world" and accepting his adoptive family and their culture is a variation of the struggle children usually resolve in adolescence. But Adrian's problem becomes exaggerated by the fact that he has not yet developed a sense of belonging to either the biological family he vaguely knew or the family that has raised him but to whom he has not yet committed himself. His phone calls to strangers may be seen as part of his continuing search for belonging. Like many other abused and neglected children in foster care, Adrian still feels the pull of emotional identification with his biological family of origin. Adrian's struggle with "getting the call" revolves around his decision about whether he wishes to belong instead to his adoptive family, the Mennonite community, and God. Smets understands that Adrian needs information before he can make that commitment. By supporting rather than supplanting the adoptive parents, he joins the family in supporting Adrian's right to make his own decision.

We are especially impressed with Smets's attempt to introduce Adrian to his biological father, after initially focusing on Adrian's yearning to know his mother. We agree that while it is inappropriate for adopted children to reconnect with the biological parents at this age, it is important to validate and support their search for understanding of the past.

Perhaps the most moving part of this case is Adrian's unsuccessful attempt to convert his therapist. Smets both graciously accepted Adrian's gesture and clearly says "no thank you," which allowed Adrian to learn a vital lesson about individuation—one can value another and also value differences. This enables Adrian to shift his focus from Smets's conversion to his own issues, recognizing himself as having value separate from his therapist and both his biological and adoptive family. In order for Adrian to accept his place in his Mennonite family and community, he first has to be given the opportunity to learn more about "the world" and to willingly "get the call" from God. As the old AA phrase puts it, "In order to keep something, you have to give it away." ■

STUDY QUESTIONS

1. What are some of the key differences between doing therapy with the whole family and inviting the family to a session as part of one person's individual therapy?

2. According to Perel, how might family therapy have helped Adrian resolve his anger toward his adoptive father?

3. Do you agree that it is inappropriate for adopted children to reconnect with their biological parents? Why or why not?

4. What does a therapist need to know, or do, when working with clients from different ethnic, cultural, or racial backgrounds? In your opinion, what helped this therapist form a successful, crosscultural therapeutic alliance with Adrian and his family?

CASE STUDY

JOINING THE FAMILY
COUNTERTRANSFERENCE CAN BE THE THERAPIST'S COMPASS

David E. Scharff and Jill Savege Scharff

The Jansen family had been in therapy for almost two years. Mr. and Mrs. Jansen first came to see me because their son, Tom, nine years old, had broken into and electrical store and destroyed quite a lot of equipment. They explained that, although he was basically a good kid, Tom was regularly the butt of teasing at school. At home there was endless fighting with his two older brothers—Tom bullied *them,* even though he was younger.

In the initial family session, Tom erupted at his two brothers and then ran out of the room to the car. Mr. and Mrs. Jansen were unable to persuade him to return. When I met with the parents the following week, Mr. Jansen said ho would not allow Tom's brothers to come to family therapy. He said, "One of our sons has gone to the dogs; we aren't going to let him contaminate the ones who are okay."

Mr. Jansen readily agreed to individual therapy for Tom, but he participated in monthly parent-guidance meetings with his wife on the condition that we only focus on Tom. He warned me that "this is not to be therapy for us!" Since this was the only contract Mr. Jansen would allow, I accepted it with the hope that the Jansens would trust me more over time and together we would eventually expand the work.

Working with the Jansens, I had the uncomfortable sense that certain topics were off limits. Mr. Jansen had a brittle quality that left me apprehensive. He alternated between despair and pride in Tom's aggressiveness and I imagined that if I said the wrong thing he would permanently drop out of therapy.

In individual sessions, Mrs. Jansen told me that she and her husband had sexual problems and fought often, mostly about Tom, sometimes

---

The session reported was conducted by David Scharff, while the commentary was written by both authors.

about the other sons. In sessions together, however, the Jansens never discussed their relationship. The weight of unexpressed feelings in the family sat heavily on me and I regularly found myself not saying the things I felt should be said.

While my feelings toward the Jansens could be understood simply as a natural response to difficult or controlling clients, they also could be used as a means of understanding the family's inner experiences and charting a therapeutic path. Therefore, I saw Mr. Jansen's distrustful, controlling style as representative of a shared family difficulty. He expected anyone in authority, including me, to harm him and his family. Consequently, he had developed an effective way of keeping people he found threatening at arm's length. Although more open on the surface, Mrs. Jansen feared that if I pursued issues too directly with her husband he would leave therapy and not allow the family to get the help she felt they needed. Both husband and wife secretly believed that outsiders would do them harm. And they could not acknowledge their own fear that they themselves had harmed Tom.

I recognized my feelings of discomfort and uncertainty working with the Jansens as my reverberation with their own emotional experience of living in a world in which it was hard to know where to walk without stepping on a land mine. In other words, I had learned how to feel like them. I became sensitive to the fear they all shared of being victimized—a fear lived out in Tom's being picked on at school. Feeling bullied by them in sessions, I eventually understood their fears that I would bully them and that each member of the family would in turn bully the others.

This case illustrates the way countertransference—a therapist's emotional resonance with a family's struggles—can be used to understand the family more deeply. The process starts when the therapist notes the way a family enters the office for the first session and continues throughout therapy. By making sense of his or her own internal experience with families, the therapist is able to achieve an emotional understanding that can invest the therapeutic encounter with deeper relevance.

After several months of therapy, things improved in the Jansen household. Tom was no longer the scapegoat for marital difficulties. We had been able to discuss his self-destructive penchant for diverting attention from the strain in his parents' marriage and the family to himself. (It turned out that the break-in at the electrical shop had occurred when his mother was having gynecological surgery and the marriage was in crisis.)

Unraveling this bit of the family process led us to talk about projective and introjective identifications. Though we do not use such theoretical terms with clients, these ideas organize our own thinking. The term "projective identification" was coined by psychoanalyst Melanie Klein to denote the unconscious process of projecting parts of oneself onto others. These may be hated parts of the self—a sense of badness or weakness—or treasured parts that feel too endangered inside the self to survive. "Introjective identification" is the complementary process, in which a person takes in and identifies with the projections of the other.

In projective identification, the intolerable painful parts of these internal, unconscious relationships are put outside the self and onto another person. For the process to be complete, another person must take on the projected parts, usually without quite knowing it. That is, there will be a complementary introjective identification in another person. In this way, projective and introjective identification become the vehicles for unconscious communication and understanding in all intimate relationships. They also can be vehicles for shared unconscious misunderstanding and for unconsciously collusive pathology.

Thus Mr. Jansen projected his unconscious sense of weakness onto his wife and son Tom. Mrs. Jansen projected her strength and stubbornness onto her husband. And Tom projected his inner goodness and strength onto others, taking in through introjective identification the sense of weakness and badness for the family. This was his unconscious sacrifice, by which he hoped to leave the rest of his family better off. At least, this was my sense of the Jansen family dynamics when Mr. and Mrs. Jansen and Tom entered my office one evening about a year after we had begun weekly family sessions. By then, the two older boys had been attending regularly and the focus had expanded to include the role of all three boys in the family dynamic, but they had just left for a month of summer camp. Mr. Jansen said that all of them, even Tom, were missing the older boys.

"Sure I am," said Tom. "They're my brothers."

"But you used to fight so much!" said Mrs. Jansen.

"Well, we love each other. That's just the way brothers are," said Tom. "But I also like having the house to myself."

I felt this was a sort of interesting byplay, and noted that Tom did indeed seem fonder of his absent brothers than he would have admitted a year earlier. Still, I felt uneasy about the way his parents were getting him to show off his progress.

A moment later, Mr. Jansen announced that they had gotten Tom's excellent school report card. As he said this, Tom began to get silly and noisily blow in the air while turning around in his swivel chair. Both parents got angry at this and told him to stop, but he refused. This was the kind of thing that led to family battles at home.

Finally, Mr. Jansen said, "Tom! No ice cream if you don't stop!"

"That's blackmail!" yelled Tom.

"Sure it is," said his father, "and I mean it!"

Tom continued to spin in his chair and also to pout. He was daring his father, who threatened again, "Tom! I mean it. No ice cream!"

I saw this was a well-practiced routine between them, in which Tom would give in just in time to ge his ice cream. I felt both frustrated for Mr. Jansen that Tom would not stop and annoyed with him for setting up Tom in the first place. I had confused and contradictory feelings about the report on school progress and on Toms' growth: It seemed to me that Mr. Jansen had gotten away with showing off Tom's increased ability to express love for his brothers. Why did he have to rub it in about school? And I thought Tom was embarrassed about doing well at school.

Though I could not quite formulate it then, I later realized that Mr. Jansen's showing off mirrored Tom's way of getting in trouble at school. Tom's obnoxious clowning in the session expressed his own wish to show off his brilliance. He knew better than to do it, but in this instance he was being provoked by his father.

During the session, however, I was unsure of what was happening and felt vaguely uncomfortable. I was uneasy with Mr. Jansen's use of empty threats and was reminded of my annoyance with Mr. Jansen in an earlier session when he had encouraged Tom to slug kids who teased him. Although initially sure that was not a good solution, I had found myself persuaded by Mr. Jansen and Tom that perhaps I was wrong. My own unhappy history of childhood peer relations made this an area where I felt vulnerable myself—and distrustful of my own immediate re-action. So I had ended up slightly confused. Of course, it is not uncom-mon for a therapist to be uncertain, or to need to wait for a while to figure out what is happening. But my confusion was different: It repre-sented the therapist emotionally losing his way inside himself.

From the viewpoint of object-relations family therapy, these are es-pecially valuable moments. In writing about Shakespeare to a friend, the poet John Keats described a quality he called the "negative capabil-ity," the ability to allow meaning to emerge form an experience, rather than imposing ideas before the richness of the experience has blos-somed. Being tolerant of not knowing and confusion allows the thera-peutic to emerge from within, adding a dimension of richness to the encounter. In that session, I knew that my discomfort was a time-tested sign of conflict and confusion in the patients, and that this was the time to explore it. While I was feeling some immediate anger at Mr. Jansen, I had come to like him more and more as therapy progressed. I also no-ticed that Mrs. Jansen was letting the struggle between her husband and her son go on without comment, as she often did. At that moment, I imagined her leaving things to Mr. Jansen but slightly smirking as she did so.

As I thought these things, Mr. Jansen again praised Tom for his report card, I interrupted, hoping to help the family stay with the themes of blackmailing and difficult behavior. I wanted to enlarge their capacity for observation, and help them understand what had led to this mo-ment. I began with a question that might link the events in the therapy hour with Tom's difficulties elsewhere: "Is this exchange in here be-tween Dan and Tom anything like being picked on at school—which Tom really doesn't like Dad or Mom to discuss—but which together you may be recreating in the session?"

Mr. Jansen was thrown off stride by my question. My own discomfort had led me to intervene less smoothly than I would have wished. But Mr. Jansen was not too thrown off to respond. "I blackmail him because I don't know what else to do," he replied. "But I can see that it might re-late to school." He paused, looking down, then he looked at Tom again and said, "Tom, did you know that I used to get in a lot of fights when I was a kid? And I used to lose!" And as he said this, Mr. Jansen's tone softened and he seemed less belligerent, more the loving father. This was a new way for Mr. Jansen to present himself. I felt relief, and hoped that this new opening might signal a breakthrough.

Tom replied, "No. I didn't know that." He stopped swivelling in his chair and looked straight at his father.

Inside, I felt a tectonic plate shift. I realized how much I had felt bullied by Mr. Jansen's rigid stand about who in the family would participate in the therapy. Suddenly I found myself liking Mr. Jansen again. I knew how hard it was for him to let down his guard and felt respect for his newfound courage.

I was also very pleased at the opening Mr. Jansen gave me for using a basic technique of object-relations family therapy—asking a family to share past experiences that resemble current problems. These moments offer more than history; they actually describe the way past relationships determine the present as they are carried alive inside individual family members, greatly influencing current relationships.

I asked Mr. Jansen to elaborate. He did, sheepishly, but willingly: "I was athletic, which helped. But when the older kids would come by, it would always be me they picked on. I couldn't beat them up. It wasn't quite like with Tom. It wasn't the kids my own age who did it, but I did get beat up—often."

I was thinking, still a little angrily, that I understood how he got them to do this so regularly. I imagined him taunting the older boys until they ganged up on him. In having this fantasy, I identified partly with him and partly with the older boys, and I saw it also from the perspective of my own childhood. I felt a surge of sympathy for Mr. Jansen and for the boys.

As I was pondering this, Mrs. Jansen said to her husband, "I wonder if you didn't do something to provoke them?" Picking up on her comment, I added that Mr. Jansen often seemed to want Tom to fight as a solution to being teased. I wondered if his own experience as a child might induce him to encourage Tom's troublemaking, even though he was worried about it.

Mrs. Jansen smiled and said, "Oh, my husband can be provocative himself, you know. Of course, he does it with me, for a start."

Another new direction was opening up. Mrs. Jansen had taken the lead in linking the work so far in the hour to their marriage. In an object-relations approach, as in other schools of family therapy, the dynamics of the entire family are understood to be built on the foundation of the marital relationship. The mutual projective identifications between the parents set the tone for the overall pattern of the family. When a link can be made in therapy between a parent-child object relationship and the parents' relationship, the family's understanding is greatly enhanced. At this point, the Jansens were willing not only to attempt this work, but also to initiate it—a sign of progress after Mr. Jansen's refusal to participate in the early months of our work.

"Can you give me an example of how you feel provoked?" I asked Mrs. Jansen.

She thought for a moment, and said to her husband, "There was the time you were supposed to pick me up and we got our signals crossed."

Mr. Jansen filled in the story: His wife had come home in a blue fury after having to walk home because she had no money with her. When she walked in the door, he knew she was mad.

"Yes," she said, "but instead of even saying you were sorry I had to walk, you accused me of stupidity in not knowing which corner was which, and said it served me right. I overreacted to begin with, but that's not the point right now. You used it to provoke me." She smiled fondly, and finished, "And you know it, Honey!"

"It's true," he said. "I do that to her, and I kind of enjoy it. I shouldn't, but it's true that I do."

Having gotten the fact of provocation within the family onto the table, I felt we could try to link it to Tom. So I turned to him and asked if he knew about this part of his father's life.

"Well, I know he can tease Mommy and me," he said. "But I never knew about the fights with the older kids. That's pretty interesting, Dad."

A barrier had dropped and I now felt emotionally included in the family. We were working together in a new way. I was emboldened to make a new kind of interpretation without expecting the usual family reluctance.

I said, "I wonder, Mr. Jansen, if you think you might want Tom to pick off a few of the tormentors for you, a sort of vicarious victory over the kids who use to beat on you?"

"I never thought of that," he said. "Perhaps so."

Mrs. Jansen now put her arm around her husband's shoulder. She did not rub in that she also often felt picked on and bullied by Mr. Jansen. I sensed that in the future we might be able to talk about the ways people felt picked on in the family as the original version of Tom's being picked on by his peers at school. So I said, "The two issues—feeling picked on at home and at school—are related." Then speaking with the conviction gained from understanding my own feeling of being bullied in this therapeutic session, I added, "Understanding feeling picked on at home ought to help figure out what happens at school."

Tom was interested. At the door he said an unusually cheerful "Good-bye."

In object-relations family therapy, countertransference is used to enhance and guide therapists' understanding, and to inform their interventions, which differ significantly from those of other forms of family therapy. We join the family, allowing their emotional experience to get inside us, and then work with members of the family to understand its meaning. When therapists have been able to make sense of their own countertransference, which is the source of their understanding, they clarify the effect that the family produces. This helps the family interpret its experience.

Interpretation has gotten a bad name in family therapy, largely because it has been understood as an imposed pronouncement that should be taken on faith, and as though the interpretation itself should produce understanding almost in a magical way. The Jansens' example illustrates the way interpretation, whether by the therapist or by a family member, is a building block in the joint construction of family reality. Interpretation is not a pronouncement from above, but shared information, to be tested, modified, and slowly accepted or discarded in favor of other ways of looking at the problems. In this sense, interpretation is not an end product but a catalyst for shared understanding of how difficulties arise and may be resolved.

What about the value of understanding itself? For family therapists who use object relations, understanding is a crucial word. We mean by it a cooperative attitude of thinking in response to feelings. Understanding stems from family members' appreciating one another's needs, much as a courting couple or a mother and baby do. In object-relations family therapy, the therapist joins with the family using a shared understanding of the experience to guide the therapy. In other words, countertransference is used to enhance and shape therapists' understanding, and inform their interventions. It is the guide the therapist uses to join the family in the work of restoring them to emotional flexibility and growth.

REFERENCES

Fairbain, W.R.D. (1952). *Psychoanalytic studies of the personality.* London: Tavistock.

Klein, M. (1946). Notes on some schizoid mechanisms. *International Journal of Psychoanalysis, 27,*(3) 99–110. And in *Envy and gratitude and other works, 1946–1963.* London: The Hogarth Press and The Institute of Psycho-Analysis. U.S.A.: Delacorte Press (1975).

Murray, J.M. (1955). *Keats.* New York: Noonday Press.

Scharff, D.E., & Scharff, J.S. (1987). *Object relations family therapy.* Northvale, NJ: Jason Aronson.

Scharff, D.E., & Scharff, J.S. (1991). *Object relations couple therapy.* Northvale, NJ: Jason Aronson.

Scharff, J.S. (Ed.) (1989). *Foundations of object relations family therapy.* Northvale, NJ: Jason Aronson.

Segal, H. (1973). *Introduction to the work of Melanie Klein.* New, enlarged edition. London: The Hogarth Press.

CASE COMMENTARY 1
BY JEROME PRICE

This case demonstrates how a therapist's subjective reactions dramatically affect the therapy he or she does. It also shows how a clinician's theoretical assumptions influence the length and expense of therapy as well as determining whether it will normalize or pathologize clients.

The approach in this case was structured by the therapist's assumption that the treatment would be "a gradual unfolding." The therapist's object-relations orientation led him to contemplate for several months what he learned about the Jansen family in the first few sessions. He retreated into individual therapy with an adolescent rather than immediately try to make use of this information to bring about family change more quickly. I am still not sure whether this retreat into individual therapy resulted from a theoretical orientation that made the therapist more comfortable seeing individuals than families, or from his induction into the family myth that bullies have to avoided and therefore he must walk on eggshells around the family bully, Mr. Jansen.

As a strategic therapist, I wondered why it took so long for the therapist in this case to make clinical use of his sense of being bullied by Mr. Jansen. Addressing this would have made the individual insight unnecessary. The therapist was concerned that alienating the father might have caused him to pull the family out of treatment. But, had he used this knowledge actively rather than reactively he might have instead identified Mr. Jansen as the family expert who knew a great deal about dealing with bullies and enlisted his help as the one person who could solve his son's problem.

After months of therapy, "the Jansens were feeling better" and "Tom was no longer the scapegoat for marital difficulties," by the therapist's report. Even if we were to assume that the therapy was completed at this point, "several months" was a very long time to spend addressing this concern. Whatever one's attitude toward the use of individual therapy in a case such as this, it is hard to argue with reported change. Nevertheless, the authors seem to think that nothing important happened during these months since they neglect to describe what the therapist did to being about what appears to be a complete cure.

Then came the pivotal session in which Tom's report card was discussed. Rather than seeing this incident as a turning point, I thought of it as the kind of relapse families sometimes use in order to prolong their relationship with a therapist on whom they've come to depend. true to their object-relations orientation, however, the authors saw the relapse as proof that the "deeper issues" still needed resolving. Assuming that the parents were happy with the progress, I would probably have tried to disengage at that point while supporting the family's ability to handle their problems on their own. Where the authors saw the remaining therapy as providing important insights, I saw the report-card session as an example of humiliating parents in front of their children and as undoing of what had apparently been accomplished earlier in the treatment.

This case demonstrates the work of an obviously accomplished object-relations therapist. While I admired the therapist's skill and patience, I was left wondering why a problem that hardly seemed very serious required more than two years of treatment. I was left with a clear sense that the case's "gradual unfolding" was not necessary, but was a manifestation of the therapist's assumptions and was of questionable value, especially when it results in therapy being prolonged at the clients' expense.

CASE COMMENTARY 2
BY ALAN S. GURMAN

There are few references to the "C" word in the family therapy literature. Most family therapists seem to believe that countertransference is a phenomenon confined to the intense, one-on-one relationship of individual therapy and does not occur when the therapist is more a consultant to the entire family than the focal point of clients' emotionality. Nevertheless, acute countertransference (the kind that occurs in limited situations, not across the board, and over and over again) is just what family therapists are referring to when they talk about "the use of self in therapy," "induction," and the "blurring of boundaries" in treatment. When a therapist brings up a taboo subject with a couple, and their anxiety spills over onto him, making him blindly move on to some other topic, this is a clear example of countertransference. In this case, Mr. Jansen tries to steer the therapist away from his own vulnerability by initially decreeing who would be seen in therapy, how often they would attend, and what would be discussed. The therapist is put in the position of either challenging him or losing what master therapist Carl Whitaker calls the initial "battle for structure." Here, out of fear that the family would drop out of therapy, the therapist allows the family to set the early structure of their therapy by going along with Mr. Jansen's demands. Fortunately, his respectful and sensitive approach allows Mr. Jansen eventually to reveal his vulnerable side and breaks through the family's collective defenses.

What if Scharff had been working within the constraints of an HMO, with more limited clinical services available? Might the Jansens have been helped in, say, 12 or 15 sessions? Consider the following alternative approach to how early awareness of countertransference collusion might have affected the choice of interventions in brief family therapy. First, the therapist might have used his own discomfort with the Jansens as a clue to their mistrust of outsiders and he might have recognized the need to empower them in a concrete way, like coaching the parents in using behavior management techniques with Tom. By beginning with the focus they requested— strictly on Tom—the therapist might have quickly facilitated their trust in him.

Another possibility would have been, earlier on in the therapy, challenging Mr. Jansen's projection of his wishes and fears surrounding aggression. While some therapists believe that early interpretation will result in early dropout (as the Scharffs believed), the actual result depends on the strength of the therapeutic alliance. While it does take a year or more to develop such an alliance with some families, this is the exception rather than the rule.

Here, the therapist was obviously on target about the family's fears of being "bullied." The Jansens might well have fought an attempt at behavioral coaching, a call for more frequent sessions or an earlier interpretation of projective family processes, regarding such interventions as his attempts to bully them. Such direct interventions, in fact, often do lead to intense transference reactions, but these are to be welcomed, not feared, for they quickly bring to the surface client families' fundamental dynamics. In fact, once they are brought to the surface, these dynamics are far easier to deal with than when they are played out indirectly and the therapy focus shifts from the therapist's countertransference to what makes symptoms persist in a family and what keeps its members disconnected from one another.

AUTHORS' RESPONSE
BY DAVID E. SCHARFF AND JILL SAVEGE SCHARFF

Unlike strategic family therapists, object-relations family therapists do not expect swift resolution of presenting symptoms and a speedy exit from therapy. Instead, we are creating an emotional environment where deeper anxieties—including the therapist's resonating anxieties—can surface and be understood. The therapist's unrecognized anxieties often lead to what could be called mistakes in technique, but when we work with the discomfort, it can open us up to profound insights about the family. In our view, paying attention to countertransference reactions during a session, and then reviewing them alone or with colleagues, broadens the clinician's range of therapeutic responses.

In the Jansen case, another therapist either might not have been vulnerable to being bullied or, if bullied, might have reacted with a bullying prescription, a premature interpretation or a rapid retreat. Of course, the Jansens could have been helped in fewer sessions, but the same degree of working through could not have been achieved. It is a fact of life for those of us working in managed-care situations that the task is to offer as much help as possible in the shortest amount of time. But we would prefer to admit the limits of the available service rather than delude ourselves, the families, and their health-care planners into thinking that the minimum is all that is necessary simply because it is all that we are authorized to provide.

Family therapists share a common goal in seeking to improve technique so that more families can be helped more economically. A few sessions can be effective in crises and for families with short-term goals. But some families, recognizing that their presenting symptom is part of a broader dysfunction, choose to make it a financial priority to work for more fundamental change in the family system and in their internal object relations. These are the families who move from short-term, focused methods to in-depth family therapy. The Jansens moved from infrequent behavioral management coaching for the parents and individual sessions for the child to fully committed family therapy. ∎

STUDY QUESTIONS

1. Do you agree with the therapist that countertransference can enable the therapist to achieve an emotional understanding of his or her clients? Why or why not?

2. Why do object-relations therapists believe that the therapist's becoming emotionally lost during therapy is a valuable moment?

3. Given Price and Gurman's responses, how do you think the therapist's theoretical orientation impacted on his interpretation and treatment of the presenting problem? Do you agree with the commentators that the therapy could have been briefer and just as effective?

CASE STUDY

NUNNA YER BEESWAX
NO-TALK THERAPY WITH ADOLESCENTS

Martha B. Straus

Any therapist who has ever tried to engage an anxious, sullen, or confused adolescent who refuses to talk knows the meaning of frustration and futility. When the old standards of "joining" with clients—active listening, supportive reframing, miracle questions—provoke little more than furious silence, toneless monosyllables, or dripping contempt, therapists need an entirely new clinical language that doesn't depend on words. If teenagers won't talk in family therapy or refuse to have therapy with their parents present, we need to find other ways to make systemic changes.

No-talk therapy, which emphasizes individual connection, competence, and creativity, goes beyond traditional approaches. It works when we give up on our obsessive need to dwell on problems and find, instead, something to cheer about.

There are times when not talking is the only form of communication available to an adolescent. The silence can have so many sources—lack of skill, boredom, powerlessness, feeling trapped, alienation, shyness, control issues, even terror. These are all potent reasons not to talk. The seemingly barren therapy hours that follow can cause even the most seasoned therapist to feel like a first-year grad student. And, as our anxiety increases, so does the possibility for a head-on struggle in the therapy room. This kink of confrontation is even more likely in family therapy, as we juggle alliances between parents and kids. Before we know it, we've become another threatening, cajoling, nagging, and pleading control agent in a teenager's life. Teenagers rarely resort to silence as a first option. By the time they refuse to talk to therapists, adolescents usually have many other people in their lives reminding them of their ineptitude. Their wordless tenacity as parents, teachers, doctors, and therapists command them to speak merits both empathy and respect. After a while, silent kids can usually learn to tolerate family therapy and more active

121

problem solving, but first they need something to be proud of and someone to whom to feel close.

Eliza Bennet is a fierce and wary 15-year-old girl with long, dusty dreadlocks, a pierced eyebrow, and an attitude. Following a Tylenol overdose, she had been admitted to the mental health unit at the local hospital. Her 10 days there had been remarkably disruptive and unproductive. She had, by all accounts, turned the place upside down, staging sit-ins at the nurse's station for more cigarette breaks and refusing to attend family meetings. Staff had to lock the unit after learning she had been organizing an escape of her fellow patients. She would not speak to adults about how she was feeling, but filled notebooks with raging diatribes about the assault on her dignity there. The referring social worker told me that Eliza had finally signed a contract that included participating in outpatient treatment and taking antidepressants. However, she had added a couple of conditions of her own: She would not "do" family therapy and she had to regain all the freedoms she had lost before the suicide attempt. But, with her insurance used up, there had been little time for prolonged negotiations.

I agreed to treat Eliza, although I insisted on beginning with the whole family; if Eliza did not want to talk while we discussed their concerns, that would be okay with me. I needed to hear what her parents had to say and wanted to see how she acted with them. Even if I ultimately decided to do mostly individual therapy with Eliza, I still wanted to establish a precedent for parent or family sessions early on, remaining flexible as the work progressed. My first assumption about Eliza was that her terms for therapy—not talking, not wanting her parents present—were a last-ditch effort to preserve self-esteem. She knew that the focus would be on her failures—she was smart to want to avoid that discussion.

Eliza came with her parents to our first meeting. When I went out to meet her, she was sprawled on a couch in the waiting room looking at *People Weekly* while her parents and other patients were squashed together in the remaining chairs. When I introduced myself, she glanced at me briefly from under piles of hair, her hazel eyes disarmingly intense. She then returned to her magazine. Eliza's father told her firmly to get up. I offered her a cup of coffee or tea. She poured herself some coffee, dumping six teaspoons of sugar into it while her mother silently grimaced, and sauntered down the hall into my room. Knees tucked under her chin, Eliza glowered at the floor as we discussed her parents' concerns, the hospitalization and Eliza's development over the years. True to her promise, she did not speak.

The Bennets shared a familiar litany of disappointment that typically precedes this level of alienation—poor grades, acrimonious family relationships, probable drug involvement, marginal friends, few outside interests. The family had moved to town, against Eliza's wishes, the previous fall, and her adjustment to the new life had been poor. She once had been a helpful oldest sibling, a good student, and a nice kid, but had spent the year floundering. Her parents at first had been sympathetic to the difficulty of changing schools during her sophomore year. Gradually, though, they became less willing to indulge Eliza's griping and began to clamp down on her. Three younger siblings were all doing well. Her suicide attempt had followed being grounded for a failing report card. Starting off with all of this anger and pain can reinforce a teenager's determination not to talk. In hindsight, I might have done better to have the family meeting later, or just held the first session without Eliza.

I asked Eliza's parents to leave and spent the remainder of the time with her alone. Concerned that she now thought I was "out to get her" like everyone else, I began by asking, "Why do you think I asked your parents for all that information?" she shrugged and replied, "I have no idea." Like most furious teenagers, Eliza operated under the assumption that, as a group, adults act in cruel and senseless ways. The past six months of Eliza's life had led her to feel she had no say over things that mattered to her; the hospital had left her feeling even more powerless, despite her wild protests. Given this recent history, my first priority was to set the record straight—I was different. I told her I believed I could help her and that, while I admired her spirit, I thought we needed to work a bit on her style. This was *her* therapy and I was not going to take ownership for what happened here—together we needed to come up with a plan. I also said that I hoped we could have fun and that I wanted to get to know her. I then sat back, telling myself to keep breathing.

After several geological epochs passed, Eliza sighed, wearily, "It's all so pointless." She stared at the clock and wedged her coffee cup between two puppets so it looked as if they were sharing it.

"That's completely true, and you can still have some fun in the next 70 years," I replied, unwilling to be diverted from a more positive opening chord. "What do you like doing?"

Eliza looked at met for perhaps the third time since we met and said she wanted to be lead singer in a band someday, even though she knew it wouldn't happen. I wondered out loud why she wasn't starting her own group right now; she had free time and friends who also played guitar. Eliza picked at her sneaker and said softly, "Maybe I will." A few minutes later, she walked out without saying good-bye or indicating whether she would return the following week.

In no-talk therapy, there is, of course, some dialogue, if only now and then. The conversation seldom, however, concerns problems and their solutions. When kids don't want to talk, they are typically both bored and degraded by the discussion of their problems. Rather, we talk about, and do, things that build a sense of competence, comfort in the therapy room, and control over their own behavior. In that first session, my primary aim was to find out about one thing Eliza enjoyed and felt good about, and get her to do more of it. I did not ask about her depression, her family problems, or her hatred of school.

This is not flashy work. Change in no-talk therapy is usually incremental; no presto, change-o here. It is, more than most therapies, about unseen and unspoken connections. A few weeks into the treatment, the relationship feels stronger. The adolescent who has kept tenuous control by remaining mute may at least be playing five-card stud or sharing a bowl of popcorn. She may even start talking. With the basic needs for competence and connection in place, change can follow quite steadily. In this therapy, kids are involved in finding out about those aspects of their lives they can control and the contributions they can make.

The next week, Eliza brought a *People* magazine into my office and asked if she could copy an article about a musician she particularly liked. I followed up with a couple of questions about the music, which she answered briefly, but without much irritation. Encouraged, I asked her to being in a tape of the group so I could hear it. She did not respond. We then launched into silence. The no-talk dance is a two-step, with the adolescent always leading. In this, we are both clumsy; we approach and retreat not knowing where our feet are all the time.

A few minutes later, Eliza, glancing around the room, noticed her coffee cup still sitting on the puppet shelf. "Hey, is that mine?"

I was embarrassed at the obvious chaos of my life. "Yes, I suppose it is. I guess I didn't do such a good job cleaning my room."

Eliza seemed delighted for the first time. "Cool," she said, looking right at me. She gulped down her current coffee, then put the second cup inside the first. The seedling of a relationship began to grow at that moment. We fell silent again for several minutes, but this time something new was in the air. I couldn't have planned this intervention, but had the sense to appreciate it. Each week for the next few months, the stack of cups grew alongside us.

Part of the early work with teenagers is aimed at making a connection at a safe developmental point—perhaps before life gets so difficult. I willingly support regression; if kids don't talk, they still can play. When I pulled out a deck of cards the next week, Eliza looked at me, surprised. I shuffled for a few minutes, engaging her slyly in a conversation about games she liked "as a kid." We played cards in companionable silence for the next three weeks. She taught me several new card games, patiently going over the rules as necessary. I continued to avoid questions about her life outside the room. I did ask, during the early weeks, about suicidality, as I informed her I had to as part of my job. Her responses were monosyllabic, but reassuring. In no-talk therapy, teenagers may be able to tolerate an occasional foray into more typical inquiry, especially if it is brief.

From time to time, I also sent Eliza silly greeting cards in the mail to let her know I was thinking about her when she wasn't with me. I have found that this small effort has tremendous significance to teenagers. One of the challenges of no-talk therapy is finding other ways to communicate. Writing notes works on many levels here, including providing constancy to someone whose world is in flux. I also encouraged Eliza to keep writing in her journal, and offered to write her back if she wanted to keep one to share with me. Other no-talk kids have written with me this way, and, at the very least, my offer told Eliza I was interested in what she had to say. Toward the end of treatment, she brought in some songs she had written, though she never took me up on my offer to read other writing.

At the end of the month, Eliza came in and announced she had signed up, along with four friends, to perform in the high school talent show, and she was going to be the lead singer. She excitedly described in great detail what she planned to wear. For a new kid in the school, and one very much on the social fringe, this was a huge and daring step. I was, naturally, very enthusiastic, though, looking back, I may have been expecting changes too quickly. Teenagers who have made such a huge mess of things seldom just snap out of it.

Eliza's mother called a few days later and asked if she could attend a session to discuss the problems Eliza was still having at school and at home. She had been suspended for smoking in the parking lot during class time and had stayed out all night drinking at a friend's house with several boys, some of whom had dropped out of school. Her grades were improving and she seemed much less depressed, but she was still making some bad choices. I agreed that we needed to meet, but this time I wanted to strategize with Eliza to see how to make it helpful to her.

"Your mom called. She wants to come in," I opened the next session. "What should we do?" Eliza was not surprised; her mother had told her this already.

"I'm not coming."

Here we go again, I thought, quickly running through how I felt about all of this, I could simply meet with her mother, but the prospect of discussing Eliza behind her back felt all wrong. If our goal was getting her more in control of her life, she'd have to be a part of this. On the other hand, if I aligned myself with her mother too much, I would lose the fragile connection I had worked so diligently to achieve.

"I want to hear about how you see all of this, but I hope you can also brainstorm with me about how we'll handle it," I said, making an effort to get on the same team.

She slowly responded, "I already got grounded for staying out. I don't see the need to talk about this anymore. She wouldn't have let me go if I had told her about it, so, of course, I lied. What would you have done?" Eliza was mad, but she was telling me about it. I let the silence simmer a minute. I was thinking to myself, "Spending the night with drunken, drop-out boys, are you nuts!?" But I spoke cautiously. We'd been playing a lot of blackjack, so I described what I knew about her gambling style: "You've had a few good hands, now. You're feeling better and doing better. People start expecting you to play for higher stakes when you're doing well. But, sometimes you gamble way too much and lose most of your savings, you know?" Staying in the playful language enabled us to talk more safely. I let the image sit there, afraid, really, to say more. If I kept at it, we would have entered lecture mode before long. I'd be dishing out gratuitous advice like that Kenny Rogers song about knowing when to hold 'em and fold 'em, and Eliza would probably be entering her no-talk zone.

"I could still get a better hand, you know. You saw me do it." Eliza was in the conversation. We still hadn't resolved anything, but I was determined not to push her any further. Nonchalantly, I grabbed the deck of cards and started shuffling. I was ready to stop the discussion if she needed to back of here. She made no gesture toward the poker chips and did not seem to want to play. I kept shuffling. She scowled. Minutes passed. I put down the cards and breathed on.

"So," I finally ventured, "she'll come next time. And . . . ."

"I am doing better." Eliza looked tearful. I hadn't seen that face before.

"Okay, that's right. I can tell her that. But how else will you get more chips? If you come, you can say this, too. Otherwise, we'll be deciding it for you." Again, I resisted the urge to solve this for Eliza. We were, briefly, into problem talk, and I didn't want the discussion to replicate her past experiences.

"She treats me like the little kids, It is ridiculous to expect a 15-year-old to be home by 11:00 on the weekend. I'll just stay at Sarah's when I want to go out late; her parents don't care when she comes in." Eliza stared at me, challenging me. I decided to summarize what I thought we were saying. We expect bright and oppositional young adolescents to have abstract reasoning abilities and logical thoughts, but in my experience, they seldom do. Notably, refusing to talk does little for the development of negotiation skills. I saw little percentage in discussing curfews at this pint. Eliza lacked the skills and confidence to advocate thoughtfully for herself; it would be an ugly scene. And, without a working relationship, I was in no position to impart negotiation techniques to her. So, I kept to a plan that incorporated no new issues and had a straightforward strategy.

"Okay, how about this, then? Your mom will talk about the stuff you've been doing. I'll say I can see why she'd be worried, since I'm a mother, too. It's in our job descriptions and we're supposed to fret. If you come, you could then say that you have been doing better. I'll completely underscore this. Since I'm such a big fan of yours, this will be easy for me to do. I'm going to ask her to describe some of the changes she's seen. Do you think she's so mad at you she won't be able to do that?"

Eliza shook her head. "She liked my progress reports and she picked me up at rehearsal, so she'd better say that I'm doing more things. And, the contract—I'm coming here and taking my happy pills."

"Money in the bank. Are you in agreement?" Eliza shrugged, but seemed to concede she could handle it. I said, "I think you're brave to do this. I know how you feel about family meetings."

The following session went according to our strategy. Mrs. Bennet was able to quite enthusiastic about Eliza, after confirming that I knew about what had been happening. Eliza knew I was going to be sympathetic to her mother, so didn't have to worry about my taking her mother's side. While not talkative, Eliza dutifully mumbled out her part about trying harder. I reiterated my sense of her efforts and told Mrs. Bennet she had a great kid. Clearly more worried than angry, Mrs. Bennet even bought Eliza's proposal to stay at a friend's house that weekend when the grounding ended.

After this session, our individual therapy resumed, though not exactly as before. Eliza was more willing to talk, particularly after the successful talent-show performance. We still played cards and drew pictures, but these were background activities to our talks. By the ninth session, three months into our work, we were able to begin to have some of the problem-solving and planning discussions that characterize more traditional therapy with adolescents. A family session with both parents was also quite up-beat. They had visited relatives over spring vacation, and Eliza had been for former, helpful self. She exhibited greater confidence, her grades were improving, and she was staying out of major trouble at home (though mostly by being smart enough not to get caught). When, a few weeks later (and under pressure from managed care), I suggested we take a break from therapy, Eliza agreed that she was ready. I asked her what I should do with the 12 cups stacked neatly on the shelf. She said, "Keep them here. Put flowers in them." She then looked straight at me and smiled.

CASE COMMENTARY
BY RON TAFFEL

All treatment with teens should go this beautifully. Straus's no-talk therapy skillfully combines a group of classic family therapy techniques—joining, reframing, structural reorganization, emphasis on competence, and connection. Several aspects of her handling of the case stood out for me as representing the best of family therapy's clinical tradition:

Starting the Relationship: At the beginning of treatment with untalkative teens, it is particularly important not to undermine the potential for connection by dwelling on problems. Family therapy has always emphasized what clients *can* do rather than focusing on what they can't do well. True to this tradition, Straus refused to pathologize and instead gave Eliza "something to feel proud of and someone to feel close to." The well-chosen words Straus used reflect the great works of Cloe Madanes, Mara Selvini Palazzoli, and Michael White: she strategically put Eliza in charge of the therapy, paradoxically prescribed the presenting problem by telling Eliza it was fine not to talk, and deftly reframed the focus of treatment from Eliza's "irresponsibility" into helping her with her "style."

Finding a Common Language: Once the basis for a relationship was established, Straus needed to create a mode of communication that would not itself become a power struggle. She turned to an approach we family therapists tend to keep at the bottom of our therapeutic bag of tricks—avoiding the distractions of language, Straus played cards, shared popcorn, discussed music, and encouraged journal writing. Developing a "space for play," as child analyst D.W. Winnicott put it, is helpful to kids of all ages.

The Transformative Moment: With the structure of a good relationship in place, only one or more therapy ingredient was necessary. Straus had to show Eliza, as psychiatrist Harry Stack Sullivan once said, "that we are all simply more human than otherwise." Untalkative patients feel so belittled and compromised that such a discovery immediately levels the psychological playing field. Family therapists Nathan Ackerman and Carl Whitaker were pioneers in the art of transforming treatment into an unpredictable exchange between imperfect beings. Straus joined this notable group of joiners with her wonderful self-revelation: "I didn't do such a good job cleaning my room." Eliza must have thought, "Ah, a nonhypocritical adult, a fellow traveler willing to admit that not everything about her is always right."

Metaphor and a New Narrative: Triggered by Eliza's acting out, Straus considered holding a family session. To handle Eliza's discomfort, Straus dipped into the creative soul of family therapy: metaphor. Appealing to her client's scoundrel self, she deftly chose the image of playing poker. Once drawn into this imagery, Eliza agreed to the family meeting. Straus artfully sided with the mother, strengthening and humanizing the parental subsystem. Salvador Minuchin or Jay Hale could not have done it better. Eliza now feels safe enough to continue reworking her life narrative from troubled revolutionary to a savvy poker player who is much more effectively involved in the game of school and remains the good-enough daughter.

Even reticent adolescents inadvertently reveal much about unspoken family legacies through their behavior. In the same vein, the techniques Straus used without a lot of fanfare wonderfully display our most treasured clinical heirlooms: tried-and-true interventions handed down by generations of therapists. This is an excellent teaching case precisely because it demonstrates how certain classic interventions and family therapy skills can still be used to connect with postmodern clients. ■

STUDY QUESTIONS

1. Why do you think avoiding talk about Eliza's problems was helpful?

2. How did the therapist address Eliza's problems without demanding conversation?

3. What are some of the reasons adolescents don't want to talk in therapy?

4. In what ways did the therapist avoid being patronizing to Eliza? In what ways did the therapist address her client's age-related cognitive abilities?

5. What is a therapist's ethical responsibility when dealing with a client who has recently attempted suicide? How did the therapist address the client's safety?

CHAPTER 3

Psychotherapy and Modern Life

Hᴀᴅ ᴀ therapist in the late 1970s been able to time travel two decades into the future to a session in today's therapy office, he or she might scarcely recognize some of the therapeutic territory. Traditional graduate school curricula did not prepare us for dealing with the emotionally charged issues of cultural diversity, sexual orientation, memories of child abuse, and AIDS, so we had to find our way and develop new approaches to previously unacknowledged problems. And as the field responded to demands of subcultures once excluded from mainstream society, our responses sometimes created their own raging controversies. At the very least, therapy in the 1990s has not been stagnant.

The following cases demonstrate therapists at work in the trenches working with growing sensitivity to issues new to our awareness. In "No Time to Waste," therapists debate how to help a woman whose cultural beliefs put her health at odds with her traditional role as wife and mother, and face the question of what to do when therapy does not fit the client's value system. "Quandaries of a Heterosexual Therapist" exemplifies need for heightened sensitivity and knowledge of therapists who work with issues of sexual orientation. Therapy in the 1990s has not only changed by including previously ignored subcultures; "Lost in America" illustrates that even therapy with a seemingly ordinary middle-class family is more complex and nuanced than ever. In it, therapists Judith Friedman and Ella Lasky help a multiproblem family move through the emotional minefield of the stigma of AIDS, marital difficulties, and school problems. The last two cases, "Avoiding the Truth Trap" and "Resolving the Irresolvable" turn the spotlight on the huge controversy about recovered memories that has focused attention on some of the excesses in the world of therapy itself. What started out as a debate among a few specialists in the field has exploded into a national controversy over the validity of repressed memories, the responsibility of therapists, and the real impact of child abuse.

CONSULTATION CORNER

NO TIME TO WASTE

When Culture and Medical Needs Conflict

EDITED BY H. CHARLES FISHMAN

Therapists today are becoming increasingly aware of the issues that arise when they see clients from cultural backgrounds very different from their own. For most of us, it has become impossible to escape the realization that many of our traditional theories and techniques are ethnocentric and not universally applicable. At the same time, many clinicians have also been busy adapting their methods to work within the medical system, exploring the interface between family dynamics and physical illness. What does traditional family therapy look like when cultural and medical issues intersect? The following case, in which a family's cultural values seem to put a member's health at risk, raises some challenging questions about our role and responsibilities in such cases.

H.C.F.

Sira is a 43-year-old housewife who was referred to me by her physician because of hypertension that could not be controlled through medication and exercise. Her doctor thought that she was under considerable stress and suggested that psychotherapy might be useful in lowering her blood pressure, since nothing more could be done medically.

Sira emigrated from India 15 years ago with her husband and two children, now ages 8 and 11. Her husband is an engineer and has an important position at a local high-tech company. Sira and her husband had an arranged marriage and met only a few months prior to their wedding.

In the initial interview, Sira wore traditional Indian dress. She was moderately overweight and visibly stressed and sweating, although it was cool in the room. Tense and tearful, she said she felt that she was suffocating at home.

(Continued)

133

(Continued)

"My husband and kids treat me with disrespect," she said. "I am required to do all the housework. I am also totally responsible for raising the kids. My husband is home very little. And the kids, as they are getting older, are more and more disrespectful. My husband thinks they are right—I am not a very tidy homemaker. I would rather read."

When asked why she does not challenge her husband, Sira stated, "I want to be a good, traditional wife. I feel guilty if I disrespect my husband. I am afraid of him. And I have nowhere to go—no money, no friends, and I do not want to leave my children."

At the end of the session, I asked Sira if she could bring her husband and children, if possible, to the next session. She responded by becoming anxious and saying, "A woman does not do such a thing." Nevertheless, Sira called after the session to give me an update on how she was feeling, and agreed to try to bring her husband to an appointment. However, when she appeared for the next session, she informed me that her husband had refused to come.

What do I do next? How do I respect Sira's cultural values while recognizing that her medical condition is dangerous and there is no time to waste? Can I respect her cultural values while also challenging them? If I cannot involve the family, how should we proceed?

COMMENTARY 1

BY SUSAN H. MCDANIEL

Sira's initial appointment revealed a stressed and unhappy woman caught in cultural transition, but I would begin by concentrating on the hypertension since it was the initial referral concern and the involvement of a physician may be less threatening and more acceptable than a therapist to Sira's husband. In addition, Sira's physical health is likely a problem that the whole family is concerned about and wants to change, and Sira, herself, may tend to somatize about her emotional problems because she feels it is unacceptable (or disrespectful) to complain directly.

To establish a more collaborative relationship with the physician, I would ask him or her for more information about Sira's hypertension. The medical literature suggests that the vast majority of cases of poorly controlled hypertension are the result of noncompliance with medication. Since it seems likely that Sira is not exercising or eating a low-salt diet, her problems with her family may be manifesting themselves in her not taking proper care of herself. Even if she is one of those rare patients who is taking antihypertensive medication but not responding to it, I would want to make sure that her depression is not partially a side effect of the medication. I would suggest a joint session at the physician's office with the physician, Sira, her husband, and myself to discuss Sira's medical condition. I would ask the physician to invite Sira's husband and I would define my role as being a consultant on the impact of the health problem on the family.

I remember vividly a home visit I did with a resident physician several years ago for a 35-year-old woman with out-of-control hypertension who had emigrated with her family a year before from Puerto Rico. The physician was convinced she was taking her medication, yet her blood-pressure readings were dangerously high. After her large family piled into the small living room to meet with the doctors, and the physician stated his concern about her hypertension, the patient's sister said, "She tells you she's taking those pills? She hardly ever takes those pills!" Further conversation made it clear that this noncompliance was an act of protest about her role in the family—she had no other permissible avenues to complain. Once she was able to express herself more directly, she allowed the family to help her with the medication and her hypertension quickly came under control. I would want to rule out a similar hypothesis in Sira's case.

I would also raise the issue of the stress in Sira's life, although how much was discussed directly would depend on the receptivity of Sira and her husband. Sometimes I will focus entirely on the somatic aspects of a complex problem for several sessions to allow a suspicious partner like Sira's husband to gain trust in me and in the therapy process. Initially, I might ask how Sira's problem would be treated in India, and whether there are any traditional Indian methods (like yoga or meditation) that might be useful relaxation techniques for Sira.

As a good treatment alliance developed, I'd explore with Sira and her husband what each saw as the stressors at home. For example, could the couple agree that the children are at times "disrespectful" to each of them? If so, the problem of respect might be a way to help this family deal with the difficulties of cultural transition. I would then try to help them find some common ground for dealing with their children.

I might use a family session to focus on the impact of Sira's illness on the children. A discussion of the role of stress could lead into the conflicts about respect at home and the cultural transition issues. I might ask the couple to describe what is expected from children— as well as mothers and fathers—by their families in India. They could list the Indian values and rituals they want to pass on to their children, and eventually discuss what they wish to incorporate from their new culture as they develop their own unique blend of old and new. Hopefully, Sira's husband would be drawn into a more active parenting role through these discussions.

Having collaborated on the medical problem and on the problems with the children, the couple may evolve a new and more healthy relationship with each other. If not, or if Sira's depressive symptoms continued, I might ask the couple to address the issue of respect in their marriage and how it was influenced by Indian and American culture. Questions might include: What is respect in an Indian marriage? How are husbands respected? How are wives? What do they wish to incorporate from the United States? What kind of marriage do they want to have? How does Sira want to define herself as a woman? What kind of wife does her husband want? This approach would elicit any remaining marital problems, test out possible changes, and allow Sira and her husband to decide what they are willing to live with and what is unacceptable.

Throughout, I would collaborate with Sira's physician and monitor Sira's hypertension to see if emotional improvements have any effect on her blood pressure. As a medical family therapist, I would continually try to understand and address the interaction between the biological, psychological, and social aspects of Sira's case.

COMMENTARY 2

BY ELIANA GIL AND KIRAN STAROSTA

While many believe that it is best to match clients with mental health professionals of the same cultural background, this is not always possible or realistic. Furthermore, even when two individuals share a culture, there is no absolute guarantee of mutual understanding and respect. I remember my first meeting with clients from my home country of Ecuador and their mistrust and concern about my ability to respect them and understand them because of the class differences between us. Their family came from extreme poverty, mine from privilege and financial comfort. I remember struggling with how little we had in common—we didn't even know the same parts of the city in which we had both lived. I was never allowed to visit their neighborhood, and they were not welcome in mine.

Early on, I purposely made grammatical errors and asked them to tell me how to say a word in Spanish, so they felt like they were capable of helping me and knew things I did not. Eventually they learned to trust me, although they often remarked that I was more American than Latin (I had lived in the United States since I was 15). However, they were very grateful when I canceled an October appointment in commemoration of Ecuadorian independence. "We thought you might remember," they noted, with apparent camaraderie.

When I receive a referral of an individual from another culture, I first try to get as much concrete information as possible about the culture's gender roles, family structures, childrearing practices, extended family involvements, and other relevant information. I also like to contact a mental health professional from within that culture to get an insider's perspective on the client's presenting problem and how to best approach the family.

After I read the consultation question regarding Sira, I contacted Kiran Starosta, an Indian colleague I had met through my association with the Multicultural Clinical Center in Springfield, Virginia. Had I not been able to find a professional with whom to consult, I would have visited a library or sought out professional articles. I might also have asked the family to tell me as much about their culture as they could, although I believe clinicians should first take the responsibility of doing their own research.

Kiran noted that therapy for Indians is a foreign concept that is seen as a last resort. It is more likely that Indians under stress will seek medical consultation, and one of the best ways to ensure they will follow through with psychological treatment is if the referral is made by a physician. Kiran pointed out that it is highly unlikely that an Indian husband would agree to attend therapy—traditionally, emotional problems are addressed only within the family system. Consequently, Kiran believed that asking Sira to bring her husband to therapy, particularly so early in the treatment, would be a mistake, since her failure to get her husband to participate would be yet more evidence that she is helpless and ineffectual.

A better approach would be to assume the father's nonparticipation initially and focus on strengthening Sira's sense of power within her family. The first step would be helping her to begin to construct a social and family situation more to her liking, perhaps delegating more of the housework to her children and using her time more constructively. Sira currently sees herself as powerless, blaming her problems on her "disrespectful" children and absent husband. However, these are conditions that would not be questioned if Sira were in her own country, because there they would be status quo—wives take care of family business and husbands devote themselves to work. The difference is that, in India, Sira would have a large family support system, as well as servants who would likely take care of the household tasks and child care.

The primary disciplinary approach in India is corporal punishment, often to the point of abuse. Children are perceived as disruptive and challenging, and parents are likely to see this behavior as within the father's control when he comes home from work. Given the fact that corporal punishment is the norm and produces short- rather than long-term results, and also given the fact that Sira was raised with the expectation that others would care for her children, she would probably benefit from parenting education. Since she likes to read, it is possible that she might be interested in some materials regarding discipline, as well as an array of other useful topics, such as emigration and acculturation, time management, and marital negotiation.

Kiran notes that Sira is caught between the demands and expectations of two cultures. She feels fatigued, isolated, and despairing—she sees no sign of relief and no support systems around her. It is possible that both Sira and her husband might view her physician's referral to psychotherapy as some indication that the problem is in her head, therefore minimizing the medical emergency and putting more pressure on Sira to cure herself. The symptom represents a metaphor for her underlying concerns: She cannot take care of herself and cannot change things.

There would be a great benefit to referring Sira to an Indian therapist, particularly because her sense of isolation from her culture would be quickly addressed by meeting with another woman from her country who shares her language and understands (and is not alarmed by) the fact that arranged marriages are commonplace and that husbands focus on work, leaving women to care for the house and children.

If such a therapeutic match was not possible and I was working with Sira, I would rely on my own bicultural and acculturation experiences to create a bridge of understanding and empathy. I would draw from my personal experience of the tremendous change in status when a well-to-do family comes from another country and must suddenly fend for itself, while feeling grossly unprepared to do so. Although I would not insist on seeing the husband, I would send a letter thanking him for his support and telling him that Sira's therapy would be confidential, and that at some later time, I would be honored to make his acquaintance. My earliest interventions would focus on helping Sira arrange her day so that when her children and husband were out of the house, her time could be used in more productive ways. Since Sira has been in the United States for 15 years, I would find out about her level of acculturation, not only her ability to negotiate the English language, but also her attitudes about the two cultures and whether she finds aspects of Western culture more or less desirable.

Sira will need to take risks carefully. Sudden, unfamiliar behaviors may seem threatening to her husband and children, so she may need to engage in new activities quietly. My initial goal would be to help Sira identify her own desires and encourage her to make choices in order to combat her feelings of helplessness and entrapment. As she feels better about herself, she may make new demands on her relationship with her husband, and it is at this juncture that I might make some home visits so that her husband might see me as an ally rather than a rival or an intruder. If, in fact, Sira's medical condition improves, my position as a helper will be established and it is more likely that Sira's husband might be receptive.

I would assume Sira has unique expectations of her relationship with her husband because theirs is an arranged marriage, a practice that continues to be common in India even today. Consequently, Indian women don't necessarily view this as unusual or negative. I would need to keep my countertransference in check so I did not inadvertently impose my Western values on her marital situation. A consultant like Kiran would be extremely helpful in making sure I maintained my perspective on both clinical and cultural issues. ∎

STUDY QUESTIONS

1. Do you think it's possible to practice family therapy with only one family member in the room? Why or why not?
2. What roles do you think gender, ethnicity, and culture play in this case?
3. How important do you think it would be to get Sira's husband to participate in her therapy?
4. What does McDaniel say about how the therapist might collaborate with the medical system to intervene with Sira and her family?
5. What kind of information about other cultures do you think a therapist needs to have when working cross-culturally?

CONSULTATION CORNER

QUANDARIES OF A HETEROSEXUAL THERAPIST

When Should Sexual Orientation Be the Focus of Treatment?

EDITED BY H. CHARLES FISHMAN

Heterosexual therapists frequently find themselves doubting their clinical judgment when working with clients who are gay, lesbian, or bisexual. They may feel as if they are visiting an unfamiliar culture, fearful of sounding homophobic or politically incorrect and uncertain about the relevance of a client's homosexuality to the presenting problem. The following case and the commentaries on it highlight not only the treatment decisions involved in work with a young woman who is both bulimic and a lesbian, but also the power of the therapist to define problems and impose labels on the complex concerns clients bring to us.

H.C.F.

Twenty-six-year-old Pat, a college dean, came to our eating-disorders clinic for treatment of bulimia. She seemed nervous and said she felt "fat and unattractive," although she looked only about 20 pounds overweight. She told me she was a lesbian, under stress at work and in her relationship with her lover, Gloria, a 30-year-old police officer. The two women had been involved for about a year. Pat had been referred by her individual therapist, also a lesbian, who had refused to continue to see her unless Pat got treatment for her bulimia. The therapist had seen Pat and Gloria together several times. Pat told me her father was alcoholic and that she suspected she had been sexually abused as a child, although she had no clear memories. Her bulimia had begun when she was about 16 and often occurred when she was angry and unable to express it directly.

(Continued)

(Continued)

She expressed a great deal of shame about having been "promiscuous" with men when she was younger. While in college, she had been raped and, at about the same time, had begun exploring relationships with women. She had had two lesbian relationships that ended badly, leaving her feeling rejected and upset enough to seek therapy.

In her present relationship, Pat was unhappy because Gloria had not come out as a lesbian, partly out of fear of losing her job. Gloria wouldn't take Pat to family parties or work-related functions, and Pat felt rejected and abandoned. She wanted their relationship to be out in the open, but she was unwilling to push the issue, out of fear that Gloria would leave her.

Pat refused to invite members of her family of origin to come to treatment, saying she feared they would feel blamed for her bulimia. She had a conflictual relationship with her divorced parents, but they were aware of her sexual preference and included Gloria in family gatherings like any other relative or in-law. Pat did agree to ask Gloria to come in for couples counseling, although couples sessions were hard to arrange because of Gloria's shifting work schedule. Gloria agreed to come only to "help Pat." In individual sessions, it had become clear that Gloria felt responsible when Pat overate and out of fear of losing Gloria, Pat would secretly go to the bathroom to throw up.

But directly addressing Pat's bulimia or other sensitive issues in couples sessions proved extremely difficult. Pat and Gloria held hands and touched each other for the entire hour, which seemed to undermine their expressing any strong emotion. Pat did most of the talking in the first session in a pleading tone. Gloria listened and agreed with everything, but nothing was resolved. Both came from conflict-avoidant families and focused on the nurturing part of their relationship to alleviate any conflict and maintain peace and calm in their relationship.

This failure to resolve conflict, I think, often resulted in Pat's bingeing and purging. She felt she had no right to speak up, that things were her fault anyway, and that if she confronted her, Gloria would leave.

(Continued)

(Continued)

The second couples session left me feeling similarly stymied. We were unable to arrange further sessions because of Gloria's work schedule and I left the clinic about three months later.

The case raised several questions for me. Pat and Gloria were the first same-sex couple I worked with, and I wasn't sure whether to address their lesbianism or treat them like any other couple with problems. My inclination was to look at the problems—communication, boundary issues, and power struggles—that they shared with couples of any sexual orientation. But I later wondered whether I had been insensitive to the issues of their being lesbian in a heterosexist world. Should I have pushed harder on the issue of Gloria's not wanting to come out?

I also felt doubtful about Pat's sexual preference. She so insistently and repeatedly defined herself as a lesbian that I wondered if she didn't protest too much. She said that she was still sexually attracted to men but was afraid of getting involved with them because of her fear of being "promiscuous" again. She also seemed to fear men's rejection and once said, "It doesn't matter what you look like as a lesbian." I wonder if Pat's sexual preference was a response to a history of real and suspected sexual abuse rather than a true sexual preference for women. I think she felt safe and nurtured in a female relationship and accepted in a lesbian culture. The repeated statements of her lesbian identity seemed like a personal cry for validation from someone deeply uncertain about who she was.

I felt that these issues needed further exploration with Pat, but she was very reluctant to look at them. I wondered how—and if—these issues should have fit into the couples therapy. And are there other issues I need to be aware of in working with a same-sex couple that I might have overlooked?

COMMENTARY 1

A Gay-Affirmative Approach

BY JULE MENCHER

This clinician is to be applauded for asking critical questions about how she should understand her clients' lesbianism. Historically, gay men and lesbians have been either pathologized or simply ignored by mental-health practitioners. For therapists trained before the historic 1973 American Psychiatric Association decision to remove homosexuality from the rolls of diagnosable mental illnesses, treating gay and lesbian clients meant helping a client achieve heterosexuality. Today, there are probably still therapists who would look at this case and see Pat's lesbianism as the source of her bulimia.

In contrast, many clinicians trained in recent years, as the gay and lesbian liberation movement has become increasingly visible, have adopted something like the color-blind approach white therapists often use with people of color. Such therapists would be likely to try to ignore Pat's lesbianism, focusing on her bulimia but studiously avoiding the topic of her sexual identity unless *Pat* flagged it as a salient issue. Motivated by a genuine desire not to pathologize or be homophobic, these clinicians are still unsure about how to gauge the relevance of the client's homosexuality, so they simply avoid discussing it.

Does the fact that Pat is a lesbian make a difference in this case, even though the problem is bulimia? Of course it does. In a social climate where one is constantly assumed to be heterosexual, a lesbian's personal life becomes uncomfortably invisible, and when this is compounded with the rampant fear, hatred, and negative stereotypes of lesbians—even active oppression and discrimination—then Pat's lesbianism must affect every part of her life, whether subtly or overtly. Therapists must not forget that the pervasive stigma of being homosexual inflates the importance of sexual orientation in the overall identity of gay men and lesbians.

The therapist wonders whether Pat is "truly a lesbian" or has come out because she was sexually victimized in the past and fears she will be "promiscuous" with men again. The clinician's suspicion is based on a commonly held myth about lesbians, but the reality is that there are no greater numbers of survivors of sexual abuse in the lesbian population than in the heterosexual female population. It is improbable that Pat has come out because of having been abused. Also, I have frequently seen lesbians, frightened about having sexual feelings for women, launch into a period of compulsive sexual activity with men, as if to prove to themselves that they could be heterosexual.

I would wonder whether Pat is protesting too much because she wants the therapist to pay attention to the issue of her lesbianism, which does not mean she wants the therapy to help her change her orientation. Accepting one's sexual orientation *begins* with acknowledging feelings for other women, but is actually a lifelong process of integrating a stigmatized identity, both intrapsychically and socially. Pat may be sure that she is a lesbian but unsure about what that means—how she should live, work, couple, and relate to the world as a lesbian. In the absence of peer or ancestral role models or images of lesbian life, lesbians often feel like they're making it up as they go along. I would explain to Pat that being attracted to certain men is common among lesbians, just as many heterosexual women find themselves attracted to certain women. Even though Pat has come out as a lesbian, she should be allowed to be confused, unsure, and even homophobic in therapy, without the clinician coming to any dramatic conclusions.

While it is possible that Pat is denying her heterosexuality, it is at least equally possible that she began to experience and then deny her feelings for women at age 16, launching instead into bulimia as a way of managing conflicting feelings about herself. This does not mean that her lesbianism *caused* the bulimia; the eating disorder may have been a way of coping with a number of highly charged issues at play in her life at that time, including her father's drinking, her sexual victimization, and the social and familial stigma around the forbidden sexual feelings she was experiencing. Therapeutic exploration could focus on two issues: First, how was the original function of the bulimia a way to manage this full array of adolescent difficulties? Second, did the all-consuming symptom of bulimia serve to truncate or postpone her lesbian identity development? If so, where are the gaps that need attention in the therapy?

Couples therapy seems premature to me at this point in Pat's treatment, given that her bulimia long preceded the relationship. I would spend more initial time with Pat to build her self-knowledge and relational skills. The individual therapy could also explore the ways in which (unbeknownst to her) Pat's struggles are further complicated by being a lesbian in a homophobic world.

Although I think couples therapy was premature in this case, the therapist's concern about the amount of physical contact between Pat and her partner during couples sessions deserves some comment. If Pat has experienced this therapist as one who ignores her sexual identity unless Pat brings it up, she may be using physical contact as a way, quite literally, of putting it in the therapist's face. Lesbian couples are often made invisible by mainstream (i.e., heterosexual) society, which regards them as friends, roommates, or sisters, and their couplehood often remains unrecognized unless the women go out of their way to assert it directly. Pat and Gloria's handholding may be their declaration of couplehood to the therapist, a way of pleading for its inclusion in the therapy.

COMMENTARY 2

A Structural Family Therapy Approach

BY DAVID WATERS

It is both the bane and the fascination of our profession that, if you present the same case to seven different therapists, you are apt to get at least three or four different treatment plans. In this case, I count no less than 15 significant issues that could be the focus of Pat's therapy. And that doesn't even include the possibility that Pat may not need psychotherapy, as many insurance carriers considering picking up the treatment expenses of a successful college dean with a moderate weight problem and relationship conflicts might conclude.

We have all seen therapists whose work reflects their personal and political beliefs more than objective clinical judgment. For these therapists, *every* case ends up being about sexual abuse, or substance abuse, or low self-esteem, or family of origin, or whatever they know is the fundamental issue in our society. Such therapists often wind up treating their own belief systems, not their clients. But we are doing the same thing when we treat clients because they were sent to us, and not because we have developed with the clients a shared notion of what they wish to accomplish.

Pat came to a bulimia clinic at the insistence of her individual therapist rather than out of any obvious concern for her bulimia. Pat doesn't want treatment for bulimia; the receiving therapist isn't sure she needs it; and—no surprise—she doesn't get it. Instead, Pat ties another therapist in self-doubting knots and continues a life of apparent unhappiness. Something in Pat seems to pull people into trying to decide for her what she needs and then produce it for her. She keeps casting herself as a perennial victim, overcome with problems and incapable of focusing on a solution, who takes down her frustrated helpers with her.

As the supervisor in this case, I would want to stop the fusillade of therapeutic misfires, in which professionals try to organize Pat's life for her, and see if she could get interested in her own patterns. Instead of just accepting the referral, and the responsibility for Pat's life that apparently accompanies it, I would push hard on the question of what Pat wants. Is *she* content with her sexual orientation? Her weight? Her relationship? Her eating disorder? Where is her natural concern for herself? What does *she* want to accomplish?

Therapy is, for me, fundamentally about mastery. Pat has managed to get everyone else to take responsibility for her progress. Even if they succeed—a long shot, given her passive stance—where is the mastery in that? The only mastery she achieves is leaving in her wake defeated therapists second-guessing themselves: a Pyrrhic victory, if ever there was one. I would alert Pat's new therapist to Pat's deft way of dodging responsibility for her life and how she offers her array of problems to willing helpers like bait for them to bite on. The main issue of Pat's treatment, as I see it, is how to help

Pat to understand her pattern of retreat from responsibility, and her terror of taking a stand on her own behalf. Even if therapy became a fight between Pat and her therapist about his or her unwillingness to script her life, that would be a good start.

Not everyone who shows up at our door needs the therapy they think they came for, or the therapy we know how to do. Not every bulimic is ready for therapy that treats bulimia. Until her therapy is based on a healthy partnership that helps Pat take responsibility for her own progress, I don't think it really matters which of her many symptoms we focus on. ■

STUDY QUESTIONS

1. In your opinion, is it a good idea for the therapist to ignore sexual orientation and treat Pat and Gloria like any other couple with a problem? Why or why not?

2. Do you agree with Mencher that Pat's experience of social stigmatization and discrimination as a lesbian is likely to have an effect on her bulimia? Why or why not?

3. Do you believe past sexual abuse can cause women to become lesbians? Discuss your views on how sexual orientation is shaped—heterosexual, bisexual, and homosexual.

4. Waters challenges that Pat needs to take responsibility for her own life. How might the therapist help her do this, and how can a therapist ascertain when a client is ready for therapy and when he or she is not?

CASE STUDY

LOST IN AMERICA
OVERCOMING THE ISOLATION OF A MULTIPROBLEM,
MIDDLE-CLASS FAMILY

Judith Friedman and Ella Lasky

The multiproblem family presented in the following case—whose difficulties include school phobia, AIDS, clinical depression, and the economic consequences of divorce—are not members of the underclass,
but of the well-educated, urban middle class. In the midst of the vast
turmoil and social isolation of the 1990s, family therapists are seeing
more and more cases like this and need to go beyond traditional family
therapy and the insularity of our therapy rooms to include adjunctive
treatment and sources of support that the therapy relationship, by itself,
cannot provide.

Thirteen-year-old Ann was excited about being admitted to the seventh grade of a special school for the gifted, and did quite well during
her first few months. Then, in December, after months of complaining
of stomachaches that had begun the previous spring, she refused to go
to school at all.

After Ann had missed 10 weeks of classes, the school psychologist
called a meeting with her family. She pressed Ann's parents to get Ann
a full medical workup and to make a commitment to family therapy.
They were told that Ann had to be back in school in six weeks in order
to be promoted to the eighth grade. When the meeting failed to get
Ann back to school, the frustrated psychologist referred the case to our
center.

Our first step was to get a full family history. Ann was the only child
of separated parents. Her father, Jack, had been diagnosed with the
AIDS virus two years ago. A bisexual, Jack had contracted the virus
from homosexual encounters; eight months before Ann began refusing
to go to school, his sexual partner of many years died from AIDS. While
Jack himself was asymptomatic, the loss of his friend had sent him into
a tailspin of fear and a preoccupation with death and dying.

Ann's mother, Betty, had been struggling with recurring clinical depression for five years. She was still grieving the loss of her parents, both of whom had died within the past two years. Although the antidepressants Betty had been taking were not making her feel any better, she had not gone back for a psychiatric follow-up. She had not gone to work for an entire month earlier in the fall.

Jack's HIV status had been kept secret from Ann and from the extended family. Refusing to seek evaluation or treatment, Jack was clearly in the grip of massive denial and Betty was dealing poorly with the secret. In turmoil themselves, Ann's parents were at an impasse about how to deal with their daughter's symptoms with the result that they had sought neither medical nor psychological help for her.

Jack and Betty had been living apart for six years but were not yet legally separated or divorced, unable to resolve issues such as custody, visitation, or finances. Jack had come to rely on the emotional and financial security of his marriage and did not want a divorce; yet, at the same time, he wanted the freedom to enjoy his homosexual encounters. Although Betty, the full-time worker and financial supporter of the family, had initiated the divorce, she was adamant in her refusal to pay alimony or offer a financial settlement to Jack, who had almost no income of his own. They had unsuccessfully tried divorce mediation. Each time divorce was discussed in our sessions, Jack threatened to drag Ann into a nasty custody battle in family court.

Ann was permitted to move freely between her mother's and father's apartments without prior arrangement or structure. Typically, this occurred when Betty's boyfriend, whom Ann said she despised, came to visit and Ann escaped to her father's apartment.

Betty presented as a cold, precise person, well organized to the point of compulsivity. She worked as an accountant and provided the family with a reliable income. Jack was a freelance writer and hobbyist (gourmet cooking, painting, gardening). Unable to market his writing or his hobbies, he picked up a little money as a part-time salesman but contributed almost nothing to his daughter's support. He appeared helpless and disorganized but, most of the time, warm-hearted. Emotionally expansive and impulsive, he could erupt with a violent temper at both his wife and daughter.

Ann presented as sweet, anxious, and somewhat defeated. In the first few sessions, she sat between her parents on the couch, slouched down, smiling uncomfortably at their endless arguments as they either ignored her or out-talked her. In individual sessions, Ann said she felt hopeless, sometimes thought about suicide, and was overwhelmed in her new school. She confided that she felt very worried since she learned that her father was HIV positive.

The therapist inquired into Betty's and Jack's families of origin to understand what kinds of experience they each had brought to their marriage. Disputes in Betty's family of origin resulted in beatings and led her to avoid conflict at all costs. Jack, on the other hand, was ignored in a chaotic home and now, in his dramatic fashion, made every effort to seek attention; his daughter and estranged wife grew tired of his endless melodrama and often did not take him seriously. Both Betty and Jack were raised in relative isolation within their nuclear families and now, in adult life, they continued to live isolated lives. They had few close friends and little contact with extended family.

Being in the same room with Betty and Jack was an overwhelming experience, even for an experienced therapist. They brought unending crises and arguments into the sessions and disagreed on everything. They rarely listened to each other or to Ann. Jack would make many bids for attention in the sessions by going off on tangents; it was hard to keep him focused on the central issues. Betty would often retreat into silence, unwilling to share her feelings. Ann was frequently overrun and ignored by her parents, especially her father. Family members would constantly speak for, or interrupt, the others.

After consultation with a seven-member team that reviewed the case weekly, the therapist told the family in the fourth session that she guaranteed them that Ann would not return to school soon. She explained to Betty and Jack that Ann could not possibly return to being responsible for age-appropriate activities until they took care of their own problems. The therapist insisted that Ann needed a thorough medical investigation of the cause of her stomach pains, Jack needed a complete medical examination with an AIDS specialist, and Betty needed a reevaluation of her antidepressant medication. She explained that it was unfair to ask a teenager to act more responsibly than her parents. If the parents failed to seek appropriate treatment for themselves, Ann simply would not return to school in the foreseeable future.

The therapist explained that Ann, a loyal and devoted daughter, had become the watchdog of the family's troubles and, as a good watchdog, she felt she needed to stay home to watch over her parents. They were told that excessive worry is exhausting and stressful, another reason why Ann had taken to her bed. The therapist shared with them that she, too, was exhausted by their story and by her feeling of responsibility for their physical and mental well-being. The family reacted with shock and silence. The therapist had finally gotten their attention—or so she thought.

After three more weeks had gone by, only Ann had been to a doctor. She was diagnosed with a preulcerous condition and had started to take medication. The therapist reiterated the basic formulation of the intervention: until the parents took care of themselves, Ann would remain a watchdog and would not return to school. In frustration, the therapist gave them each a list of appropriate resources: for Jack, the names of three AIDS specialists and for Betty, the names of three psychiatrists.

We felt, after these initial sessions, that we were faced with a multi-problem family on the brink of disintegration. Ann had dedicated herself to preserving at all cost the rigid pattern by which her family had accommodated to its problems, and by her sacrifice had aborted her own development. We developed a treatment plan involving a variety of strategies, giving equal valence to the child's and the parents' symptomatologies. We scheduled sessions according to the family's shifting needs: full family, just parents, individual, and back again to full family. Our insistence on adjunctive treatments (medical and psychiatric evaluations) and outside supports (peer groups for AIDS/HIV-positive patients and their families) reflected our belief that this family's problems had far more medical urgency and social significance than could be addressed by traditional family therapy alone. No single intervention, no reframing, no paradoxical task, no restructuring would be sufficient to deal with the scope of this family's difficulties. We viewed the classic symptom of school phobia through the widest lens possible and gave as much attention to the whole collapsing family context as to the child's symptoms.

Each week's sessions were divided so that Ann was seen alone for a half-hour, the parents for a half-hour, and the family for two half-hour sessions. This structure reflected the need to create boundaries so that grown-up issues were discussed only among adults, family issues by all three, and Ann's issues given private time. For example, issues of family finances, visitation arrangements, the management of Jack's HIV disease, and Betty's chronic depression were discussed only in sessions with the parents. Our thinking was that Ann had already been flooded by worry and that it was our job to guide her parents to shield her from the toxicity of their issues.

In full-family sessions, we worked on the restructuring of one family of three into two families of two, clarifying the rules and guidelines for each family. We encouraged Ann's input into family decisions: how she should divide her time between her mother's and father's homes; what school she should return to when ready; how to negotiate typical adolescent-parent conflicts involving such issues as bedtime, curfew, allowance, and choice of friends.

In these sessions, Jack and Betty began to work somewhat more cooperatively, but the fight to be right often took precedence over Ann's well-being. The therapist battled constantly with Jack over his efforts to dominate the sessions and with Betty's tendency to withdraw into silence, working to create more productive communication. Ann became increasingly angry at her parents' fighting and inattention to her needs and became more animated as she was encouraged to speak up clearly for herself.

The therapist expressed confusion over Ann's real age. She explained that when Ann stayed home with stomachaches she was acting like a worried parent, adding 30 years to her age; when she was having a tantrum she became 5-years-old; and when she went to a girlfriend's house, she was acting like a 13-year-old. Through the therapist, the team predicted that Ann would start to get well and return to school when she was able to give grown-up troubles back to the grownups, leave 5-year-old behaviors behind, and take on 13-year-old interests.

In the individual sessions, Ann discussed her feelings about having a father with AIDS, about knowing that someday he would become very sick and eventually die. Ann was full of questions about her father: Was he gay? Was he bisexual? Was he an IV drug user? How long did he have to live? The therapist moved slowly and carefully through this material as Ann would back off, clearly afraid of her own strong emotions.

Concerned about Jack's explosive and potentially damaging reactions, the team decided to address these questions with Ann alone instead of with Ann and Jack together. We decided that Jack would not be able to tolerate hearing about his daughter's sense of shame about his disease and lifestyle and, of course, about her grief. When the therapist did discuss with Jack, individually, how to talk with Ann about these issues, he was at best tangential and avoidant and at worst impulsive and rageful. We hoped that with the help of a support group for patients with HIV disease, Jack would eventually come to terms with his diagnosis and be able to tolerate his daughter's reactions to it.

Six weeks and 12 therapy hours after the family work began, Ann returned to school, just meeting the deadline for receiving credit for the academic year. Ann's return to school was precisely nine days after Betty began taking a new antidepressant medication and seven days after Jack's doctor reported him in good health despite his HIV status. Ann remained in school for the rest of the school year with only two short periods of absence.

At this point, the family sessions were reduced to once a week, splitting the time between Ann and her parents. In the ensuing months, much of the time in sessions was spent preparing the family for the inevitable decline in Jack's condition. Nevertheless, the family resisted dealing with it, rejecting the idea that Jack would become symptomatic. For months, we urged all three of them to participate in support groups for AIDS patients and their families. We felt that in such groups they would meet patients and their families in similar circumstances, thereby decreasing their isolation and fear of exposure about the disease. They did not follow through at this time, but since they had made so much progress, we did not press the point.

Eleven months into our work with the family, Jack was hospitalized for 10 days with pneumonia. Not surprisingly, the family handled the crisis poorly. Jack asked no one except Betty for help and never allowed Ann to visit him in the hospital (a misguided effort to protect her). Betty became seriously depressed and stopped taking her antidepressant medication. For one month after Jack came home from the hospital, Ann stayed home from school and began to isolate herself, remaining silent in sessions (when her parents could get her in), and ruminating about suicide. The family started to unravel as Jack's condition worsened.

While our work with the family had been successful during the months Jack had not been symptomatic, we were now losing the therapeutic handle. We realized we had not challenged the family's denial system vigorously enough. Perhaps we ourselves were inducted into ignoring the horror of the AIDS epidemic.

The therapist and the team began to process our own sense of loss and grief in the face of terminal illness. With a renewed sense of purpose, the therapist, with continuous support from the team, insisted that each family member join a support group: Jack for AIDS patients, Betty for spouses, and Ann for teenage children. After several weeks of hammering away at the point and continuous pessimistic predictions that Ann would never return to school unless they joined these groups, Jack and Betty complied. Unfortunately, Ann's shame prevailed, preventing her from joining a group herself. She adamantly remained isolated with her secret for weeks after her father's pneumonia.

In a series of painfully intense individual sessions, Ann addressed her anger and sadness about her father's illness. She finally was able to verbalize that she could not imagine what life would be like without her father. Immediately after this session, Ann took many photographs of her parents, unconsciously preparing the photo memories she would treasure after her father's death. This breakthrough into her denial was critical in getting her back to school after just one month.

This family has made good progress over the year of therapy; Ann is back in school and functioning better socially; the parents have made significant steps toward being more effective coparents; all three are finally dealing with the father's HIV disease. Betty and Jack have become active in their respective support groups and conscientious about medical and psychiatric follow-up, crucial adjuncts to our treatment plan.

At this point, our plan involves reducing sessions to once every two weeks for the parents, with our insistence that they continue their involvement in support groups. We are continuing to encourage Ann to join a teenager support group, but, to date, she resists the idea. We believe that the issue of a legal separation or divorce will remain unresolved, for the ultimate separation represented by Jack's inevitable and untimely death hangs over the family.

We concluded that the seemingly never-ending conflict, lack of resolution, even the serious symptomatology of their teenage daughter all served to distract this family from the humiliation and grief surrounding Jack's disease. When we went off course in our treatment, we realized that we, too, were distracted, unable to come to terms with untimely loss.

Social isolation and a collapsing social matrix are all too often the reality for families with a member suffering from HIV disease. To work with such families, therapists need to draw on a wide range of family therapy theories and techniques as well as the largest network of community resources available. In this case, our team was forced to use approaches we had never tried before, including linking a child's symptom to the family's resistance to using community resources. By so doing, we were able to restructure a family on the brink of disintegration and free an extremely unhappy teenager from the isolation of school phobia.

CASE COMMENTARY 1
BY LEE COMBRINCK-GRAHAM

I was struck by several things about this case—the perseverance of the therapists through very difficult times, the emotional burden they had to bear from this family, and the successful outcome of the work. Faced with the courage and commitment of these therapists, I offer these remarks with humility.

As a child and adolescent psychiatrist, I feel strongly that a child's not going to school is a developmental emergency, and so I tend to focus on that as the sole issue to be dealt with by the family. While focusing on the mother's untreated depression, the father's HIV status, and their unresolved marital relationship may provide a working hypothesis about why Ann needed to stay out of school, I wonder whether such hypotheses are necessary to give her the help she needed.

Since, in this case, Ann's schooling is what the family went in for, I would offer them three options regarding ways to help her (leaving open the possibility that they might come up with others). The first option would be for the parents to arrange to take Ann to school and to stay with her there so school personnel would not have to send her home when she complained of stomach problems. The second option would be to take Ann's insistence that she is really too ill to attend school seriously and keep her in bed with one or both parents at home to make sure she rests until she feels ready to return to school. This regimen would, of course, include evenings and weekends. The third possibility, if the parents didn't feel that Ann could go to school even though she was not physically ill, would be to provide home-schooling for her. I do not mean a home-bound program for which a school is responsible for providing the teacher, but home-schooling, where the parents provide the education themselves.

Each of these approaches requires a reorganization of the family in order to be implemented. The initial therapy session would be to emphasize that whatever the parents' decision, getting Ann to continue with her education was the primary goal. The therapist's major function would be to help the family make a decision about an action plan. If Ann interferred with the decision-making process, she might be excused from therapy for a brief time so the parents could come to a decision on her behalf (as good parents usually do). Or, Ann could be asked to remain quietly in the room while her parents made this decision. This alternative depends upon Ann's cooperation in keeping out of her parents' decision making and how effectively the parents could negotiate without involving Ann.

After choosing their approach, Ann's parents would need to decide how they would implement it. For example, where would Ann live? Which parent would be in charge of the plan, or how would they share responsibility? Implementing this plan would require the parents to consider the relative importance of work, income generation, and the sacrifices necessary to make sure that their child got back on an appropriate developmental track.

In the course of the negotiations about properly caring for their daughter, the mother's lack of energy from her depression might become an issue. Similarly, the father's fears for his own viability and his grief and loneliness might also arise and have to be reconciled with his commitment to posterity in the form of a successful daughter. But the therapy would remain focused on caring for Ann and advancing her education.

Ann is likely to test her parents' resolve by upping the ante in some way. If they decided to take her to school, she might actually vomit to demonstrate how ill she was. If they decided to keep her on bed rest, she might sneak out or cajole them to let her do something like go to a movie or a sports event. Actually, Ann might be encouraged to take some action to test her parents' resolve to convince herself that they are really committed to caring for her properly.

While Ann is also likely to actively dislike the therapist who is proposing such unpleasant options and to try to sabotage the entire plan, this is not germane to the outcome of the therapy. If she needs to confide her feelings to someone, it might be one of her parents; or it might well be a peer (but of course, she isn't seeing her peers since she isn't going to school). If the parents feel that they are doing the right thing for their daughter, they will proceed despite Ann's dislike for the therapist.

This kind of approach frequently works quickly and offers the advantage of not shifting the burden of the family's life dilemmas to the therapist. On the contrary, the family is forced to bear its own burden, but family members are also given the opportunity to experience competence by accomplishing the return of their child to school, which may reinforce their ability to manage other difficulties in their lives.

CASE COMMENTARY 2
BY MICHAEL SHERNOFF

This case is, unfortunately, an excellent example of how the drama of HIV infection can overwhelm clinicians and draw the focus away from a family's underlying problem. At the same time, it is an example of how nontraditional family relationships may be completely invisible, even in the offices of well-intentioned, caring therapists.

Friedman and Lasky start off by practically ignoring, and certainly underestimating the importance of Jack's decreased sexual partner. We never find out anything about him—including his name—beyond the fact that he and Jack had sex. Was he a live-in partner? Did Jack love him? Did Ann spend time with him when she was at Jack's house? Was he a stepparent figure to her? Did she witness his physical deterioration and death? Was this in some way connected to the onset of her school phobia? Did she think her father needed her help to care for him? Is this one reason she refused to go to school? Did his sexual partner's illness mean that Jack became less emotionally available to his daughter, exacerbating Ann's feelings of stress and insecurity? If Jack has no income of his own, and Betty refuses to support him financially, was he a full-time homemaker being supported by his now-deceased sexual partner? Did Ann learn how to be a parent to her parents from this deceased sexual partner? The therapists confidently assert that they obtained a "full family history," but obviously one family member was left out. I can't help but wonder whether they would have been so vague if Jack's sexual partner had been a woman.

I believe the team would have found important insights into Ann's school phobia as well as Jack's violent temper and Betty's depression by asking direct questions about how well each family member knew the sexual partner. How did each one find out about his illness, and ultimately hear that he had died? I would have liked to hear Ann talk about whether she had grieved and how she felt her parents did or didn't acknowledge the loss of this family member. A better picture of this sexual partner's illness and death may have helped the therapists anticipate how the family later dealt with Jack's bout with pneumonia and responses to his own symptomology. Like using the multigenerational scheme to understand family patterns, having the story behind the death of the sexual partner would have given the clinicians important reference points about how this family deals with sickness and death.

When a family member has HIV or AIDS, there are inevitably questions that loved ones have difficulty asking, and I can imagine that Ann, witnessing the decline of her father's sexual partner, may have been full of questions about her father's condition, and worried about who would take care of him. It seems to me that an important goal of therapy would have been to coach Jack—and Betty, too—to reassure Ann that her parents can take care of themselves and release her from her parent role. But instead of focusing on some good old-fashioned structural therapy, the team becomes distracted by the presence of the HIV diagnosis and ends up reinforcing the idea that Jack is too fragile to be held accountable. By deciding that Jack needs to be protected from his daughter's feelings and her questions about his life and illness, the therapists collude in his evasion of responsibility as a parent. How can this little girl get on with her 13-year-old life if she believes her feelings can destroy her father? Did the therapists' attempt to shield Jack, reinforce for Ann that there were terrible secrets in her family that she could never address directly, and serve to drive her thoughts and feelings further underground? Why haven't the therapists made it clear to Jack that Ann will have difficulties in her later life if he doesn't learn how to parent her? Betty, too, is not pushed to take responsibility for Ann. At times, I felt that this was a case about three siblings in competition with one another, with Ann emerging as the most parental of all!

Why are the therapists regarding this man, whom the doctors state is in "good health," as so fragile? Because he has HIV? I wonder if they were afraid to confront him because the process of change can be emotionally painful and they viewed him as close to death anyway, and therefore gave up on doing any real family work with him. Overwhelmed by the drama of AIDS, the therapists seem to simply give up on the underlying dynamic, which is that neither Betty nor Jack knows how to be a parent and Ann is suffering because of this. It is premature for the team to talk about his inevitable decline—in this day and age, that might be years away. The result of putting all their focus on Jack and his HIV status is that, once again, the attention is drawn away from Ann, who desperately needs the care of the adults around her. Because of their own reactivity to Jack's having HIV, the therapists are blind to the fact that HIV has become a screen for the family and themselves, a way to avoid dealing with all the problems that existed long before Jack was diagnosed.

Any life-threatening illness, especially one that is wrapped around issues of sexuality and lifestyle, presents itself with an urgency that can be seductive to clinicians. But in this case, it is without justification. There is no medical crisis around Jack's illness, particularly, in the early stages of the case. When there is a medical emergency—Jack's bout with pneumonia—the clinical team once again allows him to push his daughter away and think only of his own needs rather than his child's. I wish they had told him, "This is your daughter. She has every right to be here, to see that you are okay, and to talk to you about her feelings about this." It would have been important for Ann to talk directly to Jack about why she was taking pictures of him, perhaps to say to him, "I care about you, Daddy, and I don't want to be in this alone, isolated, as I have been in so many instances in this family."

Jack is not dying. The therapists are prematurely mourning him. They neglect to keep the therapy focused on the structural component and then refer the family members to other professionals who deal with AIDS. In their good-hearted desire not to ignore AIDS, they forgot their training as family therapists and became reactive to the family drama without confronting what really needed to be confronted. Although Ann does return to school, I don't consider this case a success because real structural change in the family never occurred—the clinical team did not succeed in getting Jack and Betty to take on the job of parenting their child. In fact, I predict that the family's next medical emergency will once again leave Ann in the role of parent in her family.

AUTHORS' RESPONSE
BY JUDITH FRIEDMAN AND ELLA LASKY

We appreciate Combrinck-Graham's suggestions about keeping the emotional burden of the family's dilemmas on the parents rather than shifting them to the therapists. Yet, while her approach is certainly provocative, we wonder about its viability in this case given this family's long history of parental dysfunction. Betty and Jack were deadlocked on every aspect of parenting and had no ability to negotiate their differences. We strongly believe that the combination of Betty's depression and Jack's hysteria would have made it impossible for them to implement any of Combrinck-Graham's three approaches.

Shernoff raises some interesting questions about the strong emotions HIV/AIDS evokes for the therapist and the family, as well as the role of Jack's deceased sexual partner in this case. Unfortunately, he then proceeds to be prosecutor, judge, and jury without pursuing the answers to these questions.

Shernoff's comments are based on the assumption that Tom, Jack's sexual partner, had a large role in the family, which the therapists ignored. In fact, although Jack was friendly with Tom for many years, their relationship was kept private; neither Ann nor Betty ever met him or was informed of his health problems. He did not live with Jack, support Jack, or have any relationship with Ann. Unfortunately, Ann found out about Tom's death in the worst possible way: One day, Jack blurted out the information while in an angry rage. Although Shernoff believes the therapy would have been conducted differently had Jack's partner been a woman, our concern was respecting the privacy with which Jack chose to conduct the affair. His lover's gender was irrelevant.

Shernoff states, "Instead of focusing on some good old-fashioned structural family therapy, the team becomes distracted by the presence of the HIV diagnosis." In fact, it was exactly "good old-fashioned structural family therapy" that shaped the therapy. As we clearly stated in the article, we told the family that Ann would not be able to return to school and/or resume other age-appropriate activities until Jack had a complete medical evaluation with an HIV specialist and Betty went to a psychiatrist for a medication reevaluation. Boundary-setting was not only discussed with the family but it was modeled by holding separate sessions with Ann individually and with the parents together as well as with the whole family.

Shernoff believes that we were distracted by the HIV diagnosis and ignored family therapy work. He argues that this is reflected in our encouragement to each family member in this case to join an HIV support group. He ignores the purpose of having the adjunct therapy, which was to give everyone a place to discuss their feelings about the illness with peers, learn correct information, and meet new people for emotional support. The use of support groups was absolutely necessary to achieve the goal of getting the school-phobic child back on track quickly and effectively.

We disagree with Shernoff's conclusion that the treatment was not a success because real structural change did not occur. Betty and Jack progressed from a chaotic, ineffectual duo to a well-functioning parental team. Ann returned to school within six weeks and remained there. Our ability to correct the flip-flopped family hierarchy was as structural as family therapy can get. ■

STUDY QUESTIONS

1. Why do you think Combrinck-Graham proposed a structural intervention for Ann and her parents? What hypothesis does she and the therapists have about this family's organization and Ann's reluctance to go to school?
2. Do you agree with Shernoff that the therapists ignored a vital piece of information in this case by not discussing Jack's partner? Why or why not?
3. In your opinion, should the therapists have had Ann and Jack talk directly about Ann's fears concerning Jack's HIV status and her confusion about his sexual orientation? Why or why not?
4. Discuss what you think was most helpful to Ann in this case.

CASE STUDY

AVOIDING THE TRUTH TRAP
RESPONDING TO ALLEGATIONS (AND DENIALS) OF SEXUAL ABUSE

Henry Schissler

I have seen enough clients who were sexually abused to understand the reality of incest and to know that fathers who are confronted often deny that anything happened. But I recently saw a family whose members may have been victims of false memory syndrome, a case in which another therapist jumped to the conclusion that there had been childhood sexual abuse, isolated the client from her family, and provided some very bad therapy.

The family came to me through the oldest daughter, Donna, who had first come to see me two years earlier because of a tumultuous, three-year relationship with her boyfriend. She eventually ended that relationship, met another man she later married, and successfully terminated therapy with me about a year before this contact. But now Donna sounded stunned and upset on the telephone. Her younger sister Jane had recently told their mother and two sisters that their father had sexually abused her when she was a child.

Donna didn't believe Jane, and when she asked me what to do, I suggested she come to see me. I was quite surprised that not only Donna, but her mother, Betty, and her father, David, also showed up for the appointment. Betty immediately sat down, opened a file full of papers, and told me she had been "appointed by the family" to tell the story of what had happened since Jane had had her baby a few months before. Donna nodded in agreement. I asked Betty to begin.

After her baby was born, Jane had cried constantly and said things that Betty claimed didn't make any sense. For instance, Jane thought a former boyfriend was following her. She feared her newborn son would suffocate in his sleep and demanded that her husband stay up with him. She was anxious; she heard voices; she thought about hurting herself. She spent seven days on the psychiatric unit of the local hospital, where she was placed on three psychoactive medications and referred to a local human services agency for counseling.

At the first session with her new therapist, Jane recounted a dream in which her father got on top of her and had intercourse with her. The therapist told Jane that the dream could very well be an important childhood recollection that had been buried for years. That day, Jane called her mother and her two sisters to announce that David had sexually abused her. When Betty told Jane that she didn't believe her, Jane angrily said that her therapist had supported her call to her family, but had also warned Jane that the family might turn against her.

Over the next couple of weeks, Jane told Betty and her sisters about additional memories: Her father, she said, had once carried her upstairs "like a sack of potatoes" and sexually abused her. On another occasion, Jane said, her father had gone from bed to bed in the room she shared with her two sisters. Jane vividly remembered her father lying on top of Donna and Debby. She also said she had told her fourth-grade teacher about the abuse.

Betty clearly didn't believe a word of Jane's story, and she was convincing as she pulled out Jane's hospital records documenting her daughter's paranoia and delusional thinking. Betty said that when she had telephoned Jane's therapist with this information, the counselor had told her that she might very well be "in denial" and that David needed "professional help."

Donna regularly punctuated her mother's story with short bursts of outrage: "Jane's so full of it, that never happened," she said, and, "Can you believe that jerk?" Throughout the session, David just sat there passively, sweating and smelling of alcohol. He seemed to be just as Donna had described him during her year in therapy with me—lethargic and completely unavailable emotionally.

Betty and Donna were building a case to support David's contention that the abuse had never happened, but I wasn't so sure. As I watched Betty lay out her case and protect her alcoholic husband, I wondered whether I was watching another classic story of sexual abuse unfold.

I told Donna and her parents that I had an open mind about what had happened, but that we needed to take Jane seriously and gather all the available information. I suggested they talk about the past, and think of what in Jane's life had been unusual and potentially traumatic. I also suggested that Betty invite Jane to our next session, and talked about the possibility of family therapy.

"That's fine and dandy," Betty quickly responded, "but Jane won't talk to her father. She told me I was in denial because I wouldn't acknowledge the abuse, and worse yet, Jane's therapist told me David needed professional help."

"Her therapist's acting like it happened. Like it's a fact," Donna chimed in. "Jane will not come here." That was confirmed when Donna called Jane's therapist and was told that Jane would not attend any sessions with the family. I had invited Jane's therapist to attend the session as well, but she declined my invitation.

I met alone with David the next day and asked him to tell me everything he could about his life. I told him I was not taking sides and would reserve judgment. When I asked him about his drinking, he told me he drank to ease the pain of severe colitis that started when Jane was 2-years-old. The pain, he said, had been indescribable, but he had kept it from his family and had not even told his wife for five years. He said he had had three operations—two related to the colitis and one for colon cancer—that would have made it impossible for him to carry Jane upstairs "like a sack of potatoes." He claimed he never had a good night's sleep, or a comfortable day.

David described himself as distant and uncommunicative during his daughters' childhoods—he was so removed, he said, that he rarely spent enough time with his daughters even to hug them, much less abuse them sexually. His marriage had not been good. He and Betty would go months at a time without talking. After finishing work, he would go to a bar to drink until 1 A.M. He said he was still asleep when his kids left for school and was out of the house before they returned home. On Saturdays, he worked in a friend's liquor store. He said that in their entire childhood, he'd only gone into his daughters' bedroom a handful of times. "That's why this whole thing is so incredible to me," he said. "I never, ever went near any of the kids. And my wife used to be furious at me for being a crappy father!"

As David talked, he seemed remorseful, almost resigned to the fact that he was incapable of being a better father. He had been raised in an emotionally cold family and his mother had undergone four psychiatric hospitalizations, which his family had never discussed. As a child, he had learned that he must never talk about what bothered him. It was completely reasonable to him not to tell anyone about his illness. He was "sparing his family" from the worry of his physical problems—just like he was "spared" from the worry about his mother's illness.

Later that day, Betty came to see me alone and corroborated what David had said. Her marriage, she agreed, had been unhappy. David had usually been lost in an alcoholic fog, but she said she had not left him because she was a good Catholic. She had been very protective of her daughters because of her husband's "noninvolvement," but if there had been even a hint of abuse, she said, she would have divorced David in a second.

More significantly, Betty also told me that both her mother and David's mother had undergone psychiatric hospitalizations after the birth of a child. Betty said during Jane's pregnancy, Jane seemed self-absorbed, hyperactive, and sometimes delusional. Betty was often reminded of her own mother during that time and prayed that history would not repeat itself.

After Betty signed legal releases, I looked at the hospital records of both grandmothers. I was struck by the similarities between their behavior and Jane's. I decided that, based on the family history, it was crucial that Jane be assessed psychiatrically. Perhaps she needed to be on medication. Anything less than a full assessment and therapy that explored the possibility of delusional thinking would be mistreatment.

I suggested that Betty call Jane's therapist again to try to arrange a session including the whole family, but the therapist would not hear of it. Betty tried to tell the therapist about Jane's grandmothers, that Jane might have inherited something that would be relevant to her treatment. Jane's therapist responded that family members could meet when Jane was ready. That would, perhaps, be the appropriate time to discuss the grandmothers. The therapist also told Betty that she was unwilling to talk with me and that no releases of information would be signed to allow the therapists to discuss the case.

Betty told me that Jane's therapist had referred her to a therapy group for survivors of sexual abuse at a sexual assault crisis center at the local YWCA. The group leader there had told Jane that if she felt she had been abused, then she had been.

As time passed, Jane's stories about her childhood began to change. She stopped saying she had seen her sisters abused. Originally, she claimed to have told her fourth-grade teacher about the abuse, but recanted and instead said she'd been "scared silent." She still insisted she had been abused. During a telephone conversation, she told Donna, "I'm a survivor, and he abused you, too."

Because I felt that family therapy could help the other sisters clarify their relationships with their father and hopefully lead them toward healthier relationships with other men in the future, I held a family session without Jane. David, Betty, Donna, and the youngest sister, Debby, came in. For the first time, David talked to his children about his colitis and apologized to them for not being a very good father. He told them about his operations and the fact that he was physically incapable of carrying Jane upstairs to abuse her as she had claimed. But his disclosure fell flat, somehow; he didn't show any real emotion, and, as usual, he smelled of alcohol.

Donna told her father she was furious that he hadn't told her about his colitis or his cancer. She confronted him about his drinking and called him an alcoholic. She said his noninvolvement in their lives had been devastating to her when she was little and had contributed to her problems with male relationships. "For years I thought you were an unfeeling drunk who didn't care about anyone but yourself!" she said.

David shrugged. "I don't know what to tell you," he said. "I never meant to hurt you or any of your sisters. But that's the way I was raised."

"Look," said Donna, "things weren't good when we were kids. We're sitting here talking for the first time ever because of Jane. I know I wasn't sexually abused by you, but I became an emotional wreck because of you." She thought for a minute and continued, "And I'm afraid for Jane, too. This is happening as a direct result of your problems." Donna began to sob. Betty walked over to put her arms around her daughter. "Don't!" Donna cried. "This is about Dad and me. Stop trying to get in the middle all the time. You can't fix everything!"

The next week, a series of events brought things to a head. That Sunday was Father's Day, and Jane sent David a card, thanking him for being her father. Betty called Jane and asked her what she meant by the card; Jane replied that she loved her father, but couldn't see him until she was stronger. Jane then invited her mother and sisters over for supper, without their father.

Betty lost her temper and accused Jane of playing games with her father's emotions. Jane, equally angry, replied that her survivors group had warned her not to send the card. "I should have listened to my real family," she said.

When I heard this, I decided things had gone far enough. I could not be sure, of course, that this was a case of false memory, but Jane's therapist, who would not communicate with me or the family, was blocking me and the family from getting enough information to make a responsible assessment.

At the same time, the therapist of the survivors group was advocating Jane's complete exile from her family of origin. Jane, I felt, needed to be evaluated properly, and the option of including her in family therapy explored. I advised David and Betty to make appointments with the executive director and clinical director of the mental health agency where Jane was going, and to request a meeting with the Board of Directors of the YWCA where Jane's survivors group met and to inform them all of what was going on. David and Betty, on their own, have decided to retain an attorney to explore legal options if their complaints to the YWCA board are not responsibly handled. David has also agreed to begin an aggressive, structured outpatient program for alcohol dependence.

As I reflect upon this complex, difficult, and ongoing case, I am struck by the way we, as helpers, can exacerbate the problems our clients face and how we can confuse our clinical formulas with the truth. While the debate about recovered memories continues to rage, it is especially important to be careful about the damage we can do in the name of protecting clients from their own families.

CASE COMMENTARY 1
BY MARY JO BARRETT AND WAYNE SCOTT

This case highlights the issues that typically need to be dealt with in the beginning stage of a case involving allegations of incest. Here, treatment has stalemated into an unresolvable debate between Jane and her parents—Did it or did it not happen? Mired in a preoccupation with the truth, family members avoid directly confronting the toxicity that has permeated all their relationships and led to Jane's accusation, whether an act of sexual abuse has taken place.

While situations like this one often prove destructive for everyone involved, they can also provide adults who have grown up in a psychologically oppressive household a chance to confront and move beyond the past. But to accomplish that, it is important that they not simply cut off from their families. The goal of my work in cases such as this is to discourage everyone involved from becoming overfocused on whether or not particular incidents of abuse took place. It is far more important to get beyond polarization and create a third reality in which all family members together can explore how family relationships led children to grow up feeling powerless, disconnected, and haunted by the pain of the past.

To parents who believe their daughter is making false allegations of childhood abuse, I will typically say, "If you want to maintain a relationship with your daughter, the most important question you have to answer right now is not whether or not abuse took place. It's *why* your daughter believes that it did." I emphasize that both actual sexual abuse and false allegations grow out of the same psychological environment—one in which children grow up feeling disempowered, violated, and angry. If parents insist that their child has been brainwashed by irresponsible therapists, I ask them to consider what in that child's family experience has made her vulnerable to being brainwashed. If they argue that she is delusional, I ask them what they can do to help her better deal with the pain she's feeling.

Creating a therapeutic third reality means turning the family's attention away from a fruitless inquiry into possible hidden acts to an exploration of the destructive consequences of things everybody acknowledges took place. Early in therapy, I will ask adult children and their families about behaviors around which there is no mystery: Was there physical or verbal abuse in the home? Did one or the other parent drink in excess? Was a child questioned inappropriately about her sexual behavior? Was pornography left lying about the house? The point is not to get lost in clinical detective work, but to help the family establish how a child could grow up feeling powerless and unable to protect her personal boundaries within the family.

In cases in which false memories are alleged, the therapist must take an active role. Rather than rely on embattled family members to contact Jane and her therapist, Schissler needs to become more directly involved and find a way to develop a working relationship with Jane's therapist. He needs to communicate that he has Jane's best interests at heart and is not taking a position regarding the truth of her memories. He also needs to let Jane's therapist know that he wants to help Jane find ways to move out of her present disempowered position in the system so she can experience some appropriate measure of adult power and control. Clearly, none of these goals is served by Schissler encouraging Jane's family to contact lawyers or the board of directors at her treatment center.

In cases that involve abuse allegations at my facility, we typically try to meet with all family members first. We explain to each member our understanding about the relationship between family dysfunction, individual vulnerability, and allegations of abuse. There are times that certain members refuse our invitations, but we usually extend a standing invitation to allow people to change their minds. One survivor refused to come in and talk with us because she knew her father had contacted our clinic. But after we met her mother, now divorced from the alleged perpetrator, and another sibling, both of whom invited her in, she agreed to come to a session. She then signed a release for us to contact her extremely resistant therapist. After reading our literature, talking on the telephone, and having lunch with us, the therapist eventually participated in a number of very productive joint sessions in which she supported her client while a member of our staff served as family therapist.

The damage from sexual abuse comes not only from a discrete act of exploitation, but also from living in a world in which boundary violation and narcissism are the norm. When someone raised in a psychologically oppressive family suddenly recalls being molested as a child, it can be difficult for them to establish whether the recollection was a dream or an actual occurrence because, in their experience, the sense of victimization is all too real. But once this underlying experience is crystallized into an allegation, the world begins to respond in a different way. They can no longer be ignored. Suddenly they have words to describe what they have been feeling. Now they must be heard.

The goal of family therapy in cases of alleged abuse is not to magically reconcile the survivor and her family. It is to validate the perspective of the adult child by having other family members hear what her experience has been without anyone needing to deny or redefine it. Instead of an adult child's decision to avoid spending holidays with her family or being alone with her father being regarded as strange or paranoid, it becomes accepted as a necessary means of self-protection from her perspective. Sometimes, the outcome of this approach to treatment is a cautious, distant relationship that may, in time, evolve into something more.

But whatever the result of helping families explore the third reality, it is almost always preferable to leaving family members locked in their battle stations, carrying on an unresolvable debate that leaves no room for change.

CASE COMMENTARY 2
BY BILL O'HANLON

Periodically, therapists become enamored of a new diagnosis, theory, or clinical issue—multiple personality disorder, bulimia, borderline personality disorder, brief therapy, gender issues, diversity/cross-cultural issues. Then, to counteract the fact that we either ignored or denied the issue in the past, we overemphasize or overvalue it for a while. Eventually, we find a middle ground between denial and overemphasis and the field is richer and better for it. With all this in mind, I'm glad about the current debate over recovered memories of abuse. I think it will make us better therapists and clarify that we need to be cautious about our influence with clients and our need to explore the possibility of unacknowledged abuse issues.

Clearly, this case highlights some important issues regarding recovered memory. Clinicians are *not* judges, police officers, or legal experts. We cannot make informed judgments about the reliability of our clients' reports. We do not have the investigative tools to determine the accuracy of sexual abuse allegations. When we act as legal experts, we move beyond the bounds of our expertise and our mandate as clinicians.

Accordingly, Schissler is correct in reserving judgment about David's guilt or innocence. He doesn't have enough data to determine what happened between David and his daughters. All the evidence in this case is open to question. Jane's hospital records (and those of her grandmothers) do not prove that Jane's report was false. People with delusions may also have been abused. David's denials are also inconclusive. He may have abused Jane during a blackout and have no recollection of it. In a case like this, one must be very careful about whose story one believes. In fact, I wonder why, if Jane's family does not believe her memories about the abuse, they believe her reports about what her therapist or the group leader at the YWCA said. And I am concerned that Schissler also seems to believe these third-hand reports.

The key issue for a therapist in this kind of case is establishing what the family hopes to accomplish by coming to therapy. Is this family looking for help in confronting the abuse accusations? Do they want help getting David to stop drinking? Are they interested in changing their family interaction patterns? At the onset, it appeared that Donna called Schissler asking for help and guidance about her sister's accusations. But Schissler took things one step further—he invited her to come to therapy again, rather than giving her a few ideas or some reassurance over the telephone. Schissler should clarify what his role and the focus of the therapy should be before proceeding. Otherwise, he is in danger of doing the very thing he is upset about Jane's therapist doing—imposing his agenda on the client.

If the goal is to help this family deal with the issues raised by Jane's accusations without splintering completely, I think it's important to keep the lines of communication open with Jane and the professionals who are helping her. My best friend, a lawyer, once told me something very wise: "A lawsuit is what you do when you stop communicating with someone. Go communicate with the person you are upset with. Don't sue them. It's rarely worth it." This family is in danger of cutting off communication with Jane, and Schissler is in danger of cutting off communication with Jane's therapist. I would have liked Schissler to call up Jane's therapist and offer (with the family's and Jane's permission, of course) to meet alone with that therapist to hash things out and come up with some course of action that doesn't lead to lawyers or polarized positions. I would want to find out about what Jane and her therapist are concerned.

Abuse specialists often worry that if a family meeting happens, their clients will be pressured to recant or will be further injured by the family's denial. If Schissler could convince the other therapist that he would not allow that to happen, and that the therapist could be present at any meeting to make sure it didn't happen, perhaps there could be some mutual understanding and the family could come up with a course of action that would be agreeable to all concerned. For instance, they could probably all agree that David needs to stop drinking. If Jane and her therapist saw his willingness to admit he drinks too much and to take steps to change at least *that* problem, maybe they wouldn't characterize him as being completely in denial. I would tell Jane's therapist and the family about the work of the Cambridge Public Dialogue Project, where they have gathered people on both sides of the abortion debate and created an atmosphere of understanding. If they can do that with such a polarized and seemingly intractable issue, I would argue, surely we could do the same with Jane's accusations.

The family's response to Jane's Father's Day card represents a lost clinical opportunity. I would have encouraged Betty to call Jane and thank her for taking the time to send the card. I would advise the family to avoid blame and accusation, and encourage anything that leads to more communication and contact (as long as Jane isn't abusive or threatening). If Jane was, initially, only willing to see Betty, Donna, and Debby, I would have encouraged that. Using the family's belief that Jane's memories were delusional, I would encourage them to show compassion (rather than contempt or anger) for her. "If she were having delusions about being controlled by beams of energy from outer space, how would you respond?" I would ask the family. My guess is that they would respond quite differently than the way they are currently dealing with her. Perhaps under the influence of this more loving, understanding response, Jane would change her story or she might even convince Betty, Donna, and Debby that her story of abuse is true.

One last note of caution: Jane's therapist has allegedly spoken to several family members about the fact that Jane is in therapy and Jane's family has copies of her psychiatric hospital records. If Jane is unwilling for her family to be involved, how did this information get released? If Jane were my client, no family member would know whether she was or was not in treatment with me without Jane's explicit, written permission to release such information. In a case that may involve litigation, I would be extremely cautious of my actions, especially regarding confidentiality.

AUTHOR'S RESPONSE
BY HENRY SCHISSLER

The commentary by Barrett and Scott contains a statement that captures the fundamental issue in cases where memories of childhood sexual abuse are called into question: "Both actual sexual abuse and false allegations grow out of the same psychological environment— one in which children grow up feeling disrespected, violated, and angry." In such cases, family members need help to move through their fear, resentments, anger, and finger pointing. I believe that is what is happening in this case, even without Jane's participation. David has been confronted about his drinking and is beginning to deal with the problem, and Donna has finally challenged her mother's need to orchestrate relationships within the family.

In his commentary, Bill O'Hanlon does not seem to notice the progress this family is making. While he identifies the serious difficulties in this case—the family's lack of clarity about its goals and the blocked communication between Jane and her family of origin and among the therapists involved in the case—his solutions fail to point toward useful new directions. I was troubled by O'Hanlon's assertion that if the family started showing compassion toward Jane rather than contempt, things would be different. The bewilderment, petty lashing out, and fear that he calls "contempt" are rooted in deep concern and love. It was necessary for the family to move through this mix of emotions in order to begin their therapeutic work. O'Hanlon doesn't seem to understand that and accuses me of encouraging their "contempt." I disagree.

The commentators were all troubled by the lack of communication among me, Jane's therapist, and her counselor at the YWCA. I was troubled too, but the point of the case is how the survivor-based counseling rules can cut off the necessary communication in a case such as this by placing a protective wall around the client. As a postscript, I am happy to report that the wall may have been breached. Betty and David did speak with the YWCA executive director and a meeting between all the therapists involved in this case is being planned. While the commentators may not approve, the power play of the parents' going to a higher agency authority may still enable the members of this family to get the help they need. ■

STUDY QUESTIONS

1. Do you think Schissler's criticisms about the way Jane's therapists handled her case are justified? Why or why not?

2. How might Schissler have created a third reality, as described by Barrett and Scott?

3. What does O'Hanlon say the role of the therapist is in cases dealing with allegations of abuse? What do you think?

4. Based on this case, do you believe therapists can create false memories of abuse in their clients?

CASE STUDY

RESOLVING THE IRRESOLVABLE
CONSTRUCTING A WAY OUT FOR FAMILIES TORN APART BY STRUGGLES OVER RECOVERED MEMORIES

Mary Jo Barrett

Joe, the CEO of a large textile company, called me from Boston. He told me he had two business cards in front of him on his desk, one from me and one from a malpractice lawyer. He planned to meet with the lawyer, fly to Chicago to see me, and then decide whether to sue his daughter's therapist or try mediation with me.

Two years earlier, Joe's 32-year-old daughter, Laura, had written to him (and to her mother, two sisters, and brother) saying that during the process of therapy, she'd remembered her father's sexually abusing her as a child. She made it clear that she didn't want him to write or call, and wouldn't be home for Christmas or Thanksgiving. Within months, she'd stopped talking to her mother on the telephone as well. All this had put much of the family into an uproar, and Laura was now only in touch with one sister, the sole family member who believed her.

Joe insisted that he'd never abused Laura, said he'd been in touch with the False Memory Syndrome Foundation and told me he thought his daughter had undergone recovered memory therapy that had made her even more depressed and convinced her to cut off from her family.

Since 1992, I have conducted mediations with more than 50 families like Joe's. I begin with something like shuttle diplomacy, meeting with both sides separately to see if negotiations are even possible, and then to clarify goals and ground rules. The dialogue usually culminates with family members flying or driving to Chicago, often from halfway across the country, for one or two joint negotiation sessions in my office in Skokie, Illinois.

From the first contact, I do my best to be neutral. I have worked with incestuous families and traumatized adults for more than 20 years, but when I work with these divided families, I take no position on either parental innocence or childhood victimization. It is my hunch that some long-forgotten memories of abuse reflect realities and others may be metaphors for less physical forms of familial violation. Be that as it may, my goal is not to change anyone's mind about the past. My primary goals are those of a mediator—to explore how people with very different working assumptions about reality can nevertheless organize meaningful, safe, and respectful contact with one another. This is partly a matter of crafting agreements that cover what might seem like niggling details, like who sits next to whom at Thanksgiving dinner or what topics can be addressed in a letter. These nuts-and-bolts agreements are most easily reached when family members can agree on a third reality—often an emotional truth about the family that transcends disagreements on details.

In one family dialogue mediation, a daughter who had not spoken to her father for eight years agreed to sit at the same table at a family wedding, on condition that her father would not hug her and that their conversation would be limited to safe topics, like their careers. Other families have reached agreements permitting Hanukkah celebrations, visits with grandchildren, exchanges of letters, and telephone calls within carefully defined limits. No family has magically entered a paradise where all is forgiven and understood, the prodigal daughter returns or the father confesses and charges of sexual abuse are dramatically clarified, validated, or retracted. All have more contact than they had before we began and most have reached agreement on at least some aspects of their shared pasts.

I told Joe that I would not expect him to admit to things he believed he did not do, nor would I urge his daughter to recant or ply her with information about the nature of memory. I would not go to court and testify against his daughter's therapist nor would I even hold the mediation if he was actively pursuing a lawsuit. I could offer him nothing more than a peaceful way to establish some contact with his daughter, however minimal. This was not therapy but negotiation. No one would be a winner, I told him, and yet both he and his daughter might win something.

Two weeks later, Joe and his wife, Diana, flew to Chicago and we tackled the first logistical issue: How could they ask their daughter to take part in mediation when she'd forbidden them to write or call? If they began by violating the limits she'd set, I said, they wouldn't get anywhere. I suggested they ask Laura's most sympathetic sister to be a go-between, and, through her sister, Laura agreed to receive a letter from her parents limited to the question of mediation. That letter, drafted with my help, said that I was a family therapist with experience in treating trauma as well as in mediating with families after allegations of abuse. It included a variety of ways Laura could contact me.

A week later, Laura's therapist called me. Sometimes the dialogue ends right there: Some therapists apparently fear that I will be manipulated into drawing their clients back into abusive or invalidating family relationships. But after Laura's therapist became satisfied that I did not intend to turn Laura into a scapegoat or urge her to recant, Laura called me twice, the first time with her therapist on the speaker phone. When she understood the limits of the mediation, she agreed to meet with me.

After a preliminary meeting, Laura and I got together to set goals and explore what she wanted out of the mediation. She was the manager of a photographic gallery in Chicago, and she told me that she was tired of being gossiped about within the family as "the problem" since sending her letters. She resented that the focus was on her behavior rather than her parents' actions, that she didn't want to have much to do with her father, and that she really missed contact with her mother. She wanted an acknowledgment from her parents of family difficulties that had nothing to do with sexual abuse or recovered memories.

Joe and Diana wanted more contact than that. In a separate goals-setting session, they told me they wanted to be able to call Laura on the telephone and have her come back to Boston for Thanksgiving and Christmas. They reiterated that they wanted a chance to defend their position that no sexual abuse had taken place, and I reminded them to set aside that question for the mediation. I asked them to think about something else instead: If they were so sure Laura had been brainwashed, what was it about Laura's childhood, and her role in the family, that might have made her vulnerable to "brainwashing"? Could they acknowledge that theirs hadn't been a perfect family?

On the morning of the mediation, all moves were carefully choreographed. Joe and Diana arrived in my office as planned, 15 minutes before Laura arrived, so that there would be no awkward meetings in the waiting room. By prior agreement, Joe and Diana did not rise from their seats or move to hug Laura when she arrived. Instead, they briefly shared their feelings of excitement, fear, and hope. Then all three of them burst into tears, and Laura said, "It's really good to see you, Mom."

The next three hours were as full of time-outs and caucuses as any heated labor negotiation. Whenever anybody needed a break or needed to consult with me outside the presence of others, we made time. Sometimes I offered someone a glass of water, a Kleenex®, or words of encouragement, but I would then go over to the other side and do the same thing. I regularly asked Laura whether she felt safe and asked her parents whether they felt heard by me. It was my job to stay as neutral as possible, to keep the room safe by calling everyone on any disrespectful communication, and to design and offer alternatives that might meet everyone's needs.

Laura began. She believed she'd been abused, she said, partly because of memories she had never repressed: memories of lying curled up under her bed at night, listening to her father shout, beat her brother, and break dishes against the wall. Often, she said, she feared for her mother's life. She remembered coming home to find her mother drunk and depressed on the living room couch, while her 13-year-old sister stood in the kitchen making dinner. She had tried to play the role of the "happy little girl," and she wasn't willing to do that anymore, she said. As an adult, she felt her father had badgered her about her career, asked her too many nosy, personal questions, and commented too graphically on her physical appearance. "I don't care if you deny the sexual abuse," she finally said. "Will you at least admit these other things?"

Laura's mother cried and wept. "I hate hearing this," she said. "I don't remember it all. But yes, it was terrible, and we are ashamed."

Then her father—a huge, imposing, man who'd been an Olympic swimmer—broke in. "I'm different now," he said. "I've changed." When Laura responded, "I don't want to hear how you've changed, I don't feel safe," he stopped.

"It was terrible," he said.

This was the turning point. I knew then that our negotiations would be successful. The parents, desperate for contact with their daughter, had adopted a nondefensive posture that created a safe context. Laura was no longer defined as the irrational "problem," and she and her parents had come to a shared familial reality. Even though they agreed to disagree about specific physical abuse, they all acknowledged that enough had happened in Laura's childhood to cause her profound distress and make her feel unsafe. Now that Laura's inner emotional reality had been validated, she was willing to continue communication and some sort of relationship with her parents. We broke for the day.

The next day we got down to the nuts and bolts. Laura acknowledged her anger and her pain. She also acknowledged what she enjoyed in her relationships with each of her parents and agreed to build on those aspects. She had sorely missed her mother, and we figured out ways for her to call her mother at set times when her mother—not her father—would answer the telephone. Those conversations, her mother agreed, would be kept private. She would not badger Laura into having more contact with her father or argue with her about her memories. Laura also agreed to begin writing to her father about photography, a shared love. Her father agreed to let Laura control the frequency and timing of the correspondence by only writing in response to a letter from her. Laura, everyone agreed, would be the one to initiate any hugs or physical contact. And over the next few months, all three would explore ground rules for a family Thanksgiving.

At the end of the session, we drew up a formal written agreement, based on my notes, and signed by all parties. The parents acknowledged that they had heard and agreed with much of Laura's historical narrative and understood her need for boundaries. Laura, for her part, agreed to have written and verbal contact with them. Anyone could request my renewed involvement if anyone broke the contract and they could not resolve things without a third party. They also agreed on what they would say to other family members—that the meeting was a first step and that they had agreed not to go into the details.

When I first decided, in 1992, that I had to do something to help families and therapists dig their way out of the angry, adversarial, cutoff state we'd found ourselves in, I had no idea that this sort of mediation could succeed. But it has. We haven't resolved the debates about traumatic memory and good therapy. But we have helped adult children feel empowered, and parents and siblings become reattached, usually in healthier ways. Every family that has chosen this process has reported that our mediations were just the beginning of safer family relationships. I continue to be humbled by these families' courage to face one another and move toward a shared and respectful future.

Case Commentary
BY ELIZABETH F. LOFTUS

As many families today struggle bitterly over recent accusations of long-ago abuse, paths to reconciliation have not been easy to discover. Now Mary Jo Barrett, with her innovative Family Dialogue Project, has stepped in to fill the void and offer a desperately needed new approach.

This case example fits the mold of many cases that have fueled the repressed memory controversy. Five years earlier, Laura, after remembering her father's sexually abusing her, cut off contact with practically all of her family. After years of silence and stalemate, Joe, Laura's father, wants what many fathers in this situation would want: contact with his daughter, vindication, and to stop Laura's therapist from hurting other families. For her part, Laura wants an end to the focus on her as the family problem and the acknowledgment that, even apart from her memories of abuse, Dad's rages and Mom's depressive drinking while she was growing up have created many problems for her.

In my own work over the past few years, as I have collaborated with mental-health professionals on finding better ways of helping families in which there are highly disputed recollections of abuse, I have suggested that therapists borrow from noted couples researcher John Gottman's excellent advice on how to make marriages succeed. Gottman believes that it is important to remind clients that negative events in their lives do not completely cancel out all the positives. Perhaps one of the most important factors in this case is that Barrett neither dwells on the misery of childhood nor digs for childhood sexual trauma as its cause. She is able to bring the daughter and her parents together for mediation, or, as she aptly puts it, "shuttle diplomacy." After fits and starts, the family appears to have made some progress in reconnecting. I was struck by Barrett's encouraging Laura to acknowledge what she still valued in her relationships with each of her parents—how she missed her mother and the love of photography she shared with her father. Her approach is particularly relevant since there is no clinical evidence that focusing on repressed memories and childhood trauma actually helps clients get better. In fact, after reviewing 40 studies of people who retracted memories of childhood abuse, H.I. Lief and J. Fetkewicz conclude in their 1995 *Journal of Psychiatry & Law* article, "Retractors of False Memories," that focusing on recovered memories "is bad therapy . . . patients get sicker instead of better, and huge sums of money are spent for years of therapy based on the erroneous assumption that the recovery of memories of sexual abuse in childhood is a healing process."

The fundamental question regarding Barrett's approach is whether it is possible for divided families to attempt any kind of reconciliation without addressing the validity of abuse accusations at all. I'm reminded of that famous line, "Other than that, Mrs. Lincoln, how did you like the play?" Can we reasonably expect many accused parents to be able to concentrate on a discussion of relatively lesser maltreatments when the large gorilla of abuse is sitting in the corner, never really out of the way? While the alarming prevalence of childhood sexual abuse is beyond dispute at this point, it is vital that mental-health professionals remain acutely sensitive to the damage that false accusations can inflict on families, as well as to the terrible psychological consequences of abuse itself. Again and again, I have encountered cases in which, after investigating the facts, I have been convinced that families have been victimized by destructive therapy in which the line between fantasy and the reality of abuse was blurred. For most of the parents in these cases, the question of their innocence of abuse accusations is nonnegotiable.

Although Barrett's case ends with the possibility of hope for the splintered family she describes (I would like to hear more follow-up information about them), the question remains of how generally effective Barrett's "shuttle diplomacy" is with families embattled over repressed memories. In this case, Joe seemed able to move past his anger, with Barrett's encouragement, to take a different position. So, perhaps, might others. Although very different mediation procedures will almost certainly be needed for different kinds of families, Barrett has presented us with a promising idea and some preliminary data as a starting point. As a first step toward thinking about helping divided families begin to heal, Barrett has done us all a great service.

AUTHOR'S RESPONSE

BY MARY JO BARRETT

I appreciate Elizabeth Loftus's encouragement and agree that the mediation process I am describing is tricky. Since the session between Laura and her family, their contacts with one another, to date, have been respectful. In fact, they have just telephoned me to set up an appointment to discuss guidelines for a Thanksgiving visit.

It is still too early to know whether families can reconcile while allowing what Loftus describes as "the large gorilla of abuse" to remain sitting in the corner. All that I can say is that, overall, 18 families have set up subsequent rounds of family dialogues, to continue the progress they have made in their initial contacts. I am very encouraged by this response and believe it offers the possibility of hope for many divided families. ■

STUDY QUESTIONS

1. How did Barrett create an environment of safety for all family members?

2. In what ways are the goals of *therapy* different from the goals of *family mediation?* How does the therapist's role differ in each situation?

3. What do you think of Loftus's point that a family that never resolves the validity of the abuse allegation can never really reconcile?

CHAPTER 4

The Tools of the Trade

NOTHING FILLS the seats in a hotel ballroom like a workshop that promises therapists a new clinical method, some secret knowledge that can produce sudden dramatic changes in troubled lives. In fact, it was the promise of just those kinds of results that launched family therapy in the first place. Through the years, thousands of therapists have been drawn to trainings in other approaches—Ericksonian Hypnosis, Neurolinguistic Programming, Milan Paradox—that also offered the hope of suddenly leapfrogging over the seemingly towering obstacles in their lives and accelerating the plodding pace of change. Even as the field has taken an increasingly jaded view of new clinical tools, innovators continue to try to interest their colleagues in the exciting possibilities of new methods.

The following cases demonstrate the range of possibilities available to therapists searching for something new and different—from simply adding new flexibility to a time-tested approach, to the high-risk adventure of embracing new paradigms for treating trauma. In "Mr Spock Goes to Therapy," Eve Lipchik breaks the rules of solution-focused therapy to prevent blind orthodoxy to a technique. Therapist Daniel Wiener works to free clients and therapists from rigid roles and expectations by using improvisation exercises in his case, "The Gift of Play," and discovers that spontaneity in the safe context of therapy can expand clients' emotional repertoire. In "Humanizing the Impossible Case," Jay Lappin and John VanDeusen describe how a network approach to the overwhelming multiproblems of a low-income family brought together dozens of frustrated public agencies to jointly create seemingly impossible solutions. Finally, the eagerness of therapists to do whatever it takes to help clients overcome the aftereffects of trauma has led to a new paradigm for trauma treatment that moves away from psychodynamic and family systems issues to a focus on the body and brain. "The Enigma of EMDR" demonstrates the use of eye-movement desensitization and reprocessing in conjunction with brief therapy, and "A No-Talk Cure for Trauma" shows how an unconventional technique involving tapping on certain points on the body can free a client of panic attacks.

MR. SPOCK GOES TO THERAPY
GOOD THERAPY MEANS KNOWING WHEN TO BREAK THE RULES

Eve Lipchik

Much attention has been focused on the straightforward and easy-to-learn techniques of solution-focused therapy: questions about times when the problem is less intense ("exceptions"); questions about hypothetical solutions ("miracles"); and questions about the quantitative differences between problems and exceptions ("scaling"). Yet despite the seeming effectiveness of these techniques, when clients are asked to explain why they feel better from one session to the next, they often refer in general terms to feeling accepted and understood by their therapist—a mark of all good therapy, regardless of orientation.

So rather than emphasizing technique when training therapists, I focus on the theoretical assumptions that lie at the heart of the solution-focused model. These include: Change is constant and inevitable; a small change can lead to bigger changes; since you can't change the past, concentrate on the future; people have the resources necessary to help themselves; and every human being, relationship, and situation is unique. By relying on these assumptions as a guide to what to ask clients next and how to respond to their answers, therapists are freed from their anxiety about "doing the model" the right way or whether a particular case is appropriate for this approach and can focus, instead, on attuning themselves to their clients' reality and developing a sense of timing that fits each case.

The following case illustrates the overarching importance of setting aside rigid orthodoxies and breaking the rules to meet a client's idiosyncratic needs.

When Lyle first walked into my office, he seemed a shy and sensitive man who wasn't sure he wanted to be there. Tall, well built though slightly overweight, he was neatly dressed, with a small gold hoop in his left ear. At 27, Lyle had recently moved to Milwaukee to "make a fresh start" after six years in the Navy. During the six months immediately following his discharge, Lyle had returned to his home town on the West Coast and had confided in his mother and a few very close friends that he was gay, but had asked her not tell his father, two older brothers, and an older sister. He had also had his first romantic encounter with a man, which had ended in their being friends but no longer lovers. To Lyle, life in Milwaukee was lonely and unexciting. Trained as an inhalation therapist in the service, he now worked the evening shift in a hospital, where he had met his only social contact, a nurse named Nancy. Nancy and her husband and child were Lyle's "family away from home." Concerned about Lyle's depression, it was Nancy who had urged him to seek professional help.

Despite his apparent discomfort, Lyle seemed eager to tell me his story, as though he had rehearsed it before coming. He said he did not feel at all settled in Milwaukee and felt like an outsider at work. He agreed with Nancy that he was depressed; in fact, he believed he had been depressed since his grandfather had died when he was eight. All he felt now, he reported, was anger, sadness, and very little else—except "when people are listening to me and accepting what I have to say as a viable point of view." When I tried to get him to expand on this exception, he tensed up and began answering my questions with "I don't know." An attempt to get him to scale his negative feelings in relation to his positive ones met with the same fate. The closest he could come to quantifying anything was to say that he would like his ratio of positive to negative feelings to be 50/50.

Since I put a lot of emphasis on the emotional climate in which the collaboration for solutions takes place, I took Lyle at his word about feeling best when people listen to him. I asked him what he thought would be most important for me to hear. The question seemed to relax him, and he began to talk effusively about his sense of emptiness, a lack of feeling that he thought related to the childhood experience of being removed from his grandfather's funeral because he was crying so hard. His way of coping over the years had been to try to emulate Mr. Spock, the Vulcan on *Star Trek* who was incapable of human emotion.

"Are you sure you want more feelings, even positive ones," I asked him, "or do you want to work on being more like Mr. Spock?"

"I want more positive feelings," he insisted, but then proceeded to recount all his negative ones in detail. Once again, Lyle seemed to be trying to tell me how bad he felt, which prompted me to check for suicidal or homicidal ideations. He admitted that suicide had crossed his mind at times, but he had never made any suicidal gestures and did not seem to have a plan in place. In an effort to move from problem talk to solution talk, I tried to focus more on how Lyle had managed to cope with his difficulties. This opened a floodgate of self-recrimination. "I haven't dealt with life. I've avoided it!" he said in disgust. I offered another perspective by saying that some people might think that he had coped well given his painful life. After all, he had finished high school and a year of college, he had spent six years in the Navy, had learned a profession there and had been honorably discharged, and he was now holding a job. He dismissed all of this with the comment, "If I don't function, I don't get things. I do it for me because no one else will." I wondered aloud whether his ability to do this could be thought of as a strength. Lyle seemed startled and said, "I never looked at it that way. I always thought it was fear that kept me going."

An important piece of the solution-focused approach is the summation message, which the therapist composes, alone or with a team, during a break about 40 minutes into the session, then presents to the client at the end of the session. It is a way of reflecting back, of supporting and reinforcing positive gains and offering new perspectives. This was my summation message to Lyle after our first session:

"What I hear you say today is that you are here because of your depression, which you remember as starting when your grandfather died. You say that you feel a lot of angry and sad feelings but little happy or positive ones. Your goal in coming is to feel happy feelings about 50% of the time.

"My response is that you appear to be a thoughtful, conscientious person who is very sensitive to what others think and feel about you. It seems pretty natural that you have a lot of anger and sadness, given your feelings that your parents did not validate you and that you lost the only person in your life who did. It was really creative of you to look to a fictitious character like Mr. Spock as a role model, yet you have managed to grow up and appear to be a much warmer, more human man—more like the grandfather you described to me. It seems to me to be a good idea that you took your friend's advice to come to talk to someone. That is a sign of strength. Since you have such high standards for yourself, I

hope you don't expect to develop new habits about feeling more positive very quickly. That takes time and works better if one goes slowly."

I then casually suggested to Lyle that he might spend 15 minutes
once or twice each day writing about his negative feelings and then de-
stroying what was written—a technique I often recommend to people
who are putting pressure on themselves to change. I added that it would
help me to understand him better if he would continue keeping track of
any positive feelings he experienced, no matter how small.

When Lyle returned a week later, he looked sad and sullen and told me
right away that he had not acted on any of my suggestions. I knew immediately that I was being tested. Lyle was asking, "Will you listen to me
and validate me, no matter what I do?" Choosing not to respond to this
tacit question, I asked whether there was anything he wanted to share
with me about what had happened since last I saw him. He shook his
head. When I asked, "Were there any questions you wish I would have
asked you?", he perked up and reported that he had generally felt more
hopeful this week. He had felt more focused and productive at work and
had been more relaxed with the people there. All his examples were described in feelings; he refused any behavioral focus. When I tried to get
him to talk about a future in which these positive changes could be maintained and increased, he responded by telling me self-denigrating stories.

Ventilation—or problem talk—is certainly not a solution-focused
technique, but I realized that if I did not allow Lyle to set the tone and
pace of our conversations, he would probably not come back. At one
point, I said, "I know this is very hard for you, and you want me to understand how much pain you felt in the past. I don't mean to discount it,
but the past is gone, and you came here to talk about happier feelings.
Is this helpful, or do you want to talk about how you can feel differently
in the future?" Lyle kept right on ventilating. What was I to do? Clearly,
he needed me to accept and affirm him just the way he was, yet I didn't
want to encourage his problem orientation. Even when I tried to use his
grandfather as a resource and asked him to consider what his grandfather would say about something he put himself down for, I could not get
a more positive focus.

In keeping with the adage "brief therapy goes slowly," I chose to be
patient and empathic, while listening for an opportunity to shift the

conversation. Finally, after he had inventoried complaints against his parents and against himself for poor choices he had made as a child and adolescent, I interjected, "As an adult you seem to have a much better understanding about how to relate to people than you did when you were younger." Lyle relaxed visibly, took a deep breath, and slowly joined me in talking about future change.

In the summation message for this session, I reflected back my understanding of Lyle's angry and sad feelings about his past. I commented on how hard he was on himself and reinforced the idea that he could reevaluate his feelings from an adult perspective. I also suggested that he might consider how the qualities he remembered in his grandfather might prove useful for him as an adult.

The next three sessions took place one week apart and followed a distinct pattern. Lyle would describe some small changes, then immediately begin venting negative feelings. The positive changes were consistent and significant, so I just kept doing what was working. At the same time, I found many opportunities to challenge Lyle's belief that he had to keep feeling the same way about things now and in the future as he did in the past.

As our conversations progressed, Lyle's ventilation turned to more intimate issues: his sense of being different because he was so angry much of the time; his belief that he was inherently bad; his premonitions about future events; his escape into daydreams and fantasies. I heard them all as one loud, fearful question: "Do you think I'm crazy?"

I addressed this tentatively by reflecting how difficult it must be to live with so many concerns about oneself and asked whether he had overcome any worries from the past. He answered, "No, I'm still not that human." He went on to tell me about his tendency to sit in a daze and not really hear what people were saying to him. I wondered whether he was talking about our conversations and decided to check it out—not because I was interested in exploring the transference, as a psychodynamic therapist might, but because I wanted to be sure that I was truly hearing him the way he was hoping to be heard. Lyle acknowledged that he sometimes felt dazed with me as well, but added, "I know what's expected of me, and I have to respond. I'm rising above my feelings to help myself." Again Lyle was indicating that he had some control over his feelings, which I reinforced by asking, "How is talking with me giving you the control to rise above your feelings to help yourself?" "There are times now when I'm more awake," he offered tentatively. "Then I handle things better."

By the fifth session, Lyle was still not ready to accept compliments when he reported positive changes or to expand on them in response to my questions. Instead of stonewalling me, however, he was now able to share with me what was on his mind. "If I keep reminding myself that I'm doing well," he explained, "an internal voice will scold me for bragging, or I might worry that I'll end up letting myself down." I wondered aloud what was worse, always feeling bad about oneself or letting oneself down once in a while. "I would choose feeling worse any time to letting myself down," he answered emphatically.

Now my own internal voice chimed in with a concern of its own. "Does this mean he can't allow himself to get much better?" Given this dilemma, I asked how he thought our conversations could be helpful to him. Lyle explained that I represented an unbiased viewpoint that he could allow himself to consider. "But I would think some people might still choose to discount it if they preferred the option of feeling worse," I responded. "No," he said. "Because it is a professional opinion, and that means something. I go home and think about it. It's very slow, but I think I've made some adjustments. I need to begin to do other things on the outside to help myself, and I'm starting to do that."

Since he recognized there had been change, I asked him to scale the difference between how he felt about himself when he first came in and how he felt about himself now, but again he would not cooperate. In retrospect, I realize that this technique did not fit with what he had just told me about being afraid to acknowledge too much change. In one of our later sessions, when he was beginning to acknowledge progress, Lyle spontaneously noted that the change had improved from 5% to 15%. When Lyle observed that progress was good but slow, I suggested that we meet every other week so he could continue to move slowly and not feel too uncomfortable about change. He agreed.

In the sixth to eleventh sessions, Lyle continued to report progress. Although he still started by talking about the positive and then shifted to complaints, the positive talk was getting longer and the negative talk shorter. The positive talk focused on professional and social successes. For example, when he was invited to attend a wedding back home, Lyle asked an old friend to accompany him so he wouldn't feel lonely and isolated. In my summation message for one of these sessions, I suggested that Lyle might consider doing an exercise in which he practiced distinguishing between what pleased him and what pleased other people. To my surprise, he actually followed through on the suggestion. It was a new idea for him to distinguish what he wanted from what someone else might want, he admitted.

One of the goals of solution-focused therapy is to help clients access and build on their own resources. But what if the client's resources are deficient in some areas? Lyle, for example, seemed to think that identity was a fixed set of characteristics. He was surprised by the idea that one could have an identity yet still make different choices in different roles with different people. "From what you have told me about yourself," I observed, "your identity has been shaped to a great extent by choices you have made, like whether to conform in the Navy or get kicked out. Whether to go to work and do what is expected of you there." "Then I guess I'm the type of person who sits and won't do anything because I'm afraid of what people think," he responded.

"That may be one aspect, but it isn't your whole identity," I countered. "Isn't who you are also the loving grandson; both the loving and the angry son; the sometimes pompous and authoritarian inhalation therapist who is always sensitive and caring with patients? Aren't you a unique combination of all these qualities?"

This perspective seemed to disturb him because it represented uncertainty rather than stability. Gradually, he seemed to begin to recognize that choices did not have to be either/or and did not always guarantee a positive outcome because of other people's choices. We talked about his power to make choices in the future based on his own values and how he wants to feel about himself. This seemed to take on greater meaning for him when I reminded him that Mr. Spock had not been free from making choices even though he had no feelings. As he began to understand this new perspective, I noticed that he gradually became more accepting of himself when he talked about being both "arrogant" and "warm" at work under different circumstances.

The eighth session veered from the usual pattern. Lyle started out by telling me that he had been so depressed during the past two weeks that he had almost packed up and moved back to the West Coast. As he vented about how lonely and sad he felt, I recognized this as a positive change and asked what had kept him from acting on his feelings and leaving. I also wondered what was different about this depressive episode than past ones. Without hesitation he said it had been less intense than previously because he never even thought about suicide. He then began to wonder whether perhaps he had just been lonely and homesick, and not depressed. Nancy and her family had been out of town and he had missed them. He also received a letter from home about his dog, whom he missed. I normalized his feelings and he replied that, given that this was his first experience living without parental or military supervision, "life here isn't all bad; I like being on my own."

After this session, Lyle's mood lifted, and it seemed appropriate to evaluate where we were. How many more positive than negative feelings was he experiencing? Although he did not want to scale his answer, he indicated that he thought he had made a lot of progress. He cited being more assertive at work, extending himself more socially and feeling generally more courageous. As he neared his original goal of having more happy feelings, however, he had begun to realize that his real goal was to have a satisfying relationship with a man. "But that feels like a lot of pressure," he added quickly. I suggested he go slowly after all the changes he had been making, and we set an appointment for three weeks later.

At this next session, Lyle focused almost exclusively on positive changes. He joyfully reported receiving a promotion at work and feeling really good about himself. He was even coping well with coworkers who felt jealous of him because they had been passed over. "I'm making choices for myself that work for me," Lyle said. Most important of all, he had come out about being gay to his father, writing a letter to both parents so his father would not suspect that his mother had known all along. To Lyle's tremendous relief, his father had phoned immediately and had been very supportive and accepting. At the end of the session, Lyle said he had been feeling like a normal person lately and had been enjoying more "ups." Lyle's only concern was that he had been waking up at night crying. When I asked him what he thought it meant, he said he was crying because he wanted a love relationship but was afraid of it as well. I also sensed that he might be releasing some of the sadness and grief he had kept inside for so long.

In my summation message, I reflected that he had been talking about so many losses since our conversations had begun—the loss of his grandfather, his home town, his childhood, his identity as a military man, his identity as a straight man. I wondered whether he might need time to grieve before he moved on to the new challenge of finding a relationship.

Three weeks later, Lyle seemed anxious and sad again. While acknowledging that he had met his goal, he worried about crying in his sleep and about some recurrent daydreaming. It seemed natural to me that he was presenting more symptoms at this time. Quite possibly he was feeling conflicted about giving up his relationship with me, and he might also have been trying to avoid talking about his longing for a love relationship. I decided to respond as I had in previous sessions when he was anxious—by giving him control over what we talked about. At first he seemed uncertain about what to say, but finally he shared that he had been putting pressure on himself to do things he was not yet ready to do. He had concluded, however, that he did not have to see it as one way or another. He could take a break from therapy now and consolidate his gains without added pressure. True, he was still lonely for a partner, but he had begun to consider Milwaukee his home, he saw himself as successful at work, he had expanded his social circle somewhat to include some women at work, and he felt more secure with his family relationships. I invited him to come back any time and suggested he could set up an appointment for four to six weeks later, but he chose to leave things open. I complimented him for recognizing his needs and knowing when to allow himself rest and when to push himself to grow.

When Lyle left, he walked quickly and did not look back, rather than lingering, as he had done in the past. I felt sad that he might be feeling pain at the loss of our relationship. But I knew that continuing our sessions would have compelled him to face what he clearly wasn't ready to face: the anxiety of finding a love relationship. I trusted that he would be able to rely on his own resources now, and I hoped that our conversations had been helpful enough that, when he was ready for the next step in his life, he might consider talking with me.

Solution-focused therapy is guided by the client's goals, not the therapist's agenda. It is useful and appropriate for clients who are motivated to make dramatic changes as well as those who need ongoing support for life situations that realistically may not ever change, such as people dealing with problems of aging, chronic physical illness, or developmental disability. Most of all, the solution-focused therapist must develop a sensitivity to the timing and pacing required in each individual case. Going very slowly at first, in order to really be in sync with the client's view of things, may lead to a quicker solution in the end.

CASE COMMENTARY 1
BY BILL O'HANLON

I can't stand to watch soap operas on television. It seems I'm always yelling at the screen, frustrated that the characters won't take simple, obvious steps to avoid the messes they are about to get in. Julie is about to marry the big-city attorney Barclay Clay (the III), and she thinks perhaps she ought to tell him about the child she had out of wedlock with the Vietnam vet drifter who came through town a few years back and is now being raised by the family down the street. She is just about to spill the beans when the phone rings. But when she gets off the phone, she chickens out and doesn't tell him. "Tell him!" I yell at the screen, "It will save us five episodes in the future." I know, and so should she, I think, that during the wedding, the little kid is going to come running down the aisle, after having just learned that Julie is his biological mother, screaming, "Mommy!" for all the shocked congregation to hear. Or the Vietnam vet will return and begin to blackmail Julie to keep quiet about the child, and so on, and so on.

I had the same feeling reading this case example by Eve Lipchik. I've seen Eve work and know her to be a good, respectful therapist who has lately been trying to expand the formerly narrow boundaries of solution-focused therapy. She stresses the importance of being flexible with clients rather than focusing solely on solutions.

In this case, I kept wondering why it took her so long to drop the rather rigid formulaic approach that characterizes much of solution-focused work, which some critics have jokingly called solution-*forced* therapy. Although the proponents of the solution-focused approach claim that anyone doing solution-forced therapy isn't practicing the model correctly, if you watch some of the students of this method doing therapy, you will find a formulaic approach in action.

If one of the assumptions of this method is that every human being, relationship, and situation is unique, why did Eve choose to persist in a method that was clearly not meeting the client's needs for so long? Since this client indicated in the first interview that scaling questions weren't helpful, why should he have to keep answering such questions in future sessions? This is a setup for soap opera drama between client and therapist: He becomes resistant; she redoubles her efforts to get him to answer scaling questions.

The crucial element missing in this case from the beginning was finding out what the client actually wanted to change. Too quickly, the goal of therapy became narrowed down to "feeling happy about 50% of the time." I would have thought that the client might want something like finding more friends, a change in his sense of emptiness, to talk about what would constitute dealing with life instead of avoiding it, or to discuss his gay sexuality and his coming out process, his tendency to sit in a daze and not hear people, and so forth. I'm not sure if any of those or something else would be more compelling for him, but "to feel happy about 50% of the time," didn't seem to resonate with this guy. (It also wouldn't resonate with many managed-care companies.) What Lyle's actual goals might be are uncertain from the case description, but again, rushing to impose goals prematurely is a setup for a soap opera.

The pattern of adhering to the model instead of responding to the client runs through the case description. Throughout, when Lyle expresses negative feelings about himself, Eve consistently tries to reframe him out of these feelings. She continues to give him compliments (another solution-forced method) until he finally lets her know that when he tries to do the same with himself, he hears an internal voice that scolds him, or he feels pressure to perform up to some standard. Finally, she begins to do what therapists often do when their clients refuse to fit their procrustean bed of theory and method: She doubts the client's motives and real desire to change ("Does this mean he can't allow himself to get better?"). When she asks him about this, he tells her that he does find therapy helpful, because her unbiased view gives him help in considering his life. Immediately she asks him a scaling question (oops, back to the model).

Carl Rogers taught us years ago that listening respectfully to clients and letting them know we can hear their perceptions and feelings and that we accept them as they currently are is a prerequisite for most people to cooperate in the change process. To refer to this pejoratively as "ventilation," as Eve does, seems disrespectful and shows her bias against expressing feelings and the past. But there are many ways to get to solutions. The important thing is to find one that fits for the client, not just for your model.

There's an antidote to solution-forced, structural-forced, psychodynamic-forced, and any other forced kinds of therapy. Get collaborative. You can still have a model, just be flexible: Ask clients what is helpful (Eve does this several times, to her credit) and listen respectfully to them without initially trying to change or mold them in a particular direction. Then incorporate their responses into your therapy.

A hallmark of a collaborative approach is asking *curiosity* questions rather than *agenda* questions. In contrast, when Eve says to Lyle, "I don't mean to discount it, but the past is gone, and you came here to talk about happier feelings. Is this helpful, or do you want to talk about how you can feel differently in the future?", she is saying, in effect, "I know you indicate that talking about the past is important to you, but my model says that you are better off talking about the future."

Clearly Eve, whose work is usually collaborative with a solution-focused flavor, wanted to use this case to highlight the very points that I've been making in this commentary: Be flexible, listen to people, and adjust your interventions based on their responses. Eve keeps having conversations with her model before she has conversations with her client. Our first loyalty must always be to our clients rather than to our models. When there is a conflict between client and model, always defer to the client. Failing to do so usually leads to bad soap opera rather than good therapy.

CASE COMMENTARY 2
BY MICHELE BOGRAD

I appreciated Lipchik's willingness, as a solution-focused therapist, to reveal that many cases using this approach do not have the easy, almost magical outcomes that we often read about or see on videotapes at conferences. Although Lyle eventually made changes, he strongly resisted Lipchik's efforts to have him focus on solutions not problems, on narratives of change not on litanies of failures. In fact, it is ironic that, although Lipchik emphasizes the importance of freeing novice solution-focused therapists from their anxiety about "whether a particular case is appropriate for this approach," the applicability of the solution-focused model was the major question I had about this case.

As a practical matter, few therapists are flexible enough to choose a model for each case that best fits a client's idiosyncratic needs. Instead, most of us (including myself) regularly use the clinical approach we find most comfortable or personally stimulating. Here, as I read about Lyle's passivity and deep sense of discouragement, I found myself wondering whether he would have responded more readily to a different model that paid more attention to his past, his passivity, his deep sense of discouragement, and his difficulty even entering into the therapeutic relationship. Most of us invest a considerable amount of time in training our clients how to work within our model. Such persistence is an important part of establishing the foundation of the therapeutic relationship. But when does persistence shade into dogmatism? Lipchik was indeed tirelessly persistent in applying the premises of solution-focused therapy even as she struggled with Lyle's lack of responsiveness to her interventions. Is her work an example of the dogged attempt to forge a therapeutic alliance or of a therapist's insistence on a preferred clinical framework in face of a client's desire for something different?

My own work typically focuses on reworking injuries of the past and on analyzing people's premises about life, on the nature of their relationship with me, and on the wider social issues that shape their lives. I believe that change takes time, that the therapeutic relationship is central to healing, and that clients' characteristic ways of being need to be challenged, even as current changes are highlighted and supported. I think I would have made Lyle's ambivalence about receiving help and entering into the therapeutic relationship the initial focus of our work. I also would have focused specifically on Lyle's homosexuality. Lipchik seemed to let Lyle take the lead on his coming out; I would have more actively tried to create a context in which he felt an openness in talking about his hidden world. If Lyle told me that he was not ready to address coming out or didn't find it helpful, I would, of course, have accepted his choice. But I assume that it is my job to take the initiative in helping clients who are part of disenfranchised and oppressed groups to normalize their struggles and to link them with larger social pressures. In this case, I would have tried to put Lyle's feelings of unmanliness into social context and support him in challenging norms of masculinity and homosexuality.

Lastly, I would have tried to hold Lyle in treatment longer. The feeling of wistful concern that Lipchik describes at the finale signals for me that her work with Lyle is not done. I certainly respect clients' feeling that they are ready to terminate or need a break, but I also want my own viewpoint to be part of the ending conversation, knowing that sometimes this kind of exchange can lead to a recommitment to therapy and a deeper level of work.

Our field is marked by a surprisingly competitive, critical, and sometimes disrespectful stance toward the wide range of ways in which therapists work and think about change. When I first read this case, I found it an interesting description of a solid, careful, and thoughtful piece of work by a skilled, self-reflective therapist. But when I realized that Lipchik was moved to write out of her sense that some might find the flexibility of her therapeutic approach controversial, I questioned not Lipchik's work but the state of family therapy. I felt dismay that a therapist still needed to argue that no model is universally helpful, that techniques should never hold sway over the human encounter, and that human connection is the crucial dimension of the therapeutic enterprise.

AUTHOR'S RESPONSE
BY EVE LIPCHIK

First of all, I want to thank Michele Bograd and Bill O'Hanlon for emphasizing that they realize the point I was trying to make by presenting this case study. I understand the process between Lyle and me as reflecting his struggle between wanting and fearing relationship on any level. My addressing this on the content and process level made him feel I understood him and was the reason he kept coming back and eventually developed some trust. In regard to Bill O'Hanlon's comments about goals, Lyle and I never defined a goal until it became clear to Lyle (in the eighth session) that he wanted an intimate relationship with a man. Yes, I reflected back to Lyle in an early session that he wanted to be 50% happy most of the time, but I did not consider that a goal. Lyle was so uncertain about being in therapy that pressing him for a behaviorally focused idea about the future would have been totally insensitive and would have either increased his depression or caused him to discontinue coming to see me.

I was trying very hard to put Lyle's needs above my chosen clinical approach. I recognized, at one point, that scaling did not fit. The idea that I should not have repeated a question once the client did not show interest in answering it (as Bill suggested) seems very limiting to me and reinforces the false notion that solution-focused questions either work or don't in a formulaic way. My experience is that clients are able to hear different things at different times. Moreover, an unanswered question does not necessarily mean it was not heard. Lyle proved that when he volunteered scaled signs of progress about his changes in a later session.

Finally, I hope no one else found my use of the word "ventilation" disrespectful. I merely wanted to draw a distinction between the dynamic technique of encouraging ventilation as a means for change in itself and my use of it as a way to maintain a safe, accepting climate in which the client can begin to be open to other perspectives. ■

STUDY QUESTIONS

1. What was Lipchik's goal in using a solution-focused model, and why do you think it did or did not work with Lyle?
2. Do you agree with O'Hanlon that the therapy did not fit the needs of the client? Why or why not?
3. Using this case as an example, discuss how clinicians must strike a balance between adhering to a model and meeting the needs of their clients.

CASE STUDY

THE GIFT OF PLAY
USING IMPROVISATION IN THE THERAPY ROOM

Daniel J. Wiener

Laurie and I are both nervous, but when our improvisation team captain motions us to get on stage, we jump out there. Laurie immediately becomes "Suzie," an attractive woman working out at a health club, easily lifting the barbell weight. As playboy "Jeff," I swagger over to her, showing off my bulging muscles, talking smoothly to impress her. I bend over to pick up the barbell—I can't even budge it! Rapidly losing confidence, I offer to shake hands with her, and sink to my knees with an astonished look as her grip crushes my hand. As the stage lights come down, the audience laughs and cheers. Laurie and I stride off the stage, exhilarated at having pulled off the scene.

It was the experience of working for a couple of years with a team of amateurs who shared my fascination with walking out on stage in front of a paying audience without knowing what was going to happen next that first led me to think about using improvisation with my clients. It taught me something about safe risk taking. As scary as it can be performing publicly on the edge, you eventually learn that nothing truly bad can happen to *you*, just to your temporarily assumed stage character.

During one practice session with my improv company, I noticed that a seasoned visiting player who smoothly cocreated wonderful scenes with some partners, regularly had trouble working with others. He reminded me of marital partners who appear likeable and engaging as individuals but not in the company of their spouses. Good improvising has a lot in common with good relationship functioning: Both require offering others a clear sense of oneself, cooperation, support, and making the other person look good.

I soon began to use improv exercises in my practice to assess clients' relationships and cut through lengthy verbal arguments about who had the problem by having them improvise. For instance, I once asked Paul and Marcie, a conflicted engaged couple, to try an improv exercise called "One Word at a Time," in which the players tell a story by alternating words. Paul's words appear in capitals:

I—am—COMING—home—TO—from   (FROM? . . . yes)   THE—green—HOUSE—which (pause) WILL—cover—UP—all—THESE (pause) curtains—THAT—are—MINE.   You—CAN'T—hope—MY—mother—WILL—free—UP—any—DISTRACTION—that—SHE—brings—ME.

Immediately following the exercise, Marcie complained that she had had to do all the hard work, that Paul had taken the "easy" words. Paul sounded irritated in describing his attempts to "keep the story on track." When I demonstrated the same exercise successfully with each of them, it immediately became clear to Paul and Marcie that they were having considerable difficulty in sharing control and that this exercise depended on their giving up their own ideas whenever their partner offered an unexpected word.

Improv can shift therapy to a more playful level, freeing individual clients to explore other selves and roles, expand the constricted patterns of relationships, and practice desired changes without real-life consequences. For this to happen, however, the therapist must establish a safe, playful context and must personally model the spontaneity that improv requires.

Micky, a gentle, depressed man with a perpetually downtrodden air, entered individual therapy attributing many of his problems to the traumatic family violence of his childhood. His fragmentary memories of these events were always recounted in a strained, frightened voice. In one incident, he remembered crouching under the kitchen table while the screaming and blows of battling parents and the wailing of his infant sister resounded around him. During one month of individual therapy, I unsuccessfully tried to use improv games to help Micky expand his range of expressed emotion. I then brought him into my improvisation therapy group.

During Micky's first month in the group, he maintained a low profile. He seldom spoke up, although he was attentive to other members when they experienced emotional distress. He sat out many opportunities to participate in exercises, and when he did participate, he invariably played tentatively. Although other members tried to challenge Micky into more emotionally demanding improvising, I supported him to go at his own pace and participate to whatever degree he felt willing. Improv is play and needs to be elective, not forced; most clients will take the risk of exposing themselves to emotional discomfort when they are ready.

Finally, some weeks later, Micky seemed ready. He had become very animated in discussing another member's improv and appeared warmed up to an enactment of his own. I set up a scene called "The Trial," in which several auxiliary players give character information to one central player, who then ties it all together in a monologue. Micky was the seated central player and three other group members stood on stage around him.

The group offered Micky the character name "Stefan," and told him he was a bank teller who had embezzled funds. (Group members seldom assign characters uneventful lives!) Then, Player B addressed Stefan as his boyhood friend from 40 years ago, reminding him of how they'd played cops and robbers together. Player C spoke as his tearful wife, deprived of a husband and having been forced to raise their children unaided while he was in prison. D played the judge who sentenced Stefan, referring to how Stefan had abused the trust of his employer. At this point, I directed Stefan to do the monologue in which he got to tell his story in the course of responding to each of the other characters.

Slowly getting to his feet, Stefan paced the stage, head down, arms folded around himself. Then he spoke to B, developing a tough-guy voice, hands now on his hips: "Yeah, Benny, you always played the copper. Left me to be the robber, so what kinda role model did I have, see? You'da done what I done if you wasn't so yeller!" Micky was now fully into the Hollywood gangster persona as he swaggered over to C. "Ahh, you was always naggin' me how the kids needed this or that, so what was I t'do for dough? You dames . . ." When he got to D, he was bellicose: "You think you can put me away and that's the end of it, eh? Let me tell you, Mister high-an'-mighty judge, I'm coming lookin' fer you when I'm out of the joint, see?" Turning to address the group audience, Stefan raised both fist and voice: "And that goes fer any of you what gets in my way, see? Nobody crosses Big Stefan!" As he folded his arms and turned his back to the audience, ending the scene, everyone applauded. It was a thunderous performance from a man who had previously seemed incapable of raising his voice in anger.

Micky had found an energizing theme of fearsome willfulness that counteracted his depressive persona of traumatized victim. It was not that he approved morally of the actions of his improv character, he explained, but that he had vitality and lived as he pleased. He contrasted this with his father, whom Micky saw as a victim who had become a bully out of frustration at his own ineffectual lifestyle. He also was able to connect his mother's message—"Men are likely to do terrible things if they unleash their tempers, so you must always keep yours under control—to his own stifling uneasiness at expressing mere displeasure, let alone anger.

While developing the clinical use of improv in my practice, I began using it to train therapists at an agency where I worked. Beyond adding techniques, improv promotes more effective use of self in trainees. Flexibility is a virtue in therapy; an effective therapist can switch stances easily. Improv used in training offers therapists practice in not being in control of the future and having to think on their feet. It can help therapists become more alive to risk taking and make them far more flexible in responding to the varied demands of their caseloads.

William, age, 9, had been living for the past seven months in a residential treatment facility because of a court finding of parental neglect. He and his mother, Dorothy, had seen their agency therapist, Inez, for nine sessions in expectation of William's return to his home when I began supervising the case.

During sessions, William, obedient and attentive to the staff of his residential cottage, became distracted and indifferent when he met with Dorothy, who would issue sharp commands whenever he fidgeted or appeared inattentive. William would then ignore Dorothy, at which point she would turn to the therapist, as if this confirmed what a difficult child William was and how hopeless it was to try to manage him.

William and his mother appeared extremely disconnected; whatever spark there was in their relationship only came out in a conflict about discipline. Even the therapist, after the first 10 minutes or so of a session, would lapse into a low-intensity mode similar to Dorothy's. When the therapist is inducted into the family system, it is time to try something else.

I sat in as cotherapist on six sessions with the therapist, Dorothy, and William. My goal was to support Inez's efforts to establish a more trusting, playful atmosphere in the sessions so mother and son could create a new family partnership. Inez had done some improv in her training with me, so I decided to introduce games and exercises into these sessions. I asked Dorothy and William what they did for fun together when William came home on weekend visits. Other than watching some television, they had no answer to this question. I then stated that I knew some games that could be fun and asked if they were interested. Hesitantly, they agreed to try.

The basis of successful improvisation is the acceptance of offers, meaning that players agree to create, cooperatively, playful adventures. This is like building a tower of blocks: If players cooperate in adding to what is already built, they can create interesting structures; if they knock down what has been built before (blocking the offer of others), playfulness evaporates and interest wanes. In this case, a pattern of blocking was already in place. Accordingly, I used games that encouraged agreement on one level while also channeling oppositional energy.

I began with "You Will!/I Won't!", a simple exercise borrowed from Gestalt therapy, in which two players face one another and repeat the dialogue (A: "You will!" B: "I won't!") with a variety of inflections and gestures. After several rounds, the players trade scripts and repeat the exercise. This game had a number of advantages—the instructions were simple; the blocking was similar to what Dorothy and William were already manifesting; and it encouraged the expression of emotional intensity. After Inez and I demonstrated the exercise (both to model it and to show them that we weren't asking them to put themselves in a position that we wouldn't take ourselves), Dorothy and William played it twice, exchanging parts the second time. While Dorothy added verbal justifications for her position a few times (e.g., "I won't, 'cause you're yelling at me") and had to be coached to stick with the minimal dialogue of this exercise, both of them seemed to enjoy the emotional variety and heightened intensity. Afterward, I asked each of them what their favorite part of the exercise was. Dorothy volunteered that she had liked saying "I won't" in a cheerful, confident tone, regardless of how intense William got. For his part, William declared he liked saying "You will" in a coaxing, cajoling way, since he then got his mother to smile. What seemed to work well was their newfound enjoyment at maintaining an emotionally intense interaction with one another.

In the next session, the atmosphere was distinctly more lively from the outset and William appeared quite eager to play more games. When Inez inquired about the latest weekend home visit, Dorothy said that they had played the game twice, once around an actual argument they were having, with the result that they were able to have a constructive discussion ending in a compromise. We had not even asked them to use the game at home. Already, mother and son had learned from the game a more playful way to argue and to agree to disagree.

We moved to a more advanced game, "Couples with Contrasting Emotions," a game for four players, divided into two pairs. I assigned each couple, who are meeting socially, a contrasting emotional mood (for example, "the Grumps" meet "the Cheerfuls," "the Anguisheds" meet "the Boreds," or "the Haughties" meet "the Humbles"). Each couple plays a short scene in their assigned mood before the main scene, in which the couples meet. The setting and the couple's relationship is given at the beginning of the scene and can be that of friends, strangers, business partners, neighbors, siblings, and so on, while the setting can be over dinner, on a double date, in a lifeboat, on a tennis court, and so on. During the main scene, the players are coached to remain in their mood, whether with their partner or in interaction with the other couple.

This game encourages teamwork, both in supporting one's partner and in being part of a team to others, something with which Dorothy and William had little experience. I selected "the Complainers," mother and son, meeting "the Cheerfuls," an adult couple they knew, in a fast-food restaurant.

I coached Dorothy and William to take the Complainer position in role while waiting in the restaurant before the other couple arrived. I instructed them to find things and people to complain about other than one another. Both of them started by saying fairly mild things, like "The Cokes are all ice here," but soon warmed up to William's "Look at that fool of a manager, always bossing people around" in a tone of contempt, while Dorothy nodded vigorously. Inez and I entered as the Cheerfuls, playing a three-minute scene in which the characters of Dorothy and William animatedly criticized the unsafe and unsanitary conditions of their building, while Inez and I fancifully made a virtue out of the building's faults.

During the scene, I suggested that their characters might be offended at our character's cheerfulness and complain about that as well. They were hesitant at first, but soon became quite supportive of one another's criticisms of our attitude. In fact, Dorothy quickly became quite eloquent, saying angrily at one point, "You people don't really know what it's like finding rat droppings over everything in the morning." William appeared happy to take her lead, chiming in with "Yeah! Disgusting!!"

In the debriefing afterward, for the first time, Dorothy and William offered suggestions that acknowledged and built on those of the other. Dorothy spoke expressively and related with both nurturance and authority to William for the first time. Inez later reported that discipline at home had greatly improved and that Dorothy had assumed a more active role in the agency's Mothers' Support Group as well. Three months later, William was returned to Dorothy's custody. Follow-up visits at three-month intervals up to one year afterward showed that Dorothy was appropriately nurturant to William, while he was respectful and attentive to her.

Of course, a great deal of other useful and necessary work contributed to the successful outcome of this case. Improv is not a complete method of therapy and needs to be woven into a coherent approach along with other modalities. What worked here was that the improv games permitted both Dorothy and William to play cooperatively and expressively, with the result that both came to enjoy their relationship.

Improv is not advisable when clients are actively in crisis; strong emotion inhibits playful experimentation. As occurred with Dorothy and William, improv enactments are best offered when progress has been halted and exclusively verbal methods appear insufficient to both therapist and client to get the case unstuck. Then, enactments offer brief, vivid experiences of alternative possibilities that the therapist must quickly use to catalyze a shift from being stuck toward growth. After verbally processing the enactment, therapy then proceeds as before, with further improv exercises used to extend or consolidate the possibilities opened up initially.

The therapist using improv must first establish him- or herself with clients as trustworthy and the context of performance as safe. Even so, improv techniques will not work well with a number of populations: many addicts, for whom play is not even in the realm of possibility; psychotics, who have difficulty in adopting the as-if stance needed for role enactment; people lacking a sense of humor; and those without positive play experience in childhood.

It takes patience, sensitivity, and a willingness to capitalize on the unexpected to apply improv successfully in therapy. And the unexpected does happen: Sometimes enactments break down; sometimes a therapist can err in choosing an exercise or mistime its introduction; and, quite often, clients behave unpredictably. Since therapy is itself improvisational in character, improv offers training in dealing with unpredictability. And it gives therapists an opportunity to experience playful and challenging encounters with immediacy, to discover other relationship possibilities, and to explore an expanded use of self.

CASE COMMENTARY 1
BY RICHARD SCHWARTZ

Most people enter therapy because they feel stuck. No matter how they try, they cannot stop fighting with their spouse, or control their depressing thoughts, or motivate themselves to make other changes they desire. Despite the family of resourceful selves that live within each of us, all too often clients' lives are run by parts of themselves that are ill suited to handle their problems. Often, that is because they have learned to cut off from the parts of themselves that contain the resources to solve a problem but would make them vulnerable to being hurt.

Dan Wiener's description of Dorothy and William is typical of many families I see at the Institute for Juvenile Research in Chicago. They seem cold and inexpressive as they gaze icily at one another from behind impenetrable inner fortresses they have constructed to protect themselves. Having hurt and disappointed one another, they are dominated by protective parts within them that communicate to other family members, either overtly or covertly, the message "I no longer care about you." "You are the problem, not me." "You are hopeless and you will not get me to try again." It is as if the loving, playful, spontaneous parts that do care and desperately want to be closer have been closed off behind thick walls of defensiveness or apathy.

How can a therapist convince clients, whose lives have been filled with trauma, betrayal, and abandonment, to take the risk of allowing the caring sides of themselves to surface? How can therapists ask clients to be vulnerable in the presence of people who have hurt them? Getting family members to talk about problems in families dominated by distrust often only increases their sense of disappointment and futility. But what can a therapist do if talking only makes matters worse?

Wiener offers a promising answer to this question. He shifts the frame of therapy temporarily from problem solving to play. The safe context of play enables clients' inner guardians to relax a little in the assurance that the session is not likely to cross into any danger zones. Further, the exercises Wiener uses elicit from clients the kinder, gentler parts of themselves, the ones that can play, that would not otherwise be revealed. Wiener knows that once clients have played together, their beliefs about their relationships begin to change. I can imagine Wiener's clients saying, "I forgot that we could have fun like that together" or "I didn't know I had that in me (or you had that in you)." Once people have tested a new potential in their relationship or in themselves, it is easier to convince them thereafter to drop their guard, even around threatening issues.

Each of the games Wiener chooses brings forth different parts of Dorothy and William. In "You Will!/I Won't!" he gets them to pretend to be defensive, angry, and controlling in a way that helps them get some humorous distance from their habitual ways of reacting to each other. Afterward, Dorothy admits that she liked being able to remain firm in her position without getting upset, even in the face of William's escalating challenges, and they wind up feeling more connected and hopeful. "Couples with Contrasting Emotions" further expanded the foundation of trust and cooperation between them and elicited still other hidden resources. It enabled Dorothy to show, for the first time, that she can be an effective parent, not because the exercise teaches her anything, but because it establishes a context in which it was safe to show the nurturing, determination, and knowledge she already had.

Family therapy has dabbled with playful techniques before. Virginia Satir was noted for her use of family sculpting and other experiential methods derived from the human potential movement. Cloe

Madanes has used what she calls her "pretend technique" to help family members take on new roles and enact new patterns under a playful as-if frame. However, these methods were closely tied to a particular theory and model of therapy that may have limited their applications. Ironically, in being less ambitious and not trying to sell us a new model, Wiener offers us some ideas that can be incorporated into any approach and may achieve even broader applications.

I would like to voice one caution about Wiener's approach. He does not mention the fact that once highly polarized and defended people allow themselves to be vulnerable with one another in a session, the potential for an explosion in the ensuing week increases dramatically. When hopes are raised, they fall much farther when it looks like nothing real has changed. When you let someone get close to you, they have that much greater an ability to hurt or disappoint you. Therapists using these techniques need to anticipate the possibility of strong delayed reactions. Perhaps the best way to avoid this backlash is to spend time up front addressing the understandable fears each person has about getting closer before trying an improv technique.

CASE COMMENTARY 2
BY DAVID WATERS

There was theater long before there was therapy, and it served a lot of the same purposes—catharsis, insight, and changed perspective. Even though therapy has superseded drama as a way of dealing with life's trials, role taking and interactive play in therapy have an undeniably energizing impact. The improv games in this case are a good example of such play. After all, the struggles in relationships, with their make-it-up-as-you-go-along quality, can be easily simulated and observed in improvisational theater terms—and improvisation provides a natural format for exploring relationship glitches.

It does not surprise me that the improvisations Dan Wiener uses with William and Dorothy produce a significant change in their attitude and behavior. What does surprise me is Wiener's specific choices of improv games. While the first exercise mimics Dorothy and William's problem rather precisely, the second invites them to be quite nasty and negative, which doesn't seem like it would help them work together more positively. But clearly the most important consideration is that improv games are 90% process; the content is unimportant compared to the impact of simply cooperating and accepting one another's offers in novel and creative ways. So, William and Dorothy find a place to work together in which, because Wiener sets it up so well and so simply, they cannot fail. It's all play, all make-believe, all fun. And it's all therapeutic.

Wiener's approach with Dorothy and William is especially appealing because of what it highlights about the possibilities of improv work with children. In working with children—within families or individually—the therapist must discover and incorporate the child's energy in a way that allows it to become part of the therapy. Sometimes this means finding out what the child is excited about and getting interested in that with him or her. Sometimes it means merely giving a child permission and encouragement to open up and cut loose a bit, removing the usual adult fetters about good behavior. And sometimes it requires a kick start, with a form of play that engages but does not control the child. This isn't easy, since most forms of play aren't play at all: They have rules, penalties, and expectations. They may be analogous to life—how she cheats at Uno® mimics how she battles her parents for control—but they're not really *play*. Finding something that is truly playful can be difficult, which is why Wiener's comfort with creating the improv scenes is so striking. These simple tasks merely set up a platform from which William and Dorothy can truly play, and anything they do on that platform puts them in the novel position of working together.

In this case, the energy that the improv brings to life is the craving for contact and connection that lies beneath the boredom and deadness of the relationship between mother and son. As director André Gregory has said, "Just beneath the thin ice of boredom, the biggest sharks swim." Getting past clients' retreat into ennui is the hardest part. And since we all project our anxiety about playing onto our clients, we will all ask, "What if they refuse to join in and play?"

Wiener's great skill is not just that he knows improv, but that he has the conviction needed to sell it to his clients effectively, and the courage to join in and go off the high board with them.

Clearly, therapy is getting more and more constrained by the demands of managed care: do it faster, don't waste a nanosecond. Yet the spirit of therapy is the spirit of play: It's safe, it's not the real world, nothing counts. We can redo and rehearse and alter things endlessly, if we choose. That spirit is *not* enhanced by a time-obsessed managed-care mentality, and we need to protect therapy from being so reduced and curtailed that there is no room left for play, freedom, and energy. At this point in our field's development, Wiener's willingness to provide the gift of play deserves our special applause. ■

STUDY QUESTIONS

1. What would you say are some of the parameters for using improvisation exercises with clients, and what kinds of clients might benefit most from it?

2. What cautionary note does Schwartz raise about potential problems that might occur after using this technique? How might a therapist help prevent such problems?

3. Discuss Waters's point that the "spirit of therapy is play." What does he mean by this? Do you agree or disagree, and why?

CASE STUDY

HUMANIZING THE IMPOSSIBLE CASE
ENGAGING THE POWER OF A FAMILY-LARGER SYSTEMS INTERVENTION

Jay Lappin and John VanDeusen

Mr. and Mrs. Peters, who were in their seventies, lived in a crowded, run-down row house along with their 12 sons and daughters and 21 grandchildren and great-grandchildren. To the dozen frustrated public agencies who had become involved with their case, the Peterses were simply and pessimistically known as "The Family."

The Peters's house was condemned two years ago by the city's fire, health, and building departments, but every time their case came to court, judges took pity on the elderly Peterses and either granted a delay or suspended the fine. The state office of Child Protective Services (CPS) also had investigated two of their daughters for child neglect, but no action had been taken. During a single month in the summer of 1992, police were called more than 50 times to investigate reports of assaults, gambling, drug dealing, noisy crowds, and a child in a wheelchair wandering the streets outside their house at 1 A.M. A drug raid netted 37 vials of crack and some heroin. Although police suspected one of the grandsons was the dealer, there were simply too many people living in the house to pin the charges on anyone, and no arrests were made.

At the Peters's house there were no boundaries. Police found 8 mattresses on the bedroom floors—the only sleeping accommodations for the 35 residents of the house. The furnace did not work; there were no smoke detectors; the refrigerator was turned off and filled with flies. Water taps were broken, and leaks dripped from one floor to the next, pooling in the basement. Human feces covered parts of the floor.

Although the Peters family did not have the funds necessary to make any repairs, they refused to leave their home and avoided all contact with city agencies. It was the sort of situation that often ends either in quiet tragedy or public disaster—police officers evicting crying children

215

and frail, elderly people in front of angry neighbors, while the local news media look on.

In July 1992, Sergeant Jim Nolan, a member of the city police department's community policing division, instituted a different approach to the Peters's case. Nolan, who has a master's degree in social psychology, but little experience with family therapy, decided to take a network approach to the case. Network interventions that bring together an extended family and the system of helpers connected with it seem to many clinicians like a quaint throwback to the 1960s. That's too bad, because larger-systems interventions can be efficient, effective, and inspiring, especially with cases that would otherwise be considered hopeless. Nolan made sure that the heads of several departments were involved, creating an unprecedented level of interagency cooperation and administrative clout.

The interagency task force soon discovered that they had their work cut out for them: Different agencies had conflicting information about the family, and there were huge gaps in their collective knowledge. Their discussions tended to reinforce stereotypes of the Peterses as a poor, multiproblem, African American family. The quality of follow-through on recommendations made in the interagency meetings was difficult to assess: Some agencies were felt to be dropping the ball, while others were judged as being too tough on the family. It appeared that their efforts to join forces in dealing with the Peterses was only creating greater difficulty.

As the task force participants struggled with these issues, Sgt. Nolan met a member of our consultation team at the city's police department and told him about his "crazy case." The team member asked Nolan to draw an ecomap to help clarify who was involved with the family. The ecomap is a basic graphic tool developed by family therapist Ann Hartman to aid social workers in the task of identifying the quality of a prospective adoptive family's social network. Just as a blueprint serves to illustrate the concept of a house, ecomapping reveals specific links between family members and persons and organizations in the larger environment. To appreciate the value of this method, just imagine trying to build a house solely from a written description!

Nolan's ecomap of the Peters family (Figure 4.1) indicated extensive contact with public sector agencies and few ties to other resources

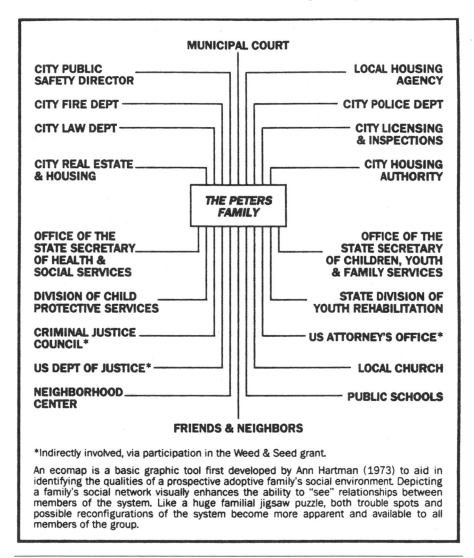

MUNICIPAL COURT

CITY PUBLIC SAFETY DIRECTOR

LOCAL HOUSING AGENCY

CITY FIRE DEPT

CITY POLICE DEPT

CITY LAW DEPT

CITY LICENSING & INSPECTIONS

CITY REAL ESTATE & HOUSING

CITY HOUSING AUTHORITY

THE PETERS FAMILY

OFFICE OF THE STATE SECRETARY OF HEALTH & SOCIAL SERVICES

OFFICE OF THE STATE SECRETARY OF CHILDREN, YOUTH & FAMILY SERVICES

DIVISION OF CHILD PROTECTIVE SERVICES

STATE DIVISION OF YOUTH REHABILITATION

CRIMINAL JUSTICE COUNCIL*

US ATTORNEY'S OFFICE*

US DEPT OF JUSTICE*

LOCAL CHURCH

NEIGHBORHOOD CENTER

PUBLIC SCHOOLS

FRIENDS & NEIGHBORS

*Indirectly involved, via participation in the Weed & Seed grant.

An ecomap is a basic graphic tool first developed by Ann Hartman (1973) to aid in identifying the qualities of a prospective adoptive family's social environment. Depicting a family's social network visually enhances the ability to "see" relationships between members of the system. Like a huge familial jigsaw puzzle, both trouble spots and possible reconfigurations of the system become more apparent and available to all members of the group.

Figure 4.1   The Ecomap.

(friends, neighbors, employers, etc.). In reviewing the ecomap, task force members for the first time began to develop a shared picture of the family's complex involvement with multiple helping agencies.

By identifying the full array of social forces acting upon the family, the ecomapping exercise was a giant step toward mastering the complexities of the Peters's case. But while the map provided us with a membership list for this social system, it did not reveal how the system actually performed, or how and where to effect useful changes. To get this missing piece of the puzzle, we advised Sgt. Nolan to throw a party and invite the Peters family to meet directly with the task force. One of the consultation team members volunteered to act as a facilitator for the meeting, in exchange for allowing our team and trainees to observe the process.

Sgt. Nolan was intrigued. Nothing like this had been tried before. He went to the Peters's house—out of uniform—and met several times with one of the sons, trying to get the family to agree to the meeting. At first, the family was dubious, but they finally consented.

Meanwhile, the task force finally brought a coordinated hammer down on the family, forcing a crisis. The fire marshal and building inspectors issued new notices requiring the family to vacate, while CPS workers informed the family that unless living conditions were changed dramatically, all of the children would be removed from the home. The workers then started helping the family make plans to place the children. Two of the Peters's daughters, each with seven children, were bumped to the top of the public housing waiting list, and two vacant apartments were made available.

The Peters family responded preemptively: Within 24 hours they had placed all 21 children with family and friends. Determined that the state would not take their children, they had, in effect, matched the state's power. The stage was now set for a crucial network meeting, to be held at a local community center.

The meeting was held in October 1992. Even before the Peterses arrived, there were more than 40 people present, including representatives from 10 agencies and the police department, and a dozen members of our own training group.

The task force members had agreed to hold this meeting only if we all met first, without the family present. Sgt. Nolan had introduced one of our team members, John VanDeusen, as the meeting's facilitator, and we began to discuss the purpose and agenda for the meeting. VanDeusen had hoped to arrive at some level of consensus before the family arrived, but the newness of the network approach, the size of the group, and the uncertainty about outcomes created sufficient role ambiguity and anxiety to keep some people firmly entrenched in their most official roles.

While one department head argued strenuously that the Peters's situation was intolerable and must be changed, another official came to the family's defense. Still another worried that the family would feel ganged up on in such a large meeting. VanDeusen challenged this last point, reminding us that only the family could judge its own comfort level, and he would ask them. This kind of polarization was unanticipated by us even though it frequently occurs in the early stages of a network meeting.

The family arrived in the hallway, and the bickering stopped. Like a classroom of kids suddenly on their best behavior when the teacher steps into the room, the members of the task force put their differences aside and adopted an uneasy wait-and-see attitude. Then, in walked six African American women, led by Leslie, the oldest daughter and matriarch-elect, a teacher who lived in another part of the city. As she and her sisters entered the room, the tension gave way to cautious hellos and smiles. Everyone spoke softly as the group attempted to come to terms with itself and the pain reflected in the family members' eyes. Pride, shame, sadness, hope, and anger all seemed to coexist—waiting to see which would win out.

VanDeusen greeted the family by asking if they were comfortable with the seating arrangements. As Leslie shook her head, "No," he asked her what rearrangement they'd like to make. "In one big circle," said Leslie. "It's more hopeful and it's friendlier." The agency representatives moved their chairs and the stage was set for the family to tell its own story; a story that had long been recorded in case files, but now would be given human voice and meaning.

Leslie, clutching reams of "official" papers, said the women were here to represent their parents. In order to set a positive, collaborative tone and deter negative finger pointing, VanDeusen asked which agencies had been most helpful. Leslie and her sisters named CPS and Sgt. Nolan. "I was skeptical at first because I've never seen the police reach out to anyone like Sgt. Nolan has to us," Leslie said. She went on to say that one of the biggest problems was getting appropriate care for her parents, who were both quite ill. Mr. Peters had suffered a stroke a few years earlier and now had difficulty speaking.

"We tried to get my parents into a high-rise apartment, but at this stage of their lives, they don't want it. That house is all they have. If they had to move now it would just kill them." She began to cry. "I visit my mother and see her sitting around the house, wringing her hands because she's got so much on her mind—and that's not my mom," she said. "My mom was always so strong for us, she was a pillar."

Than another sister, who lived in the house with her seven children, spoke tearfully. "I just want to say the reason why the house was really overcrowded. My father was adopted when he was very little and he always had this thing that he would always have a home for his kids—no matter how many of them—and his grandkids and that if we were ever in need, there was always a home for us. And I guess . . ." Pausing, she looked down and then to her sisters, ". . . that we took advantage of it, you know what I mean? We could have done better. We could have gone out there and got homes. I guess it just backfired on us." For the skeptics in the room, that moment changed everything. The Peterses shifted from being "the problem" to being real people in need, a family whose love and loyalty had created bonds they could not break.

One of the most pressing problems was that, even though apartments had been found for the two daughters, they had no kitchenware or furniture. All of the task force members reassured the family that they were there to help. To make this pledge real, VanDeusen circulated a sign-up sheet. Voluntary offers of furniture, clothes, kitchenware, and time filled the empty page. By the time the paper got back to the family, it was clear to them that people were there to help, professionally and personally.

Just as seeing the family made them real for the task force, seeing the members of the task force go beyond their official roles made the city's desire to help real for the Peterses. The meeting ended with a plan for the children to remain with family and friends until their mothers could move into the public housing apartments that had been found for them. Other agencies promised to do everything possible to find funds to repair the family home. For their part, the family agreed to vacate the house for repairs as soon as it could be safely boarded up. After the meeting, several task force members accompanied the family on a tour of the vacant apartment that one of the daughters would be moving into. Our team gave a videotape of the meeting and this tour to the daughters, to take home to their parents and the rest of the family. This videotape and the experience of those who had attended the meeting were enough to finally convince the elder Peterses to move in temporarily with their daughter, Leslie. Their house was then boarded up while the city agencies applied for funds to renovate it.

One month later, the task force met again with the Peterses at a neighborhood church suggested by the family. This time, without mentioning names, some family members alluded to the fact that others had drug problems. At a third, smaller meeting four weeks later, the daughter with the drug problem was named and arrangements were made for her to enter a drug treatment program—a sister agreed to accompany her to ensure she would get there. Connections were made between CPS and mental-health agencies for counseling with various family groups, all coordinated with the schools. In all, five meetings were held with the family over a five-month period. During this time, calls to the police declined from 50 in June to 0 in December.

By the next spring, the Peters family had received a $50,000 grant to repair their home. A furnace was donated, and plans were begun to return to the house. The daughter who entered the drug treatment remained on methadone maintenance. Two other daughters and their children were living in public housing apartments, one successfully, and the other precariously close to being evicted for overcrowding (some of "the problem" at the Peters's old house had been transferred to the new apartment). A fourth daughter continued to work and her children are doing well in school. A fifth—one of the most capable—died unexpectedly of a brain aneurism, and one of her children died of pneumonia. Her other children went to live with an aunt. CPS soon closed its several cases involving the family. For the first time in generations the Peters family was on its way to self-sufficiency.

Large public institutions set up systems of uniform rules and procedures in order to keep from sinking into the very chaos they are supposed to remedy. But to the families knit together through emotional ties of love and need, the narrow role definitions; rigid chains of command; and the floating, interchangeable faces of the bureaucracy's personnel too often seem inhuman. Furthermore, large, established organizations seem to be subject to the same laws of inertia as ancient planets; the weight of internal politics, hidden agendas, and implicit social prejudices keep them moving in the same orbit forever unless shaken out of it by a very strong, opposing force.

Paradoxically, however, both clients and agency personnel share certain similarities. Families like the Peterses are stuck in very much the same kind of inertia as big, public institutions; they, too, are unable, somehow, to transcend their own self-perpetuating system of implicit rules, roles, lifelong attitudes and habits. Furthermore, both systems—family and institution—are equally determined to survive and recognize, however grudgingly, that they are necessary to each other. Needless to say, each system is often deeply ambivalent about the other, engaged in a kind of wrestling match alternating between anxious collaboration and mutual resentment.

And yet, the force that can knock each system *out* of its inertia also exists *within* each system. However impersonal and alien each side appears to the other as an abstraction—"those people," "them," "the system"—however different the languages spoken by each culture, individually, the members of each system bring whatever knowledge, understanding, and crude working tools he or she can muster to what everybody knows will be a difficult encounter. Banal as it sounds, what is required to interrupt the mutual inertia is not a cataclysm, but a strategic and well-directed nudge that awakens the capacity for empathy and goodwill in those involved.

Leslie's demand that the task force and the family sit in one big circle was symbolically right on target. In a circle, there is no obvious authority, no stratified rows to hide behind, no clear-cut separation between public organization and private family, no beginning or ending. Everybody in a circle looks out into the faces of everybody else and discovers that they are not really so different from themselves after all—mutual recognition, appreciation, trust, and optimism become possible. At that point, the system is transcended and a human community emerges.

Although the networking meetings with the Peterses got off to a powerful start in the fall, we did not realize how thoroughly progress would be set back by elections in November. A new mayor entered office, staffs were reshuffled and, by January, nearly all of the members of the original task force had been replaced by people not present at the network meetings. While the original participants had gotten to know the Peterses, and had been deeply touched by their plight and attached to them as human beings, the newcomers did not know them at all. They were yet another anonymous, difficult, time-consuming case; an individual family had once again become part of an uncounted number of "them." Inertia once more set in.

Communities can regenerate, of course, and the strong, working coalition between the Peterses and the task force can be reestablished. But it will take time. Organizational development practitioners find that larger systems take longer to transform than do most families—two to four years on average. Faces and roles change continually, and there is no inherent appeal to ties of love or blood. As before, it will take the consolidated and determined efforts of individuals from within the separate systems to make it work. And, as before, a real conversation has to be initiated, a uniquely human talent for personal encounter, not successfully undertaken by either machines or organizations—or even people en masse. Systems don't talk to systems—only people talk to one another.

CASE COMMENTARY 1

BY EVAN IMBER-BLACK

This case is a testimony to the power of a family-larger systems intervention in a seemingly intractable situation. What the authors describe as a network meeting enabled *news of a difference* to be experienced, both by the Peters family and by all of the agencies working with it. Prior to the meeting, the family and the larger systems were locked in an unending struggle. The Peters family had no reason to believe that anything good would result from involvement with public agencies, since they had never experienced any follow-through, even from social control systems. In fact, as is typical in such cases, a set of triangles involving the various helping agencies and the family served to block any progress. Given the enormous inertia in the macrosystem, how can we understand what happened here that resulted, initially, in so much positive change?

The first step was Sgt. Nolan's decision to begin organizing the larger systems. By intervening at the level of heads of departments, he was able to gather sufficient clout within each system to make the network meeting happen. Clearly, *where* one intervenes in larger systems is crucial to producing the necessary leverage change requires.

Creating the ecomap functioned to overcome the rigid bound-aries between the various agencies, enabling them to begin to view themselves in a new way, as connected members of a macrosystem that included the family. Frequently, this shift in focus from "the family" to "we're all in this together" is a critical step that facili-tates all that follows.

A number of decisions contributed to the success of the network meeting. It was crucial to honor the various helpers' requests to meet together first without the family. In my experience, helpers often feel quite vulnerable to criticism and judgment, and a prelim-inary meeting can reassure them that the facilitator will show them respect. The gathering of the helpers also gives the facilitator im-portant clues regarding interactional patterns and core beliefs that may be attended to during the family-larger system meeting.

Honoring the family's request to sit in a circle served to tem-porarily break down the hierarchical divisions between family and helpers. The facilitator showed that he would be responsive to re-quests from the helpers and the family, setting the stage for the birth of trust and mutuality. My own hunch is that had the family's request to sit in a circle been disallowed, the meeting would have quickly disintegrated with no real dialogue or movement toward change. Beginning a meeting of this sort with all participants sit-ting in a circle is a metaphorical communication that there is now a functioning macrosystem (or at least a willingness to struggle to-ward one).

Instead of succumbing to the typical pitfall of highlighting dif-ferences, the network meeting made maximum use of the similari-ties between the family and the helpers. Perhaps as a result, two critical departures from business-as-usual occurred: The helpers were able to fully listen to the family's story, and the family was able to experience the helpers as effective allies.

Reading and reflecting on this case, I was struck by the many is-sues that I struggle with daily in my own work in the Bronx. The change process seemed to get underway because one person, Sgt. Nolan, was determined to try something different. We need to know more about what made this possible, both in the personal qualities of Sgt. Nolan and in his own working system. On a concrete level, how did he get the family to agree to come to the network meeting? The authors seem to imply that the threat to remove the children was critical, but given the larger systems' lack of follow-through, this family had no reason to believe anything its representatives said. We are not told how the helpers in this case got beyond the various constraints inherent in all larger systems. How, for instance, were they able to obtain new housing, house repairs, and a $50,000 grant for the family? What exactly made possible the follow-through after the meeting?

While, as a reader, I thought something magical had occurred, as one who works at the family-larger system interface, I know it wasn't magic and wanted more reflections from the authors regarding what they think happened *after* the network meetings. We are told the race of the family, but no information is given about the racial makeup of the helpers' group. I was left wondering about the impact of race, racial difference, and racism on both the earlier situation and the change in the macrosystem.

Finally, the end of this case, with the new elections, the new workers, the starting all over, left me wondering, yet again, about change at the macrosystems level. When I first began thinking and writing about families and larger systems in the late 1970s, I worried that the family therapy field might invent methods that would work on a case-by-case basis, thereby obscuring the need for real change at higher organizational levels in larger systems. While effective family-larger systems interventions may spring one family at a time, they do not seem to do much to change public agencies and helping systems, which are, of course, embedded in our wider sociopolitical system. While it's perhaps grandiose to imagine that the family therapy field can do anything to create significant change at the larger systems level, this case is a poignant reminder that we can and should keep working on it.

CASE COMMENTARY 2

BY LEONARD SHARBER

Having provided services to families on Chicago's Westside for the past 18 years, I am quite familiar with the paralyzing feeling of sorting through the myriad "helpers," pseudohelpers, friends, families, and bystanders typically involved in cases like this. My experience has taught me that whenever you think you have a fairly inclusive genogram or ecomap, that is your cue to look for another missing piece.

It was crucial that Sgt. Nolan had the time and support to pursue network therapy. This kind of networking is not easy, and it is very time consuming; however, it is worth the effort. Anyone who decides to take this kind of approach must be sure to have the time to carry it through. In addition, the authors write that, at first, the interagency task force "tended to reinforce stereotypes." Clearly, the success of this kind of intervention depends on avoiding old thinking and developing a new way for seeing the family.

Initially, the lack of an experienced supervisor appears to have led the team to spin its wheels longer than necessary. I wonder how long they struggled based on the conflicting and incomplete information they had before the first intervention the consultation team suggested—an ecomap. I've always found graphic descriptions helpful, especially with complex cases like this. The other benefit of an ecomap is that it tends to make all the players feel they are on the same team, reducing the feeling that some agencies are irresponsibly dropping the ball.

Even though this is where interventions like this live or die, the write-up contains no information about what, exactly, Sgt. Nolan did to get the Peters family to agree to attend the network session. Omitting a discussion of what it took to get the family to the meeting certainly heightened the drama of the daughters' entrance in the case description, but it leaves the readers without some key information.

The writers imply that the coordinated hammer of seeking placement for the children in the Peters household was an intentional intervention. But generating that kind of crisis might have backfired, making the family even more inaccessible and harder to help. Had I been involved with the team, I would have been concerned about balancing the messages to the family, combining the show of force with an equally strong message of "we want you to come to this meeting because you're important."

This case has much to tell us about the untold strengths in seemingly dysfunctional and helpless families. Who would have believed that the Peters family could place 21 kids in alternative homes in less than 24 hours? As I keep trying to tell those who downplay therapeutic interventions and insist that what the poor need most is concrete services, we must not discount the power of family rules and scripts. Once it was revealed that Mr. Peters had vowed never to leave one of his progeny at the mercy of the child welfare system, the task force was able to see this case in a different light. It then became possible for it to ally with the Peters family and its goals.

Finally, wouldn't it be great if we could develop helping communities of professionals committed to the poor for the long haul, and not be replacing members every few months? This case reminds us of what can be accomplished when we learn to walk arm in arm, like the Peters's daughters, ready to face and support each other no matter what.

AUTHORS' RESPONSE
BY JAY LAPPIN & JOHN VANDEUSEN

Len Sharber and Evan Imber-Black, both veterans of larger-systems struggles, get right to the heart of the matter: What made this intervention work? Magic? Sgt. Nolan? And what about the risks of putting pressure on the Peters family by using the threat of housing summonses and the removal of their children? All these questions illuminate the central themes in the case: trust, negotiating bureaucracy, and the use of power.

The best way to describe what made the Peters family agree to attend the network meeting is to tell a little more of the story of this case.

At the time the Peters case came to a head, Sgt. Nolan was in charge of a new community policing unit. His boss at the time, the city's director of Public Safety, Karen Johnson, oversaw the development of an interagency task force as a part of a grant from "Weed and Seed," a Reagan-era program designed to crack down on the drug trade in inner-city neighborhoods by combining beefed-up law enforcement and community aid. During the 1980s, the lion's share of the grant monies had gone toward "weeding" (i.e., vice-squad activities). Johnson and Nolan were well aware that while a get-tough approach appealed to a frightened electorate wanting quick solutions to the problems of drugs, it was ultimately ineffective. They believed that with the right kinds of support, the community could do much to police itself. Other task force officials were also increasingly aware of the failure of the weeding strategy and were now open to trying something different.

The first step in making the intervention with the Peterses possible was Johnson's decision to give Nolan the time needed to build trust with the family and coordinate the task force's involvement. Early on, Nolan learned that one of the task force members knew the oldest son in the Peters family. That member was able to convince the son to attend a meeting with Nolan, and soon a kind of shuttle diplomacy evolved, with the son serving as a go-between, linking the family and Sgt. Nolan. Eventually, however, the case stalemated as it became apparent that the oldest son did not possess the necessary leverage with other family members to get them to take any action. Seeing this, the task force members, who had begun by giving the new approach the benefit of the doubt, grew increasingly impatient.

Nolan described the stalemated case to a family therapist friend, John VanDeusen, who immediately suggested that Nolan might get better results by contacting the other family members directly. Nolan's subsequent home visits gave the family their first sustained contact with any representative of the city bureaucracy, opening up the possibility of true dialogue and a mutual search for solutions.

As for the hammer, which had already been implemented by task force members prior to our input, we agree that it could have backfired. But we had to respect it as a part of the existing situation we were entering. The hammer was based on the familiar good cop-bad cop strategy. The message was that, if the family attended the meeting, the police would intercede with the city agencies that had issued all the summonses against the senior Mrs. Peters. But things got out of control when CPS jumped ahead of the other agencies, demanding that the Peters kids immediately be removed from the home. At this point, two CPS workers whose obvious concern for the Peters children impressed the family, successfully helped them to place all of the children. The family's demonstration that it could mobilize around a genuine crisis was the first sign of hope and family strength.

The willingness of both professional helpers and family members to take personal risks eventually made the difference in this case. In effect, what developed was a chain of trust starting with Karen Johnson's trust of Sgt. Nolan and running through his relationship with the Peters's eldest son and eventually in the connection he developed with the entire Peters family that inspired hope and positive action.

We agree with the commentators about the need for family therapists to move beyond only thinking of one family at a time. In this case, we made sure to include our own trainees as participants in the first two task force meetings as our way of seeding the notions of embracing diversity, collaboration, and searching for strengths as the core values in this kind of work.

It may be hard for family therapists to appreciate how radical the idea of talking to family members was for the police. Commenting on the task force's willingness to try a new approach, Nolan laughed, saying, "We felt like we were doing God's work." But, clearly, missionary zeal by itself is not enough and cases like this are important because they show us what is possible when we take our ideas and our expertise out of our offices and into arenas where new approaches are desperately needed. ■

STUDY QUESTIONS

1. Based on this case, what do you think were the strengths and weaknesses of a network approach to systems change?

2. How was the ecomap used in this case, and for what other kinds of cases might it be useful?

3. In your opinion, was it wrong of the team to use the threat of placing the children outside the home as leverage to get family members to come to the meeting? What might have been some alternatives?

CASE STUDY

THE ENIGMA OF EMDR
AN INTRIGUING NEW TREATMENT METHOD
PROMISES DRAMATIC RESULTS

Clifford Levin

Philosophically, the kind of brief therapy we practice at the Mental Research Institute (MRI) in Palo Alto, California, has little in common with Eye Movement Desensitization and Reprocessing (EMDR), a new method for dealing with the aftereffects of trauma that has captured the attention of thousands of therapists around the country. Brief systemic therapy focuses on the present, not on history or memory. Its goal is to alter the interactions within the family system that maintain the problems clients present. EMDR, on the other hand, uses an intrapsychic, rather than a systemic, model of change, and like conventional individual therapy, it takes seriously the effects of past memories on people's inner and outer lives.

A relatively new method developed by my MRI colleague, psychologist Francine Shapiro, EMDR locates the problem not in the interactional system, but within the body and brain of the identified client. EMDR assumes that traumas have left unprocessed memories, feelings, and thoughts that can be "metabolized" or integrated if they are recalled during the application of the EMDR method, one of many components of which involves patterned eye movements. After it is over, many clients report that the memory of the trauma faded and lost its charge. It differs from conventional therapy in that it produces extraordinarily rapid results: Therapists across the country are reporting success with Vietnam veterans, incest victims, and other survivors of trauma, sometimes in a single session. Nevertheless, in spite of their differences, both EMDR and brief therapy offer complementary approaches that, when used sequentially, as in the following case, can yield results that might not be possible if either one were used alone.

Leonard, a slim, healthy-looking 50-year-old software designer who ran his own, struggling company, came to me with a problem that involved both memory and behavior. He had heard great things about EMDR and hoped it could cure sexual problems he had experienced with his wife, Sarah—problems he connected with a traumatic childhood. When he was 7-years-old, he had contracted polio, and the memories were still with him. He recalled lying in a hospital bed, breathing through a ventilator, with tubes running in and out of his body. Several times a day, in a painful process that he violently resisted, nurses would aspirate fluids from his lungs. He felt profoundly helpless. He remembered doctors standing over him, saying he was not going to survive. He developed a view of himself as having an inadequate, broken body, an attitude he carried into adult life. Although he was a personable, creative man, he jokingly described himself as "human from the neck up." He lived daily with memories of his devastating childhood illness. He also occasionally experienced a numbness in various parts of his body that is part of post-polio syndrome and feared this numbness would affect his penis.

He and Sarah had enjoyed a loving, companionable relationship for 22 years. Nevertheless, in all that time, they had never had an orgasm together. Sarah would kiss and caress Leonard; he would kiss her back; and they would lie on their bed and hug lovingly. Leonard would become aroused, touch his wife directly on her clitoris, and get an erection.. Then Sarah would begin stimulating Leonard directly and lose contact with her own arousal.

They would have intercourse. But at the point where Leonard felt orgasm was inevitable, he would shut down ("like a heavy curtain falling") and he would lose his erection. Neither one would have an orgasm, and both would feel filled with shame and disappointment. A few weeks later, Sarah would try again and the cycle would be repeated.

This had been the pattern through Leonard's six years of psychoanalysis and countless, demoralizing attempts at couples counseling and individual therapy. Nothing had worked. Even sex therapy using the Masters and Johnson model, in which Leonard and Sarah took turns at giving and receiving sensual pleasure from each other, had failed. Both had had little experience with dating or necking—much less intercourse—before they married. Neither Sarah nor Leonard had seen each other—or anyone else—have an orgasm. Their orgasmic lives were limited to private masturbation.

While Leonard said that his painful memories of childhood polio did not arise during sex, he felt they lurked in the background, influencing the way he felt about his body and his sexuality and perhaps contributing to his low level of sexual desire. He hoped that EMDR could remove his deep sense of being physically "broken" and allow him to become sexually functional with Sarah. I told Leonard that I was willing to try EMDR to help heal his traumatic childhood memories, but I could not guarantee that his sexual relationship with Sarah would automatically improve.

In our first session, Leonard decided to work on the image of being aspirated while being restrained in a hospital bed. I asked him what he associated with the memory. He told me he had thoughts of gagging and choking, of being in emotional pain and of thinking, "I'm a piece of meat and I'm going to die."

Following the EMDR protocol, I asked Leonard what he would say to himself if he were to feel better about the memory, and he replied, "I'm safe now. Those efforts were made in an attempt to save my life." Again, following the protocol, I asked Leonard what he felt in his body. He told me he experienced fear in the pit of his stomach. Using a self-reporting scale, he rated his upsetting feelings as an 8 on a scale of 0 to 10.

Then I instructed Leonard to call up the memory while he followed my fingers as I moved them rapidly from side to side in front of his eyes. As his eyes flicked back and forth, Leonard was surprised to find himself reporting not intellectual or verbal responses, but changes in body sensation. He relaxed and became less anxious. His mental picture shifted and he saw himself as his father looking down at the young Leonard in the hospital bed. He felt intense feelings of warmth in his shoulders—then panic, wanting to cry—heat moving to his groin area—coolness in his left arm moving up his body and the smell of menthol—and then nothing. His anxiety level, he said, had fallen markedly, from an eight to a three.

I asked Leonard to call up the image of being his father once again and tried another series of eye movements. He felt numb on the left side of his head, as though his jaw was being held. He felt panicky; he panted, had trouble breathing, then relaxed, and once again smelled the scent and felt the coolness of menthol, this time on his right arm. He told me he felt slightly more anxious—about a four on the scale. As he left the office, he said, "EMDR does seem to have some sort of validity for me."

At his next EMDR session a week later, Leonard told me that during the week he had felt a numb spot on his head and old feelings of abandonment. This time we worked on another traumatic medical memory. When he was 4-years-old, he was treated for a massive abdominal infection by a group of doctors who drained it with needles. After it was over, he had woken up in terror in a dark room, surrounded by cribs, crying out in vain for his parents.

At his third session, Leonard chose to begin with an image of himself as an adult, looking from his father's perspective at his 7-year-old self lying in bed, stricken with polio and breathing through an oxygen mask. He responded slowly at first to the eye movements, but soon reported a warm glow in his lower abdomen reminiscent of a sexual feeling. The pleasurable glow moved up his body, through his jaw and forehead, and then down again. He told me he had an image of someone standing behind him and cradling him.

He felt a stiffening in his cheeks, pressure on his jaw, and a feeling of wanting to cry—a poignant mixture of happiness and sadness, like someone moved to tears by a touching scene in a movie. He told me that when he was in the hospital as a child, he could not eat because his trachea was paralyzed. He begged his mother for a soft-boiled egg, but could not be given one. By the end of the session, Leonard reported his level of upsetting feelings at a three.

We did not use EMDR during Leonard's fourth session because Leonard was filled with revelations. Although he did not connect his revelations with his EMDR treatment, he said he had come to realize that he was not as financially productive as he could be, and felt responsible for Sarah's staying at a high-paying job with a boss she despised. He also told me, just before he left, that he had noticed that when he did not approach Sarah sexually, she would talk about how unattractive she felt. This, he said, increased his feelings of guilt.

The next week, we used EMDR again, and Leonard described a series of changing perspectives on the aspirator that was used on him as a child. In the final image, it had become a modern aspirator, a smaller and less uncomfortable piece of equipment. He reported that his anxiety and discomfort level had been reduced to zero. "It's over," he said when I asked him what he thought about the memory. "It's in the past and now I can live free of it."

No longer haunted by his memories of childhood polio, Leonard felt much better on a day-to-day basis. He restructured his business in order to do more of the things that gave him pleasure and less of those he did not enjoy. (He made no connection between this and EMDR, but I have often seen people make spontaneous, seemingly unconnected changes in their lives following EMDR.) However, he felt no change in his low sexual drive, and he and Sarah were continuing to have the same sexual difficulties. He wanted to work on the issue in marriage counseling.

I agreed, and moved to an entirely different paradigm of problem solving. No longer would we concentrate on Leonard's past and inner life; now we would look closely at the couple's present behavior and the past solutions that had failed them. Following this protocol, I began by defining the problem in behavioral terms, meeting with Sarah and Leonard separately and together to learn about their sexual histories and their life together. Leonard had only once tried to have sex before he married, but had not been able to maintain an erection. Sarah, who was even less sexually experienced, told me in an individual session that she did not feel attractive and needed Leonard to pursue her in order to feel desirable. When she was a teenager, she told me, her mother had introduced her by saying, "This is my daughter Sarah. At least she is very intelligent."

When I asked Sarah and Leonard to name what they would consider a small but significant positive change, neither of them could describe anything less than having an orgasm in each other's presence.

Following the MRI protocol, I gathered my data about the problems and the solutions that had failed in the past. Afterward, alone in my office, I tried to formulate an intervention that would create a small but significant positive change. Success, I felt, could occur in one of two ways—either their behavior could change, or their frame of reference could shift so that their problem was no longer seen as a problem.

I felt stymied at first. They had been through other forms of therapy that had failed and I did not want to ingrain that failure any deeper or repeat what had not worked before. At the same time, I believed I needed to include some form of sexual education. Since neither partner had ever had a fully satisfying sexual experience and Leonard did not seem to understand that few women enjoy hard, direct clitoral stimulation, I also wanted to free them from a lifetime of messages absorbed from movies and television suggesting that only conventional intercourse constituted a real sexual experience.

I decided to present an intervention that said, in effect, "I would like you to learn all that you can while you are having sex in a way that is not sex at all." So, midway through the next session, I said seriously, "I am afraid I have to give you some very bad news. After reviewing both of your histories and giving much thought to your situation, I strongly believe that the two of you will never be able to have a normal sexual relationship like those you see in the movies. Leonard's post-polio syndrome alone might make it impossible, and all the years of failure have also taken their toll. The best we can hope for is a form of altered sexuality that provide some small pleasure for the two of you."

I then instructed them to perform a series of experiments to discover what this altered form of sexuality should look like. I forbade them for having sexual contact outside the experiment, which I said must be carried out six times in the following two weeks. For experimental sessions 1, 3, and 5, Leonard was to learn about Sarah's sexuality by watching her masturbate. First he was to sit in the living room while she was upstairs masturbating. As she became comfortable, she was to tell Leonard to gradually come closer, until he stood at the foot of the bed observing. He was not to touch Sarah or himself, or say anything.

In sessions 2, 4, and 6, Sarah was to learn about Leonard's sexuality. He was to lie naked on the bed wearing headphones playing his favorite music at loud volume (in order to distract him and make sure that he kept the focus on himself rather than his wife and her needs). She was to stimulate his penis until she saw a clear secretion. I termed this secretion a "miniejaculation," in order to create an experience that could be seen as a small but significant positive change. She was then to squeeze Leonard's penis in the well-known technique introduced by Masters and Johnson to delay premature ejaculation, and make it go limp. She was to continue to excite his penis and squeeze it to flaccidity for half an hour. I hoped that this would allow Sarah to gain a sense of control over Leonard's penis, which had refused to cooperate with her for so long. Afterward, if he wished, Leonard would be allowed to masturbate to orgasm. I also was confident that this technique, usually used with men who ejaculate prematurely, had never been tried in all Leonard and Sarah's years of therapy.

When they looked at me strangely and asked questions, I said, "I know this does not seem to make any sense, but it is only an experiment and we are attempting to gather data." They agreed, but as they were about to leave the office, Leonard asked if they could express affection nonsexually, by holding hands and kissing lightly. I looked concerned, but said that as long as the experiments were carried out as instructed, they could express nonsexual affection as they normally would.

Two weeks later, I went into a waiting room packed with people, most of whom looked anxious and were deathly quiet. There, in the middle of the room, were Sarah and Leonard, engrossed in intimate conversation. As we walked toward my office, Sarah turned to me and said, "I bet you think we are the same people you saw before the holidays, but we're not."

In the office, they eagerly told me what had happened. One day after our session, Sarah told Leonard that her period had started. I believed this was a kind of serendipity, taking the pressure even further off them both because never in their wildest dreams would they have imagined having intercourse at such a time. They sat on the couch and held hands and kissed. They had not tried any part of my elaborate prescriptions. However, somewhere along the way, nature took its course, and, as Sarah told me, "We started fucking like bunnies and haven't stopped since." Later, Sarah told me, the two of them had tried conducting my experiment, but decided it was not necessary. We made an agreement that they would come back into therapy if they had any more problems, and I have not seen them since.

I am not sure whether the EMDR alone would have produced such wonderful results if Leonard had stuck with it, but he clearly wanted to try marriage counseling. Also, I strongly doubt that the brief therapy intervention alone would have worked without EMDR. Leonard held onto the idea of being a broken body so strongly that he was not going to become a sexual creature no matter how clever my intervention. EMDR freed Leonard from the hold of his old, pessimistic ideas blocking change. It also produced other shifts in the family system when Leonard reorganized his business.

On the other hand, the brief therapy intervention freed Leonard and Sarah from their oppressive sense of failure. By telling them they would never have a normal sexual relationship, I changed the paradigm within which they viewed sexuality, and they were no longer restricted by anything they had seen before. By my rules, they could only win because they were allowed to write their own rules.

Afterward, my colleagues and I tried to find some commonalities in the paradigms offered by EMDR and by systemic brief therapy, both of which we find effective. We concluded that the models seemed based on entirely different theoretical assumptions. Nevertheless, successful cases like Leonard and Sarah's simply remind me not to be wed to intellectual purity or to a single technique, but to allow synergism by experimenting with things in succession and seeing what works. Clearly, different approaches work for different people at different times.

CASE COMMENTARY 1
BY FRANCINE SHAPIRO

While EMDR has come into widespread use throughout the country, it is surrounded by controversy because clinicians untrained in the method often view it as simplistic and too good to be true. EMDR is actually a complex, interactional approach that uses a series of patterned eye movements as one component of treatment. Initially developed to allow clients to rapidly work through traumatic memories, EMDR can be usefully applied to many other presenting complaints. Essentially, if offers a method for defusing the force of negative memories that generate disturbing emotions and limited beliefs about oneself and the world. Once this takes place, clients often experience dramatic shifts in beliefs and spontaneous changes in behavior.

When the body is cut, the wound will naturally close and heal. We believe EMDR works as effectively as it does because the information-processing system of the brain has a parallel self-healing mechanism. People experience this process all the time in their everyday lives—a troubling event takes place, we talk about it, we think about it, we sleep on it, and it eventually doesn't bother us any longer. However, in the case of a traumatic event, the disturbing information (and all the feelings of powerlessness and hopelessness associated with it) are locked in the nervous system. EMDR appears to mobilize the information processing system, which may be similar to the one found in REM (rapid eye movement) sleep. Thus, EMDR enables people to rapidly process and resolve disturbing memories.

In this case, for example, Leonard went very rapidly from believing he was "a piece of meat and going to die" to both experiencing a sense of well-being and recognizing that, while his experience of childhood illness was horrible, the traumatizing medical treatment he received was part of an effort to save his life. Instead of serving as the source of painful, alienating feelings, his memory now allowed him to feel self-worth and to appreciate the concern of others. As often happens with EMDR, the structure of Leonard's memory of the painful experience was transformed: He now recalled it not from the terrified perspective of his child-self, but from the concerned, adult vantage point of his father. The past event did not change, but Leonard's experience of it did. This shift in this pivotal memory had a snowball effect, generating new, self-enhancing alternatives in other areas of his life.

It is important to recognize that EMDR is not a magic bullet; it must be used in conjunction with a full treatment plan. If a 36-year-old woman's only experience with men is as a survivor of sexual abuse, even a successful reprocessing of all the early abuse memories would not prepare her fully to begin dating. Beyond the traumatic memories, the therapist would need to address issues of personal development and social skills—including adequate education on dating in the 1990s.

While EMDR ultimately seeks to help clients develop new behaviors, it first addresses the early experiences that block change. A depressed client may have memories that convince him or her that "I am not worthy. I am not in control." A borderline client may hold memories of events that instilled the belief that "I will be abandoned." EMDR works first with those memories before trying to encourage behavior that would promote different relationships in the present. This approach is consistently effective mainly because earlier memories are the foundation of many of the relationship problems clients experience in the present. Once memories are shifted through EMDR, it is far easier to get clients unstuck and help them form more positive relationships in the present.

The key to EMDR's success is the clinician's ability to identify the appropriate targets for reprocessing. If Leonard had been my client, I would have continued to use EMDR to focus on his present sexual reactions. We would have worked with his actual sexual experiences (along with a series of suggested ones) in order to get rid of any detrimental beliefs or disturbing feelings that blocked change. To increase the possibility that Leonard would experience some degree of sexual success, we would have worked through any hesitancy or misgivings in my office first before giving him a specific sexual task.

Dr. Levin's treatment of Leonard and Sarah varied from the usual EMDR protocol. When Leonard requested couples therapy, Dr. Levin decided to use an MRI brief therapy intervention. He successfully placed them in a win-win double bind by allowing them to be sexual without having sex. While some form of couples intervention was clearly necessary, I might have used a more straightforward task assignment—having the couple mentally rehearse it in advance using the EMDR method. Just as processing a memory allows inappropriate negative reactions and beliefs to drop away, a similar, positive effect can occur with a proposed future event.

While fundamentally a clinician-assisted, self-healing process, EMDR can be viewed as tapestry work. The clinician must see the pattern in the clinical picture, find the missing or misplaced threads of beliefs and experiences, and gently and creatively weave in what is missing. Ultimately, all clinical methods are only as good as the hands that use them.

CASE COMMENTARY 2

BY DAVID WATERS

This case reads like a made-for-television movie: huge leaps each week; visible, wrenching changes; release from the fetters of childhood polio, with insights, memories, and feelings tumbling forth;

job changes, priority changes, life changes; and, ultimately, the cure of a lifelong, severe sexual problem on the basis of a single, semi-paradoxical intervention. It is what everyone *wants* to believe could come out of therapy—including us therapists. So I have two questions: How can anyone take this stuff seriously? and Where do I sign up?

Novel interventions and new paradigms in our field are very confusing. They are like a friend getting rich and famous: They make us jealous even as they give us hope. My first reaction to EMDR is to dismiss it as another fad or some zany, esoteric, nonverbal form of hypnosis. My main argument against it is, "I can't do it, and I'm a smart therapist, so how real can it be?" Of course, this is jealousy disguised as scientific rigor. (If I investigated it carefully first, and learned about it enough to accept or dismiss it on good grounds, that would be *actual* scientific rigor.)

Results that we would love if they came from our own trusted methods seem suspect and farfetched when we don't understand the paradigm that produced them. That kind of thinking has hindered our field terribly. I can recall when the psychoanalytic elite declared all family therapy results—most of them exciting and effective—as pure figments of our imagination, transference cures, flights into health, and so forth. They were saying, "It's not how we do it, so it can't be real." None of us today would say that now about family therapy, yet many of us might resort to it as a response to EMDR.

My usual criterion in evaluating new clinical ideas is the common-sense test: Where does this fit with and build on what I already know, and does it make sense? EMDR fails my common-sense test miserably. It is discontinuous with almost everything else I know; it has no theoretical basis at all; and it is viable (so far) only in anecdotal, empirical terms: It seems to work for some people, for no apparent reason. The same can be said of faith healing or scientology or many other things in which I don't believe and have long since discarded. So my skepticism is strong. But it's hard to ignore the kind of results I have been hearing about EMDR. They are certainly more dramatic and impressive than what I usually accomplish, especially in such a short time.

In some ways the most basic and vital issue in therapy is getting people interested in new possibilities and change. The willingness to explore new ground and the courage to take risks are fundamental to successful therapy, albeit frequently conspicuous by their absence. That leaves us two choices—to work only with those who already have that courage or to learn how to create it.

Using EMDR seems to be one way to create openness and courage, to effect change quickly and without much apparent trauma or resistance. Leonard went to Dr. Levin and asked him to use EMDR in his therapy. This might have made it easier to obtain results in this case, but I was nevertheless truly impressed by the impact of the intervention with such seemingly minimal effort. EMDR might make him more easily hypnotizable, but apparently no substantial suggestions were made to induce the bodily sensations or memories that Leonard experienced—the trigger seemed to be pulled by the eye movements alone. The production of the memories and sensations through EMDR seems self-curative; apparently, no processing or working-through of the memories is needed. The eye movements trigger the sensations, the sensations come and then go away, and the problem is solved. It's a bit of a black box, albeit an intriguing one.

The marital session with Leonard and Sarah seems more understandable, though it may qualify as a spontaneous remission. It seems to be a variation on Jay Haley's ordeal therapy—the cure is simply easier and less painful than the disease. It's hard to imagine Leonard and Sarah going through the awkward, embarrassing, serial masturbation routine. (And how would it make them *more* likely to enjoy sex? It was not clear to me—or, I think, to them.) I think they were offered a painful, low-yield solution and sidestepped it in a creative and gratifying way. Levin may have anticipated that sidestepping, or he may have just lucked into it as a byproduct of his otherwise complex and unpleasant treatment plan.

Despite being intrigued by this case, I am still not ready to sign on for EMDR (or paradoxical ordeal therapy, for that matter). I think it is important for some people to create these new paradigms, and equally important for others to sit back and ask skeptical questions. Our hunger for powerful, quick and easy treatments to complex problems is so great that it can easily lead us to accept them uncritically. Until EMDR scores higher on my common-sense test, I'll watch others use it—and be jealous.

AUTHOR'S RESPONSE
BY CLIFFORD LEVIN

Given my own early skepticism about EMDR, I can understand how it fails Dr. Waters's common-sense test. As a trained mathematician and a midwesterner, I had severe doubts about EMDR when Dr. Shapiro first introduced it to me in 1989. But in spite of the fact that I could not fit EMDR into any existing psychotherapeutic model, I decided to take the EMDR training with an open mind and a spirit of discovery.

When I applied what I learned in the EMDR training in my practice, I was astonished with the results I got. EMDR differs fundamentally from any other clinical approach I have used. It seems to effect change on a physiological level, not on a conscious mental level. With EMDR, the therapist's job is not to focus on psychodynamic issues or behavioral instructions, but to keep the EMDR process flowing as smoothly as possible. The healing takes place naturally.

Medical science is probably not advanced enough to monitor the myriad of physiological changes that occur during the application of EMDR, but understanding the mystery of REM sleep may help us move closer to a common-sense understanding of the EMDR phenomenon. In a recent issue of *Scientific American*, Jonathan Winson writes that the act of dreaming is the "means by which animals form strategies for survival and evaluate current experience in light of those strategies." Other researchers have found that disrupted REM sleep is a symptom of posttraumatic stress disorder and have proposed that some traumas are so powerful that the brain's natural curative process (i.e., REM sleep) is interrupted. EMDR may be effective because it reinitiates the kind of natural information processing cycle found in REM sleep. Perhaps EMDR will make more and more common sense as this kind of research proceeds. For now, the anecdotal reports are sufficiently promising for the continued exploration of EMDR.

It seems that neither Dr. Shapiro nor Dr. Waters has much enthusiasm for my behavioral prescription in this case. Dr. Waters viewed it as a form of paradoxical ordeal therapy, while Dr. Shapiro indicated she would have continued using EMDR and been more straightforward in her prescriptions. My intent in designing the intervention was not to be sadistic or overly complicated. I simply wished to avoid repeating any suggestions offered by the host of previous therapists in this case. Given the scope of previous interventions, it is not surprising that my prescription sounded a bit "strange." What is more, I was not at all surprised that my prescribed intervention was not carried out and yet was successful. Such is the life of a brief therapist!

I contacted Leonard early in May 1993 for a follow-up. He had moved his office and is enthusiastically engaged in expanding his business activities. Sarah has quit her job, helped found a new company, and is doing quite well. They are both satisfied with their sexual life and Leonard describes the relationship as being "on a new level." ■

STUDY QUESTIONS

1. In your opinion, what role did the EMDR play in Leonard and Sarah's ability to change their sex life?

2. How did the therapist's intervention—telling the couples that they would never have a normal sex life—change the nature of the therapy task for the couple? Why do you think it was successful?

3. What is your opinion of the efficacy of EMDR, based on Shapiro's and Waters' discussions? In your opinion, what should be therapists' criteria for assessing new therapy techniques?

CASE STUDY

A NO-TALK CURE FOR TRAUMA
THOUGHT FIELD THERAPY SEEMS TO VIOLATE ALL THE RULES

Fred Gallo

The traditional treatment for posttraumatic stress disorder (PTSD) has frequently been lengthy and emotionally demanding, for both therapist and client, often with disappointing results. Perhaps the most common treatment is the behavioral flooding procedure, which requires clients to relive painful memories and emotions, even though this approach often triggers panic episodes, depression, and, in some cases, alcohol-abuse relapse. But for the past five years, I have been using a method that has been consistently successful in quickly and permanently freeing clients from the effects of trauma without having to resort to medication, carthartic abreaction, or painful, protracted discussion of the details of the trauma. While the most severely and extensively traumatized clients may require additional therapeutic work in putting their lives back together, I have found that rapid, painless neutralization of the trauma is indeed possible.

The method of treating trauma that I now use, thought field therapy (TFT), is also one of the strangest I have ever encountered. Developed by psychologist Roger J. Callahan, it involves a true paradigmatic shift in the way therapy is done. TFT is not a conversational therapy, although conversation certainly takes place within the session. It does not entail challenging beliefs, inducing trance, visualizing outcomes, anchoring desired states, or anthropomorphizing disorders, like other popular trauma treatments. Instead, TFT directs patients to tap with their fingertips at key locations on their bodies, while thinking about the trauma or other psychological problems from which they desire relief. According to Callahan, the tapping alleviates psychological problems by addressing the body's bioenergy system, an approach that has also been the basis of acupuncture for thousands of years. By removing disruptions within the energy system caused by the trauma—what Callahan

calls "perturbations"—the trauma's emotional and behavioral consequences can be rapidly resolved. Tapping at specific meridian points in
sequence seems to activate the energy system and eliminate the perturbation—the initial domino that sets the whole process of emotional distress in motion. This approach is premised on the view that the trauma is
fundamentally contained within the energy system, rather than within
memory, cognition, chemistry, or neurology. By tapping on specific
acupuncture meridian energy points, TFT practitioners try to restore balance to the energy system and eliminate the symptoms of trauma within
a few sessions at most, eliminating many months or years of therapy.

Kate, a 40-year-old woman married for the third time, entered therapy on the recommendation of her sister, whom I had treated months
earlier for physical-abuse trauma and social phobia. Kate was experiencing generalized anxiety and frequent, severe panic attacks, often several
times a day, involving tension, tachycardia, difficulty breathing, and fear
of losing her mind or even dying. She was also phobic of driving and
was anxious as a passenger. She had a history of alcohol abuse and was
increasingly relying on alcohol to handle her anxiety.

Describing her first panic episode, Kate nervously related an event
that had occurred 10 years earlier. She and her second husband, whom
she referred to as "the love of my life," were attending a work-related
social event. As Kate was mingling with her colleagues, she noticed that
one woman was sitting next to Kate's husband with her hand between
his legs. The woman had been drinking heavily, and so had Kate's husband, "I was humiliated! I thought he'd get up and leave, but he didn't!"
Kate told me.

Almost matter-of-factly, Kate continued, "We got into a huge argument that night at home. We'd both been drinking. He got so mad he
took a gun and put it to the back of my head and threatened to shoot
me. All I can remember is yelling 'No!' He backed off and I ran into the
bedroom. Then he shot himself."

She described the sound of the shot and said, "I heard that and came
around the corner . . . and . . . I couldn't believe it." She added, in a
monotone, "Him, there, in a pool of blood."

She called 911, and the police and ambulance arrived in a few minutes. Initially, they arrested her for murder, before determining what
had happened. Shaking her head in disbelief, Kate sighed, "There was

a lot of confusion. I kept saying, 'What am I going to do? What am I going to do?' " Her family lived in Pennsylvania, more than 2,000 miles away.

"Did you have a panic attack that night?" I asked.

"I must have, because my sister said that when I called home, she was telling me to breathe because I couldn't talk."

Even if her other symptoms were not connected to this awful experience, I felt certain that trauma relief would prove beneficial to Kate. I began by describing TFT as a method that usually relieves trauma rapidly and painlessly. I told her, "It's similar to acupuncture, in a sense, in that you will be tapping on potent points that we believe affect the body's bioenergy system." Kate knew a little about acupressure and said that the therapy I described made sense to her. She then gave permission to be treated in this way.

Not all clients are so readily compliant with such a strange treatment approach. When I encounter a client who balks at the idea, I attempt to provide detailed information about the emotional, time, and monetary advantages of this method compared with traditional therapy. If the client still refuses this therapy, however, I generally explore other therapeutic approaches more in line with the client's expectations, advising the client to keep this option open. I usually feel disappointed at such times, since I have regularly found TFT to be rapidly helpful.

The first step in working with Kate was to help her identify a target for treatment, a significant link in the chain of events that holds the trauma together. Often this is the most painful moment, or an aspect of the experience that represents the entire trauma. Some people are easily treated as they think about the trauma as a totality, while others need to approach the event in a step-by-step, linear fashion. I begin treatment by finding out where the client wants to begin, which is especially important for clients who feel violated and need to have control over the process. Securing clients' permission and piquing their interest helps to establish a strong working alliance.

"When you think of that whole memory, there are different aspects to it," I said. "There's the part where your husband held the gun to your head, the argument, the moment when you found him dead, the way the police treated you, and whatever else." Kate nodded in acknowledgment. "But when you think about that terrible event—and I certainly do not mean to trivialize it—on a 10-point scale, with 10 being the worst level of distress and 1 being no distress at all, where would you rate that event as you think about it now?"

Without hesitation she stated, "Ten."

"And which part is the most painful feature of all?"

Kate responded, "Coming around the corner and seeing him dead."

Next I guided Kate through the initial stages of a TFT algorithm, or therapeutic recipe, that has been found to be effective in treating trauma. This involved having her tap several times with two fingers at the following acupuncture energy meridian points in sequence: the inside edge of one eyebrow at the bridge of her nose (a point along the bladder meridian); on the bony orbit directly under one eye (the stomach meridian); four inches under an armpit (the spleen meridian); and under her collarbone next to the sternum (the kidney meridian). This sequence was derived by Callahan a number of years ago by using a specific muscle-testing diagnostic procedure with a wide array of clients who had suffered from various traumas. The sequence, at times with some minor variations, has been found to be highly effective, and it is, therefore, seldom necessary to use the diagnostic procedure itself with traumatized clients.

After the first series of tapping, which required less than a minute, I asked, "Where is it now on the scale?"

"I can see it, but I don't have that fear," she said. "It's a five."

I took her through the next step in the algorithm called the "Nine Gamut Treatments (9G), which took about 10 seconds to complete. This involved her tapping repeatedly on the triple heater meridian, between the little finger and ring finger knuckles on the back of her hand, while moving her eyes in various directions, humming, and counting. (The 9G was also derived by Callahan from his muscle-testing procedure; he considers it to be an essential aspect of the TFT algorithm architecture, because it usually produces additional relief or otherwise appears to tune in other aspects of the psychological problem that requires treatment.) Again, I asked her to rate the distress level while visualizing her dead husband. With no trace of surprise she reported, "It's gone. It's a one."

I then asked Kate to identify any remaining distress. She rated the moment when her husband held the gun to her head as a 10. Within seconds, using the same sequence as before, her distress was gone. "There's no fear when I think about it. Not the old butterflies. I'm not getting them." She paused, "It's there. I can see it clearly, but I don't have the fear with it."

I asked her, "When was the last time you were able to think about this and not have fear?"

"Never, I always had it."

To be certain that we had processed all of the trauma, I had her search for anything else from that series of events that still carried distress.

"The way the police treated me," she said.

We repeated the trauma algorithm with slight changes to incorporate her anger at the police. While the sequence utilized earlier produced some relief from this aspect of the trauma, it was not sufficient to allevi-ate all of the anger. Therefore, I directed her to tap on the radial aspect of her little fingernail (the heart meridian), since TFT, as well as acupunc-ture lore, identifies this point as beneficial in the treatment of anger. "The anger is gone," she reported with a tone of astonishment. "They were just doing their job."

Finally Kate thought about the argument she and her husband had had. She rated it a 10 because of her feelings of guilt. "I was saying ugly things to him because he hurt me."

Within a couple minutes, the distress decreased from 10 to 6 to 4, then 2 and none. Again, the basic trauma sequence was insufficient to relieve all the guilt feelings, so I adjusted the recipe to include the inside tip of her index fingernail (the large intestine meridian)—another point identified by Callahan as relevant in the treatment of guilt. By the con-clusion of this session, Kate was quite calm and relaxed, with a pleas-ant glow on her face.

When I saw Kate the following week, she reported that memories of her husband's death no longer bothered her, she was feeling much less anxiety, and the frequency and intensity of panic had diminished signif-icantly. Since the panic attacks were not completely gone, I inquired about what could have triggered the recent surge of attacks. Kate re-ported that the current episode of panic began after her brother-in-law died of a heart attack, some time after she had had an argument with him about some money matters. On the day he died, her panic attacks resumed. This event was not only significant in itself; it likely stirred up the unresolved trauma about her husband's death.

Again, we proceeded with the trauma algorithm, and within a few minutes she no longer felt distress when recalling events surrounding their disagreement and her brother-in-law's death. At the end of this session, we experimented with sequences of points, deriving an individually tailored algorithm that she could use herself to alleviate any anxiety and panic that occurred before the next session.

At the third session, Kate reported that all of the traumas were still resolved and she had had even fewer instances of panic during the week. What panic did occur lasted only seconds and was much less intense. She had successfully used the algorithm she learned at the last session to alleviate the little anxiety she felt. While many patients' anxiety and panic resolves quickly with treatment, others find that repeated treatments over time, including self-treatment, are necessary for sustained improvement. However, even people with long-term, severe anxiety seldom require more than a few months of TFT treatment.

During this session, I treated Kate for her driving phobia. After having her rate the anxiety, I took her through a standard algorithm for this phobia, and within a couple of minutes she was able to comfortably think about driving. I encouraged her to repeat the algorithm as needed over the following week.

Although her sister had driven her to the office for the first three visits, Kate drove alone to the office for our fourth session. She reported dramatic improvement in her overall level of anxiety, with no panic episodes. Because she said that she still had some anxiety when driving, I used the TFT diagnostic procedure involving detailed muscle testing to determine a specifically tailored algorithm for this issue. This method, derived from Callahan's work with applied kinesiology, identifies the precise sequence of meridians involved in a particular problem.

After completing this sequence in a few minutes, Kate had no fear as she thought about driving. I wrote out this algorithm for self-treatment as needed. Since all of Kate's anxieties and panic were gone, we agreed to terminate treatment, with the understanding that she could resume at any time, if necessary.

Follow-up contacts a month later and again at four months revealed that Kate was doing quite well. She said that none of the traumatic events bothered her and that the nightmares she used to have were now gone. She was not having any panic and she was driving without anxiety.

The results Kate obtained are quite common with TFT. In my experience, trauma is easily resolved within minutes, and in the hands of an accomplished TFT therapist, abreaction seldom occurs. After the trauma is alleviated, the patient is usually able to vividly recall the event without experiencing any emotional distress, and the relief usually lasts. Additionally, results of trauma, such as panic, avoidance, nightmares, and emotional numbing, disappear. It is important to note that relieving the trauma doesn't always immediately take care of every problem the client presents. Specific attention to related symptoms is often necessary, as it was with Kate's generalized anxiety and driving phobia.

While a few studies have demonstrated the effectiveness of TFT, clearly much more research needs to be done to establish its empirical validity to the scientific community. In my practice and in the practice of many of my seminar trainees, however, TFT repeatedly has been demonstrated to be effective for a wide array of psychological problems, including depression, rage, jealousy, addictive urges, eating disorders, and even some physical complains, such as chronic pain and allergies.

One of the best results of using TFT, for me, is that I seldom find therapy as emotionally demanding as it once was. While I still enjoy relating and conversing with my clients, assisting them in achieving a greater understanding and a healthier perception, the results I realize with TFT are so rapid and thorough that I believe it is now unethical for one trained in TFT not to offer this choice as an integral part of the treatment plan.

A colleague recently inquiring about my work with TFT asked, "What's the most common question/criticism about TFT that you encounter these days?" There are two. First there is the claim that TFT is simply distraction or placebo. The second is skepticism about how long the successful results will last.

To the first criticism, I respond that distraction or placebo is seldom so consistently powerful. Distraction, in fact, can interfere with treatment effectiveness, and placebo, at best, only accounts for 30% of any treatment effect.

The question, "But how long will it last?" is also a compliment, tacitly acknowledging that change has actually occurred. In all the years that I had been doing other types of psychotherapy, seldom did anyone ask me how long the results last, since seldom did profound therapeutic results occur so quickly. Time will tell how long the results will last, but so far, my experience reveals that time is on the side of TFT.

CASE COMMENTARY 1
BY LAWRENCE LESHAN

It is impossible to evaluate this article, which, in my opinion, should not have been published. Tremendous and imprecise claims are made for a process so far from our usual ways of thinking about and conceptualizing modern therapy that we simply do not know what to do about it or how to respond.

For the size of the claims made—that TFT has been "consistently" and "repeatedly" successful in treating depression, rage, jealousy, addictive urges, eating disorders, chronic pain, allergies, and other maladies—little evidence is given, except the author's enthusiasm and one case history. We learn that he has, for the past five years, been using a method that has been "successful in quickly and permanently freeing clients from the effects of trauma." We are given references to the "bladder meridian," the "stomach meridian," the "body's bioenergy system," and other terms from acupuncture literature. And we are told that there are "algorithms" to be followed. These are intriguing references, but in the absence of data, they don't mean anything.

Either this is a new contribution of tremendous importance (in which case this report should have been sent back for supporting details and facts), or it is one of those wild therapies that depend on the therapist's personality and belief (recalling the old medical school dictum, "Use your new medicine while it still works") or, who knows? The author obviously believes in TFT, but he gives us no reason why we should.

CASE COMMENTARY 2
BY ANNE SPECKHARD

PTSD involves the continual triggering of highly emotional states associated with the preconscious, unconscious, and conscious recall of traumatic memories. These psychophysiological states can be thought of as a particular neuronal set that engulfs a PTSD sufferer in terror and helplessness. An effective treatment must somehow intervene in the system of the individual (brain, body, cognitive schema, etc.) so that the trauma is no longer overwhelming the individual emotionally and psychologically. The most effective and enduring interventions either pair some calming response with the traumatic recall or somehow manage to circumvent the cuing up of the original psychophysiological state associated with the trauma.

While TFT purports to do this in a unique way, it should be noted that the case presented here is not an example of a miracle cure for trauma. Clinicians who regularly treat traumatized individuals know that simple traumas, especially those that occur to adults, can often be treated quickly by any number of methods. The key is to calm and attentuate the emotions surrounding recall of the trauma.

Of course, that does not mean that TFT should be dismissed. In fact, I have had some personal experiences that have impressed me with the power of the kind of bodily interventions Gallo reports. About 10 years ago, after a back injury, I visited a chiropractor who practiced applied kinesiology, a discipline concerned with the relationship between muscle systems in the body that resembles TFT. After two sessions of muscle testing and manipulation, the chiropractor fixed my back. However, when I returned to the place where my injury had occurred, my pain suddenly recurred. I scheduled another session with my chiropractor.

In that session, he did something that seemed quite unusual. He told me to think about when I was hurt while, at the same time, he began tapping on the side of my forehead 8 or 10 times, telling me to try to keep the image in my mind. I couldn't! As much as I tried, I found it impossible. When I asked him to explain what had happened, he said it was a "pain erasure" technique called "temporary tapping." No one knew quite why, but you couldn't keep recall of pain in your mind when you were tapped this way.

Now, 10 years later, my hat is off to TFT's developer, Roger Callahan, for translating the concepts of applied kinesiology into a useful format for psychological treatments. I do, however, have trouble with TFT's claim that, as Gallo puts it, this method involves challenge to "the energy system, rather than within memory, cognition, chemistry, or neurology." Every system within the body is interrelated, so to claim one is working within the energy system alone is not an adequate account of what can be a very powerful intervention. Nevertheless, just because TFT's theory of change is inadequate (or false, in my opinion) does not negate its power and usefulness.

In their efforts to distinguish their intervention from others, the proponents of TFT claim that TFT is not hypnosis. However, Gallo states in this case that an essential ingredient of the TFT protocol is to gain permission and pique interest, both well-known components of trance induction. Similarly, engendering a state of confusion, which occurs when given many instructions at once—to tap, hum, count, and so on—is an alternate method of initiating trance. Gallo does not like to think of this technique as a paired-associate method either. Nevertheless, as Kate goes through the TFT protocol, there is a pairing of the state invoked by TFT and that invoked by the traumatic memory. The result is that with recall of the trauma, the calming effect of the TFT is also retrieved, which allows Kate to have access to the memory while responding to it in a different way.

As I pointed out earlier, simple traumas can be successfully treated in one or two sessions through a variety of procedures. Although I am familiar with TFT, I prefer to use my calming voice to help my clients when they enter their trance states of terrifying memory. While a similar reorganization within the system as a whole occurs as with TFT, my style of intervention is very different. It is also important to emphasize that those who were traumatized repeatedly, or extensively, especially in childhood, require more than a simple technique to help them overcome their trauma. In cases in which development was stunted or sidetracked, clients need help reorganizing themselves, cognitively, emotionally, and socially. Even in these more difficult cases, however, the ability to quickly access and move beyond the horror of traumatic scenes without reliving them is important.

One caution I have for those who use TFT is that it does have a demand component that may have negative associations for anyone who has previous experiences of forced compliance. An overly accommodating or anxious patient may report a lower rate of subjective distress simply to avoid displeasing or angering the therapist. So transference issues, especially with abuse victims, are still important to consider when utilizing this method.

While at the current time, TFT training is prohibitively expensive, I hope it can be made more readily accessible in the future. The bodily interventions involved in the TFT protocols are powerful tools. We should all welcome a promising new addition to our repertoire of interventions.

AUTHOR'S RESPONSE
BY FRED GALLO

After experiencing the rapid resolution of a psychological problem with unusual methods such as TFT, clients often attribute the change to any number of factors other than the method. Some claim that they were "confused" or "distracted," even though they continue not to be bothered after the confusion and distraction have ceased. Others wonder if they have been "put in a trance," even though they remained quite conscious and alert throughout the procedure. Still others deny that they were in distress in the first place, although pretreatment affect and SUD (Subjective Unit of Distress scale) strongly indicate otherwise. Even scientist-practitioners are wont to offer unlikely explanations for methods that produce the kinds of rapid changes often found with TFT.

In response to Speckhard's comments about the trance-inducing quality of TFT, I would reply that getting clients' permission and piquing their interest should not be confused with TFT protocol. Even in the absence of setting such a stage, the TFT procedures are consistently effective. Also, while I realize that trauma can be effectively treated with a number of methods, I have not found other methods that treat trauma with the ease common to TFT.

Speckhard faults TFT for seeming to make the theoretical assumption that the various systems within the body are unrelated. In fact, like Speckhard, I agree that we are one, interrelated system; that is, after all, the point of most methods that combine psyche and soma. While traumatic and other conditions include behavioral, systemic, cognitive, chemical, and neurologic aspects, TFT posits that the subtle electrical configurations within the patient's thought field (i.e., perturbations) trigger a disruption within the energy system that, in turn, sets the entire process in motion, culminating in disturbed emotion. The perturbation is merely the initial domino.

In response to LeShan, I respect the skepticism the research psychologist must show for unproven clinical methods. It is important for us as a profession to avoid being misguided about highly touted new tools in the absence of evidence. There are a few studies supporting the effectiveness of TFT and solid empirical research is still needed if the therapists are to view this unconventional method with any confidence. Meanwhile, during the decades required for this research to be conducted, traumatized people will continue to be in need of our assistance, and I believe that therapists in the trenches can be trusted to determine whether methods like TFT are effective in relieving the unnecessary suffering of their clients. ■

STUDY QUESTIONS

1. What is the theory behind TFT, and what is your opinion of it, based on this case?

2. What are some of the ways Speckhard cites that transference issues might affect follow-up data from clients?

3. Should it be important to clinicians to be able to explain why Kate changed for the better, or should therapists continue to practice a technique that has proven to work with their clients without knowing why?

CHAPTER 5

The Impossible Case

MANY FAMILIES seem so trapped in tangled webs of destructive relationships, mutual recrimination, substance abuse, and institutional inertial that they strain the sense of competence and self-confidence of any therapist. These are the cases that test the limits of both our theories and our clinical resources. But by examining the cases that don't go according to our preconceptions, we extend our grasp of the endless complexity of our work and expand our notion of what it means to be a therapist.

In the following cases, therapists share their experiences of success and failure in the face of entrenched obstacles. "The Resistant Substance Abusers" illustrates the challenges a therapist faces when clients enter therapy involuntarily and without motivation to change. In "The Overresponsibility Trap," Joe Eron and Tom Lund challenge the mass-media generated language of codependency by recognizing the strengths and contributions of an alcoholics supportive family members. In their case, "Is the Customer Always Right?", therapists Barry Duncan, Mark Hubble, and Scott Miller demonstrate their willingness to accept a client's theory of change, even when it goes against their own belief system, to join with her and work collaboratively. The case "One Step Forward, Two Steps Back" raises two fundamental therapeutic issues: (a) when to work with a client individually or with the family, and (b) how to help a client when getting better seems against his best interests. Finally, in "Herman Wept," Michael Murphy turns an apparently intransient conflict between the needs of the client diagnosed as a dangerous psychopath and the needs of the public agency caring for him into two narratives that lead to a resolution for everyone involved.

CONSULTATION CORNER

THE RESISTANT SUBSTANCE ABUSER

Court-Mandated Cases Pose Special Problems

EDITED BY H. CHARLES FISHMAN

Twelve-step programs and a belief in the addiction-is-a-disease model form the foundation of most established drug abuse and alcoholism treatment programs. However, many family therapists are uncomfortable with approaches that minimize family involvement and they believe that a client must hit bottom in order to become motivated for change. Consequently, substance abusers can receive strikingly different treatments depending on the theoretical orientation of the therapist involved.

The following case was sent in by the frustrated staff at an outpatient clinic working with a court-mandated client who was apparently quite unconvinced he had hit bottom. It vividly dramatizes the obstacles typically encountered in such cases. One commentary proposes an approach integrating the traditional 12-step model and the language of the disease model with a strategic attempt to mobilize the forces for change within the substance abuser's family. The other commentary proposes a more unconventional tack, arguing that both confrontation and family involvement can confuse the treatment process and undercut the prime leverage in successful therapy—mobilizing the client's own motivation for change.

H.C.F.

When Bob called our outpatient center for help with his crack and alcohol problem, he had been unemployed for more than a year, and his wife, Joy, was working two jobs to support the family. On the phone, Bob told the intake worker that he wanted to quit drugs and return to work "to regain my pride and support my family financially."

At the initial session, Bob and Joy were accompanied by their two children, Jerry, 16, and Monica, 14. Thirty-two-year-old Bob

(Continued)

(Continued)

described his drug and alcohol problems as dating back to the time he was 15-years-old. During the last two years, Bob used crack an average of three times a day and drank beer or wine every evening until he became drunk. Joy reported that she had been totally clean of all drugs and alcohol for two years. The children reported no drug or alcohol usage.

At the time he called, Bob was staying home all day watching television, while his wife worked. He had few friends and his only supports were his wife, children, and extended family members. After some probing, it was revealed that when high or intoxicated, Bob verbally abused his wife and children and on some occasions physically abused his wife.

Throughout the session, Bob's wife and children appeared very cautious about what they said, closely watching Bob's reaction after any statement they thought would upset him. Whenever any family member started to confront Bob, someone else would quickly move to defuse the tension by trying to change the subject or by reporting that Bob also had many good qualities. Sixteen-year-old Jerry sat between his mother and father and interceded for his mother when arguing between his parents became too intense. Jerry revealed that he regularly gave his father money, put him to bed when he was high and/or drunk, and helped his mother look after the day-to-day household affairs.

It became clear that many people in Bob's life treated him like an irresponsible child who had to be taken care of. According to Joy, the next-door neighbor often gave him food and money, Bob's father thought Bob "could do no wrong," and Joy's mother "adored him" and also gave him money. Only Joy's sister and father would not "give in to Bob or listen to his bullshit." Joy admitted that she was afraid to confront Bob on his alcohol and drug use.

As the family was leaving the session, Bob suddenly said, "Oh, I forgot to tell you. Here's Judge Roger's number. Would you please contact him and say that I've entered treatment." This caught me completely off guard, as Bob had said earlier that he was seeking treatment voluntarily. When I contacted the judge the next day, he

(Continued)

(Continued)

told me that Bob's case had come to his attention when Joy had requested a restraining order to keep Bob away from the home. When Bob violated that order and was arrested, Joy had sought a reconciliation. The charges were now contingent on Bob's seeking treatment for his drug and alcohol problem. If he did not, Bob could be fined or imprisoned.

Bob's court-ordered treatment plan called for placement in a voluntary drug and alcohol treatment program for at least a week to help him detoxify. A job counselor had been recruited to ascertain Bob's skill level and help him find a job. After three days in the program, however, Bob checked himself out of the hospital, claiming he was sober and ready to find a job. He never called the job counselor. Bob did find a part-time job building wooden carts, but quit after two weeks because he thought this job was demeaning.

Even though Bob had a DWI (driving while intoxicated) charge on his record and was not supposed to drive, he took the car whenever he wanted, and no one in the family confronted him on his behavior. After the second therapy session, Bob missed the next two scheduled sessions and never called to cancel. The other family members were asked, and agreed, to come for the next session with or without Bob. But as the family was about to leave, Bob hid the car so that they couldn't make the appointment. The judge told Bob that if he missed another session and did not comply with treatment, he would be held in contempt of court. Bob and his family showed up for the next session, but Joy said she was afraid to speak her mind for fear of Bob's anger after the hour was up.

Presently, Bob and the family continue to attend treatment sporadically. The family will not confront or challenge Bob. Bob does not seem motivated to change. What is the next step?

COMMENTARY 1

A Structural-Strategic Approach

BY DAVID TREADWAY

Working with substance-abusing family systems often feels like wading, hip deep, through an alligator-infested swamp in the dark. You're surrounded by the buzz of insects and other less familiar night noises. Dawn seems a long way off.

Bob and his family seem grimly determined to enact a gut-wrenching tragedy. No wonder the authors are unsure about the next step. It's a normal part of the work with substance abusers and their families for the therapist to become lost, bewildered, and ultimately frustrated.

Rather than presume to tell the therapists treating the case what they should do, I considered what steps I would follow if it were my case. There are three basic principles that I would keep in mind:

1. *Blood is thicker than therapy.* It is obvious that there are compelling loyalties binding this family together, as well as fear. It is critically important that any therapeutic interventions be consistent with the family's need to "help" and "protect" Bob.

2. *Don't be the only motivated person in the therapy.* Part of the authors' exasperation with the case may be a result of their being the only ones in the treatment pushing hard for change. Bob and his family appear to be successfully maintaining a painful status quo in spite of the therapists' best efforts. In such cases, I always feel it's my job to engage those people who really want change and mediate between family members who are motivated and those who are reluctant.

3. *Do the doable.* The treatment team seems to feel that it's their job to get Bob sober. But the only goal that seems possible to me is to help Bob and his family fully appreciate the consequences of his continued substance abuse. Then it's time to let the chips fall where they may.

Armed with these rather simple ideas, I would being in all of Bob's extended family and elicit their ideas about how best to help him. I would attempt to make an alliance with everyone, including the people who are actively enabling Bob's continued abuse (i.e., the neighbor, Bob's dad, etc.). While overtly allying with Bob, I would elicit from him a public commitment not to be abusive to his wife and children and a promise to leave the house if abuse occurs.

I would have this meeting even if Bob refused to attend. I frequently resort to calling reluctant family members and including them in the interview by phone. In this case, I would call Bob while the family watched and ask him for his perspective. I would also ask him whether there was any risk of his being abusive to his wife and kids as a result of their attending the meeting. If his answer was in any way ambivalent, I would have one of his prime supporters get on the phone and discuss the safety issue with him. If it couldn't be settled, I would encourage the wife and children to go home with someone else in the group.

After uniting everyone around their concern for Bob, I would have a follow-up meeting with this group in the judge's chambers. The judge seems to be the most motivated member of the system and thus likely to be willing to play the role of the bad cop. It would be important for the judge to be specific about the consequences of Bob's continued chemical abuse, including the likelihood of his being sent to jail. With the judge playing the heavy, I could strengthen my alliance with Bob and the family by invoking the disease model of alcoholism and taking the position that Bob doesn't need punishment, he needs help. Hopefully, this would help Bob make a commitment to either sobriety or inpatient treatment. If not, I would help the entire family accept the possibility that the severity of Bob's disease may necessitate his having to suffer the full consequences of his behavior (e.g., go to jail).

Although mandatory involvement in self-help groups is not always helpful, in this case, I would encourage the judge to use legal leverage to insist that Bob, his spouse, and his children attend AA, Al-Anon, and Alateen meetings. In the eventuality that Bob continues to drink, use drugs, and be physically threatening, I would coach the family on the mechanics of doing an intervention in which they make it clear that unless he enters inpatient treatment, they will report him to the judge. If the family is unwilling to do this, then I would notify the judge.

The authors have already demonstrated their commendable commitment to working with this family. They need to keep on keeping on. Generating ideas is easy; doing the therapy is the hard job.

COMMENTARY 2

A Solution-Focused Approach

BY SCOTT D. MILLER

Many mental-health professionals and treatment programs face the difficulty of treating clients who indicate that they do not want to be in treatment for the identified problem or that they do not have the problem for which they were referred. In such cases, professionals and treatment programs report that a great deal of time must be spent initially confronting the denial and resistance that such individuals (and their families) seem to display. This approach is usually quite labor intensive and often extremely frustrating for the therapist. All this is further complicated by the fact that insurance companies and third-party payers are now placing more restrictions on the amount of outpatient and inpatient alcohol and drug treatment services than ever before.

At the Brief Family Therapy Center in Milwaukee, we have found that clinical time is spent more efficiently and effectively when, as a first step, we work *with* clients to identify what *they* want from treatment. Based on our firm belief that *all* clients, voluntary and involuntary, want something from the therapist and/or treatment program, we customarily forgo all efforts at breaking through resistance and denial in favor of working together with clients to identify a goal that is important to them.

One useful strategy with Bob might be to start over completely and initially meet alone with him. This would serve at least two purposes: First, the therapist could work together with Bob to identify a treatment goal that is important to him. An example might very well be to "get the court off my back" or to "regain my pride and to support my family financially." With either goal, clinical time could be spent investigating what Bob believes he must do in order to achieve this goal. Clinical experience and outcome research demonstrate that clients are more willing to work on treatment goals that are personally relevant and that they choose for themselves.

This strategy was used successfully in a case treated recently at the center involving a police officer in his mid-30s who was ordered into treatment after being arrested for domestic violence. While the arrest was the first on record for this officer, it was learned through the referral source that fellow officers on the force had been summoned to his home on numerous previous occasions, without an arrest being made. In each instance, the officers had removed their usually drunken friend from the home, returning him after he had a chance to sober up.

When the young officer reported for treatment at the center, his initial words to the therapist were that he did *not* have an alcohol problem and that his wife provoked him into fighting. He quickly added that the only reason he had come to treatment was "to please [his] captain." While a typical strategy in such a case might be to set limits or aggressively confront this man in an effort to break through the obvious resistance and denial of his problem, we have found that such a strategy usually increases and solidifies defensiveness. Therefore, as a first step, we routinely begin by accepting the goal that the client has for treatment—in this instance, to "please the captain." Accepting this as the treatment goal, the therapist asked the client what he needed to do differently in order to make his captain happy. The officer quickly responded, "Not use alcohol or have any kind of problems with my wife." Resistance and denial were bypassed and the question then became a simple matter of what he needed to do to achieve the goals that he had initially denied and would have resisted if interviewed in the traditional, confrontive manner.

A second reason for starting over and initially meeting alone with Bob would be to decrease the confusion about what the next step should be. In the treatment described, so many problems and issues—and potential problems and issues—have been allowed to arise that it is difficult to know exactly where to start. As a result, Bob's goals have become obscured and the treatment process stalled. This is not an uncommon problem when family therapists require all members of a family to be present for treatment. At the

Brief Family Therapy Center, we have not found this particularly useful. Rather, we find that family therapy can be done successfully even when only one member of the family is present.

One technique we have found especially useful in doing family therapy with an individual client is asking relationship-oriented questions—a variant of what others in the field have referred to as circular questions. In this case, the therapist might ask Bob what he believes his wife would say is the problem and/or the goals that should be worked on in treatment. A similar line of questioning could be followed by asking for his perception of what the judge, his children, the probation officer, or anyone else involved might say is the problem or goal to be worked on in treatment. Bob could be asked to specify what he believes each of these other people might say would be different about him if treatment were successful.

In the case of the police officer, the therapist asked the officer to specify what he needed to do differently in order to accomplish his goal of "pleasing the captain." Later questions focused on what the officer believed his wife would say needed to be different so that he would not have any more trouble at home. The officer's answers to these and other similar questions identified a pattern of behaviors that was important to all parties involved. In subsequent sessions, other family members could be met with individually and asked similar questions about the problem drinker and themselves. Eventually, all of the family members could be brought together and asked to describe their perceptions of the views of their fellow family members.

One question we have found particularly useful in arriving at clear treatment goals with all types of clients goes something like this: "Suppose tonight, after you go to bed and fall fast asleep, a miracle occurs, and the miracle is that the problem that brought you into treatment is solved! But because you are asleep, you don't know that the miracle has occurred. When you wake up in the morning, what would you notice that is different that would tell you that this miracle has occurred and the problem is solved?" The miracle question acts to quickly and powerfully reorient the client away from the problem and toward a time in the future when the problem is solved.

The question accomplishes a number of things. It clarifies what the clients hope to accomplish in treatment and instills a sense of relief and renewed hopefulness. Typically, clients smile and even laugh when they first hear it. Most often their responses to this question have nothing to do with the problem for which they are in treatment. Clients learn immediately that little time is going to be spent rehashing ancient history or affixing psychological blame. A level of cooperation and rapport is established as the client and therapist work together to bring this "miracle" about. In the process treatment is expedited.

The response of the police officer to the miracle question can be used to illustrate a typical response. When he was asked the question some 20 minutes into the interview, he responded, laughing, "My wife and I would be able to communicate. That would be the real miracle, you know, like it used to be. We could talk . . . she could talk, I could listen, she could listen. We would touch again, you know, 'nice' touching . . . ."

The officer voluntarily asked his wife to come to the next session. Together, they worked on safety, communicating, and touching. The captain is pleased so far. ∎

STUDY QUESTIONS

1. Based on Treadway's commentary, describe the main elements of a structural-strategic approach.

2. What are your opinions of self-help groups such as AA, Al-Anon, and Alateen? Would you refer clients to these groups? Why or why not?

3. According to Miller, what happens in therapy when treatment goals are not defined? How might the treatment goals have been defined in this case, and who might have defined them?

4. How might the brief therapy technique of asking the "Miracle Question" have helped Bob?

5. In cases in which family members seem afraid and physical abuse has occurred, how might a therapist address family safety? What is the therapist's responsibility?

CASE STUDY

THE OVERRESPONSIBILITY TRAP
HELPING CODEPENDENTS CREATE A NEW LIFE STORY

JOSEPH ERON AND THOMAS LUND

Among the most challenging presenting problems family therapists face are those in which the person initiating therapy complains about the burden of a partner's out-of-control behavior—whether that be domestic violence, incest, or substance abuse. To help people deal with these difficult situations, the self-help movement developed concepts of "codependency" and "enabling." These ideas have helped many people to become more aware of their own contribution to the irresponsible behavior of other family members, which has empowered many of them to change their lives. Unfortunately, in some cases, labeling themselves as "enablers" or "codependents" may place responsibility for change on the shoulders of people who are already overwhelmed.

We believe that people who are quick to accept responsibility for others too often tend to overemphasize their contribution to their family's difficulties, even to the point of blaming themselves for the problem. Moreover, ascribing negative intention to caregiving behavior can sometimes add to clients' emotional burden while allowing their partners to continue to avoid responsibility. In fact, people who refer to themselves as "codependents" or "enablers" are often the standard-bearers for responsible action in troubled families. Consequently, we prefer to begin the therapeutic conversation with such clients by appreciating their strengths, competencies, and personal initiative. Our goal is to de-emphasize how such clients themselves contribute to the problem in order to help them find ways of holding their partners more accountable.

We have found that when we can help such clients develop another story about their problem that also manages to align with their own preferred view of themselves, they are often able to change how they think and act in relation to their predicaments. Even clients strongly committed to Alcoholics Anonymous and Al-Anon typically consider this approach compatible with the ideas emphasized in these programs. The Christopher family is a case in point.

Diane Christopher called me because she was concerned about her 16-year-old daughter, Jerrine. Once an enthusiastic student with an avid interest in sports and an active social life, Jerrine had, for the past year, seemed increasingly listless and withdrawn. Although she went through the motions of doing her homework, her grades had begun to drop. She was spending less and less time with her friends and no longer invited them to her house. And she was even showing less interest in activities like basketball and soccer, which she had once loved.

In our first session together, Diane Christopher had a ready explanation for her daughter's behavior. In her view, Jerrine had lost touch with herself and her own interests because of her worry over her father, Frank's, drinking problem, which had been growing more and more out of control. In fact, Diane reported, her daughter was now playing the role of "codependent" for her father, a role that she herself had abandoned several years before.

Both Frank and Diane grew up in alcoholic families—Frank's father died young of an alcohol-related illness, and his mother and brother were still active drinkers. Diane and Frank initially connected around drinking alcohol. But when Jerrine was born, Diane decided to become more responsible, gave up alcohol, and became an active member of Alcoholics Anonymous.

Over the past five or six years, however, Frank's problems with alcohol had grown more severe, isolating him from his wife and only daughter. After years of feeling depressed and putting up with her husband's irresponsibility, Diane had decided to seize control of her life. Diane described how she had sought help through Al-Anon and individual therapy and had even coaxed Frank into coming to couples therapy with her. Unfortunately, Frank had beat a hasty retreat when both his wife and therapist confronted him about his drinking. Diane slowly began to relinquish responsibility for her husband's behavior, shifting the focus to herself and Jerrine. As she had assumed this more self-oriented approach, her depression lifted. She became involved with Al-Anon and found ideas she heard there about codependency very helpful.

Eventually, Diane had returned to college to complete a business degree so she could become financially independent and leave the marriage when her daughter completed high school. Everything proceeded according to plan until Jerrine started following in her mother's old footsteps. In particular, Diane worried about Jerrine's habit of waiting and worrying—waiting for her father to come home while worrying that he would stay late at the bars and wind up with his car wrapped around a tree. Concerned that her pursuit of her own independence was preventing her from being the caring mother she believed herself to be, Diane begrudgingly decided to cut down on her course load to stay home and help Jerrine with her school work.

Once again caught bearing the burden of Frank's drinking, Diane could not contain her bitterness, which leaked out in sarcastic remarks about his uselessness, disgusted looks, and repeated advice to Jerrine to ignore him. Her disgust and disregard only served to deepen Jerrine's worry about her father.

When I spoke with Jerrine alone, she agreed that she had begun to assume more responsibility for looking after her father as her mother disengaged from him. Jerrine still regarded Frank as a nice guy who, despite his drinking, would drop anything for a friend or a family member in need. Recently, however, Diane had stopped asking her husband for assistance with family matters, and now the only area in which he assumed any responsibility for the family was through his job. Even that was in jeopardy due to cutbacks at work. Frank's doctor told him that his drinking would eventually kill him, just like his father before him.

Jerrine felt compassion for her father and refused to join her mother in abandoning him. As we talked, it became clear that Jerrine wanted to be "just like her mother"—hardworking, responsible, independent, and strong enough to resist the influence of alcohol and drugs. But she also wanted to be caring and sensitive to the needs of others—qualities she saw in her mother's attitude toward other family members, but not in her recent lack of sensitivity toward Frank.

In fact, Jerrine attributed the escalation of Frank's drinking problem to her mother's recent detachment. The more Diane criticized Frank and appeared to give up on him, the more Jerrine became determined to take care of him. The more Jerrine neglected herself, the more trapped Diane felt and the more resentful she became toward Frank. Now both mother and daughter were bearing the burden of Frank's problem—Jerrine by watching him, Diane by watching Jerrine, and both by losing sight of their own independent pursuits.

Diane blamed herself for Jerrine's "codependent" behavior and believed herself to be a bad mother for raising a daughter who looked after someone else's needs while neglecting her own. The notion that Diane had passed on the "curse of codependency" to Jerrine had become a fixed, unshakable view that restricted her options for change by saddling her with a burden of guilt. Despite the fact that Diane continued to participate in Al-Anon and found it helpful, the construct of "codependency," which once freed her to pursue her own independence, now took on a different meaning as she came to regard it as a personality flaw that could be passed from generation to generation. To help ease this burden, I explored with Diane her family's preproblem past, hoping to find a key story—one that challenged her current negative view of her relationship with Jerrine and offered an alternative that supported her preferred view of herself as a mother who had raised a strong, independent daughter.

What emerged was the story of Diane's persistence in trying to solve Jerrine's reading problems in grade school. When the school's psychoeducational evaluations failed to turn up anything specific, Diane had made sure Jerrine was evaluated by several specialists. Finally, a visual perception problem was diagnosed, and a series of eye movement exercises were prescribed. With her mother's support, Jerrine did these exercises diligently every day and gradually gained confidence in reading. She made up for her slow reading by working harder and eventually became an honors student.

In a subsequent conversation with Diane, I used this story to remind her that she was a caring mother who had helped her daughter to be self-oriented, just like herself. I pointed out to Diane how much her daughter admired her and aspired to follow in her footsteps, information I had gleaned from Jerrine in previous sessions.

Now that I had aligned with Diane's preferred view of herself, I wanted to emphasize her success in cultivating other-oriented attributes in her daughter, like responsibility and sensitivity to the needs of loved ones.

"The other thing that strikes me about Jerrine is her heart," I continued. "She's very sensitive about her father's well-being and tries her best to take care of him. It seems like she's also followed in your footsteps in trying to be a responsible person."

"Yeah, I guess," replied Diane. "But I'm not so sure how good all this caretaking stuff is for Jerrine. I've learned about 'codependency' through Al-Anon. They've taught me to watch out for myself and stop picking up after Frank so much. Now I see Jerrine doing what I used to do."

I had reframed Jerrine's helpfulness as a strength and credited Diane with grooming this positive attribute in her daughter. Now I wanted to encourage a different way of thinking about accountability within the family. I began by asking Diane how she imagined Jerrine experienced Diane's anger toward Frank.

"I don't think she likes it when I get angry," Diane said. "Sometimes she's even asked me to stop being so angry with Daddy. But it makes me even angrier when I see her come to her father's defense all the time."

Once again reframing Jerrine's behavior, I remarked, "Like you've said, she's a sensitive, caring person who worries about her father. I notice, though, that when Jerrine sees you getting the least bit critical or sarcastic with Frank, she feels even more determined to watch over him and to ignore herself. I can't help but wonder whether her fierce determination is getting channeled in the wrong direction. Maybe you and I can think of ways to help her get her focus back on herself. What do you think?"

"Maybe I have to control my anger more," Diane mused.

"Rather than thinking of controlling your anger," I offered, "which puts even more burden on you, I was thinking of how to help Jerrine by shifting more of the burden over to Frank. What about coming up with some creative ways to include Frank in being responsible, to help Jerrine get off the hook?"

"I'm open," said Diane. "How do we do it?"

In subsequent sessions with mother and daughter together, we explored how to help Frank feel helpful and responsible again and how to hold him accountable for his influence on others. Jerrine was receptive to this conversation because she wanted to see herself as a helpful, caring person, and she liked the idea of bringing her father back into the family fold. Since Frank, in Jerrine's assessment, preferred to view himself as helpful and available to others, an appeal to his sense of responsibility and helpfulness might be the most empowering way to help him notice the effects of his drinking on others.

In the process of brainstorming solutions, Diane suggested that Jerrine invite her father to one of her basketball games at school as a way to help him reconnect with the family. Jerrine liked this idea but wanted to make sure Frank didn't embarrass her by arriving drunk. She decided to ask him if he would please come to the game sober, and he did.

Jerrine began inviting friends over to the house again and made the same request of her father in order to protect herself from embarrassment. Again Frank complied. When Jerrine asked her father to help her with her math homework, a subject in which he felt more confident than Diane, Frank eagerly chipped in.

Diane stopped criticizing Frank in Jerrine's presence and joined in asking for his help when she genuinely needed it. On several evenings, instead of meeting his buddies at the local bar, Frank helped carpenters finish work on a ceiling that needed repair. In planning for meals for the week, Diane and Jerrine told Frank that unless he arrived at the proper time dinner would not be waiting, which again encouraged responsible participation. On his one early day, Diane asked Frank to prepare dinner so that Jerrine could concentrate on her studies. Again, Frank complied. On the other evenings, Jerrine resumed her old homework schedule and slowly returned to concentrating on her work. Gradually, Jerrine came to realize that it was far more helpful to her father for her to stay focused on her own responsibilities and ask for his participation as a parent than to worry about him and neglect herself.

Once Jerrine resumed doing the things 16-year-olds like to do, her depressed mood lifted. At that point (about six sessions into therapy), I suggested that Frank join in the conversation, as a way to continue to promote his accountability and helpfulness.

By the time I met with Frank alone, I already had some ideas about how he wanted to be viewed by others, so I could begin our conversation on terms that emphasized Frank's strengths and allowed us to talk about his problem in terms of preferred characteristics like helpfulness and responsibility. I let him know how supportive he had been in going to Jerrine's games, reviewing her homework, and encouraging her to have friends over. He seemed to appreciate the compliment and made it clear that he wanted to be helpful. Despite the daily drinking, Frank had in fact noticed that Jerrine's grades had slipped and that she had lost enthusiasm for sports. He was also aware that she was making a comeback in recent weeks.

I explained that Jerrine had been so worried about his drinking and the effect it was having on his health and well-being that she had been unable to concentrate on her school work. I vividly described how Jerrine sat alone each night in the living room, waiting for her father to come home from work, unable to concentrate on anything except his safety. I explained that, by participating in his daughter's school work and honoring her requests to go to her ball games sober, he had helped to lessen Jerrine's burden and supported her progress. Frank listened intently but made no comment about his drinking per se.

While continuing to attend sessions to be helpful to his daughter, Frank also continued to drink. He would stop for certain occasions like his daughter's ball games, but would resume his usual pattern on other evenings. Toward the conclusion of therapy, we all met together for a family session, and Diane made a direct request to her husband to stop drinking. In a matter-of-fact tone, without a hint of the old sarcasm, anger, or disgust, Diane told Frank that she wasn't sure how long she could stay with him if he continued to drink. Noting that she was encouraged by his recent participation in family matters, she said that she wanted the three of them to begin acting like a family again but could only entertain the idea of getting close if the drinking stopped. Frank agreed to try to cut out the drinking, but insisted that it was not a problem and that he could refrain if he put his mind to it. Diane looked skeptical but made no comment.

For the first time in several years, the family planned a vacation together, and Frank stayed sober as promised. In all, he maintained sobriety for about one month, during which time Diane and Jerrine caught a glimpse of the consideration and thoughtfulness that drinking had all but obscured. When he once again returned to alcohol, Diane and Jerrine didn't falter but remained focused on their own lives, their school work, their relationships with other family members and friends. Shortly after Jerrine became involved with her first boyfriend—who was responsible in school and didn't like drinking—therapy came to an end.

After 15 conversations with family members in different combinations, Jerrine was no longer depressed, and the three of them were now talking with one another in ways that confirmed everyone's preference to be helpful. If Frank's drinking continued, which it seemed almost certain to do, Diane might feel freer to make a decision that suited her own interests without seeing that as in conflict with her view of herself as a caring mother and a sensitive spouse. If it became apparent that Frank's drinking could no longer coexist comfortably with the view this family now held of itself, perhaps Diane and Frank could seriously consider ending their marriage.

About a year after our last session, I received an urgent phone call from Frank. Jerrine was still doing well in school, Diane was about to graduate with honors, and Frank had managed to hold on to his job, although he had been forced to accept a transfer out of state. The big news, however, was that Diane and Jerrine had moved out, without conflict or acrimony, and Frank was finally alone.

His voice cracking with emotion, Frank said he still hoped against all hope that his family would return, but he knew he had no control over that right now. It was time, he said, to take charge of the real problem, his drinking. I referred him to a colleague who specialized in substance abuse. He worked with Frank and helped him get involved with Alcoholics Anonymous.

At last report, Frank and his family had reunited and moved together to his new job in another state. Frank himself had maintained sobriety for a year and continued to attend AA meetings several times a week. Diane continued to attend Al-Anon. After years of divisive conversations, Diane and Frank had finally established common ground, and the family was now responsibly connected, perhaps for the first time.

In our view, the key ingredient of therapeutic conversations is that they promote how people wish to be seen by others important to them. Once people who are stuck in problems see themselves being affirmed and validated in this way, they change how they act. They also begin to talk with intimates in a way that makes problems solvable. When family members experience symptoms, and initiate therapy to resolve them because they feel burdened by the out-of-control behavior of another family member, the therapist can promote change by connecting with the positive intentions of these responsible people. Gradually, these family members are helped to engage in what we call *accountable conversations* with the person or persons whom the regard as irresponsible. As the burden of responsibility transfers from those who have noticed others too much to those who haven't noticed others much at all, the symptoms that originally brought people into therapy begin to improve. Not only that, but the stage is set for finding solutions to the more serious difficulties that lurk behind the presenting problem.

In this case, therapy ended when the presenting problem was resolved, and when new patterns of conversation were established within the family. Although Frank was still drinking to excess, the family had found helpful ways to talk with one another about this upsetting behavior so that its effects were less burdensome. Ultimately, it was a series of therapeutic conversations that took place outside the treatment room that inspired a once disconnected father to take notice and to do something different about his drinking. In the final analysis, a 16-year-old girl's unflagging commitment to hope and compassion was the basis for a solution to a problem once seen as hopeless.

CASE COMMENTARY 1
BY JAMES COYNE

Having watched videotapes of Joe Eron and Tom Lund's work, I know that they are warm and engaging therapist. In fact, they are so skilled that they can work effectively despite, as this case demonstrates, having tied one hand behind their backs with some fashionable, but constraining, assumptions about how therapy should look.

Their first assumption is that the therapist should appear nonimpositional and noninterventionist. My conterassumption has always been that to choose one's words or even to choose to be silent is itself an intervention. Since therapists intervene by their mere presence in clients' lives, the choice is not whether to intervene, but how to do so responsibly. The therapists in this case impose their values on this family with profound effects. They give the adolescent girl's welfare a priority, effectively asserts his moralistic view of drinking as a problem, decides the girl's father is "out of control," and excludes the father from the first six sessions. I see these as defensible choices, even if I disagree with some of them, but they remain impositional and interventionist. If therapists insist on believing otherwise, they run the risk of failing to see how to most effectively utilize their influence.

The therapist in this case also seems to assume that in order to avoid blaming clients, he should focus exclusively on "strengths, competencies, and personal initiative." I think there is a large excluded middle ground here. We can actively acknowledge that clients mean well, even while doing them the favor of pointing out how they may get confused and misdirected in pursuit of these good intentions or how their actions may have unintended consequences. While therapists should not blame clients for their predicaments, they should also not discourage clients from taking responsibility for their own behavior. When we portray clients as blameless angels, we run the risk of distracting them from seeing the influence that they have in a situation and choices they can make. As a result, they may be left feeling passive and powerless, or worse, entitled victims.

The therapist in this case says some exceedingly flattering things to the mother and daughter. Some of this sounds so saccharin that, unless the therapist has an exceptionally skillful delivery, he might leave this mother and daughter wondering if he can be trusted to be genuine. Personally, I would have trouble delivering such a one-sided, Pollyannaish view of clients without feeling silly.

While Eron and Lund adopt the view that therapy is a narrative conversation, it seems to me that therapy should be more than just story telling. Life is always more complicated and less coherent in its meaning than the story people tell about it. In this case, I worry that the therapists became too caught up in their own uplifting tale of a heroic, angelic teenager saving her family from Demon Rum.

Finally, therapy should also involve more than just talk, it should involve helping clients commit themselves to action and to following through. Undoubtedly, even good narrative therapists would agree with this, but I suspect the therapists' immersion in the narrative frame of reference actually slowed down whatever progress occurred in this case.

Here is my understanding of how this case proceeded: After a mother calls about her depressed daughter, the mother, daughter, and therapists tie the daughter's depression to the father's drinking. The father is excluded from the first six sessions, although he later joins the therapy. The therapists frequently intervene by saying positive things about the daughter and mother. In some instances, it seems like they bend over backward to avoid assigning blame, even when this entails discouraging the mother and daughter from accepting responsibility for their own behavior. This is particularly notable when the mother brings up the issue of controlling her anger. Nevertheless, the therapists seem to persuade the mother to stop criticizing the father in the daughter's presence. The mother and the daughter also enlist the father in such family activities as going to the daughter's basketball games, doing home repairs, and preparing dinner. The daughter becomes less depressed, at which point the therapists invite the father to the sessions.

Despite being told about his family members' concerns about his drinking, the father continues his usual pattern, albeit with some notable interruptions. Therapy terminates after 15 sessions. A year later, the mother and daughter move out and the father gets a referral for treatment of alcohol abuse. The family then reunites and looks forward to living happily ever after.

While at the end of therapy the family's situation may be as positive as it is presented (or at least as could be expected), I am skeptical about attributing the changes in the family and its subsequent reunion to the effects of therapy, which had ended a year earlier. The mother had previous indicated a readiness to move out and had proceeded with the first stages of a plan to do so. While therapy may have accelerated this process, it could also have postponed it by lulling the mother into temporarily settling for the father's minimal involvement in the family without his making the desired commitment to stop drinking.

It might be helpful to look at this case from a different vantage point: I see the daughter's depression as the explicit issue for everyone. The label itself might be used as a basis for giving the girl permission to more consistently look after herself and for developing and implementing a plan for doing so. I would review with her what it means to be depressed—that it is not just a sense of personal failure or a head trip, but a whole-body experience that saps one's energy and enthusiasm and limits one's ability to get things like school work done. I would add that it is sometimes nature's way of saying that one is taking on too much and not looking after oneself.

Unlike the therapists in this case, I would not encourage the daughter to continue to try to solve her parents' problems. I would point out that the best gift she could give her parents would be her assurance that she was looking after herself and becoming someone of whom they could be proud, despite their own problems. If she disagreed with me, I would inquire about how effective she thought she had been in solving their problems and review the evidence with her. As a more direct alternative, I would point out that she had only succeeded in becoming depressed herself. I would propose our telling her parents that it was depressing and debilitating to live in such a troubled household and ask them to get their act together. With that done, the girl and I could get back to the task of making her well-being less dependent on the parents' ability to solve their problems.

I would also educate the mother about her daughter's depression and be prepared for her disclosure that the family's situation was depressing her as well. I would be sympathetic if she did so, explore her symptoms, and similarly emphasize self-care as her solution. If the mother wanted to denigrate herself about having turned her daughter into an enabling codependent, I would listen patiently for a bit. However, I would probably interrupt her at some point and suggest that the best thing she could do for her daughter is to be a good role model, particularly in dealing with men. Finally, I would ask her to keep her daughter out of her marital problems.

I would attempt to get the father to attend the second session if he had not come to the first, probably by using his concern over his daughter's depression as a hook. If he did not, I would send him a message that we were talking about important family matters and rather than having us scheme and talk about him behind his back, he might want to take part and speak for himself. If absolutely necessary, I would proceed without him, but with the knowledge that his absence would make it more likely that his remaining in the home would not be part of any solutions we developed.

As with the mother, I would educate the father about his daughter's depression. I would quickly get to the issue of how irritating it must be to have a couple of women trying to run his life, even if he loved them and they loved him. I would probably become a bit irksome and outright annoying, trying to slip him into a position of defending them and their concern for him. I would be careful not to jump to the conclusion that he was committed to stopping drinking. After I asked him to keep his daughter out of his personal struggles, I might question why he did not pick out a wimpy wife so that he could drink without harassment.

Overall, my primary goal would be to reduce the young woman's depression. Beyond that, I would try to help all three family members be comfortable with their own behavior. The family might settle into a détente, with the father more involved but still drinking. Maybe he would prove capable of controlled drinking, but more likely he would have to discover that he was not. If he was serious about getting help in stopping drinking, I would refer him to an alcohol treatment facility. After all, his daughter's depression had been the presenting problem, not his drinking. While Alcoholics Anonymous would be an option, I would not present it as the only one.

What stands out most for me about this case is how the mother and daughter had ignored how much influence they could have on family life, even if they could not control the father. They had confused the lack of control with lack of influence. Had this been my case, I would have focused on helping them recognize their choices, particularly regarding how to be more influential in their family. I would then have negotiated plans of action with each of them and assisted them in the implementation. I would have done the same for the father if I could engage him. Perhaps the result of all of this would have been the same as what Eron and Lund achieved. However, I cannot help thinking that by confusing influence with control and wishing to avoid being controlling at all cost, the therapists here missed opportunities to exert their clinical influence as effectively and efficiently as possible.

CASE COMMENTARY 2
BY VICTORIA DICKERSON

Eron and Lund begin their case study by making a connection between the behavior of the family members and the stories they have about themselves. Diane had previously seen herself as "codependent," but as she pursued more self-oriented goals, her depression lifted and she began to act more independently. Out of concern for her father, Jerrine had subsequently taken on the "codependent" role, leading to a loss of interest in her school work and social life. The therapists explore with Diane her "preproblem past" with the intention of helping her challenge her negative view of her relationship with Jerrine. From this work, a story emerged about Diane as a caring mother who had helped her daughter be self-oriented like herself. The therapists then focused on how Diane had also helped her daughter cultivate other-oriented attributes and "reframed" the caretaking as a strength. They then encouraged both Diane and Jerrine to take steps toward including Frank "in being more responsible" and "holding him accountable." As they did this, Frank became more involved in the family while Diane and Jerrine continued to pursue their own interests (Jerrine resuming her attention toward school); eventually Frank took steps toward controlling his drinking and behaving more responsibly.

Although the outcome seems positive, I was struck by what was not addressed in this case. Because Diane and Jerrine were never engaged in a discussion around their underlying assumptions about what it means to be women in this society, they never confronted how gender conditioning might be dictating their view of themselves and their intentions to be self-oriented. Although Diane took a step for herself away from taking care of Frank, she began to feel guilty when her daughter stepped in to take up that role. The therapists encouraged them both to reaccess their "caring and sensitive" desire (as well as their interest in pursuing their own goals), which I believe, might have reinforced Diane and Jerrine's thinking that they needed to be responsible for the relationship *and* for making Frank responsible.

Although at face value this work seems to fit Diane and Jerrine's preferred view of themselves, my concern is that it never raises the question of who is responsible for what. In my experience, women see themselves as the ones primarily responsible for relationships. Thus, when women take steps for themselves in their lives, they often experience guilt, because they are not doing what the culture tells them they are supposed to be doing. When a therapist encourages women to continue to take primary responsibility for the relationship and for others, it play right into the culture's hands. This can continue to keep women trapped in a gendered role without their noticing other possibilities.

A narrative perspective regards problems in the context of how the culture shapes the problematic ways people "story" their lives. A narrative approach would attempt to separate people from these problems and their cultural meanings, thus enabling them to see new possibilities. In this case, I would have explored with Diane and Jerrine how the problem of Frank's drinking affects them. I expect that for Diane what would arise would be her bitterness and disgust and how her feeling powerless in relation to her daughter. For her part, Jerrine might describe how her overconcern for Frank comes at the expense of her own needs and interests. I could then discuss with both mother and daughter the negative effects of these experiences— a sense of loss of control for Diane and listlessness and withdrawal for Jerrine. We could then explore how the larger culture influences women to believe it is their responsibility to care for relationships and for others at the expense of caring for self. This exploring of cultural meaning often allows people to question whether their behaviors and attitudes are really how they want to be in the world.

Once there is some separation from the problem, people begin to notice possibilities that did not previously seem to exist. Diane and Jerrine might see that they could continue to pursue their own interests without loss of caring for Frank. In fact, they might also see that self-oriented pursuits could include a commitment to their relationship. This combination of caring for self and caring for Frank, without getting actively involved in inviting him to respond, could also have a powerful effect on him—he might notice that he *wants* to be more a part of the family and be more responsible. He might even be willing to explore the effects of the problem on him and how the culture might be influencing him. He might then notice other possible ways of being and acting.

My experience is that clients choose what fits best for them once they are separated from the problem and are free to notice possibilities they had not previously seen. Often their choices are counter to cultural norms, but not always. In any case, they experience themselves as freer to choose, and they make choices that support their own values, as well as their desired relationships.

When we compare Eron and Lund's work with the alternative scenario I describe here, the question arises whether it is possible to integrate a strategic approach to therapy with a narrative one. The strategic flavor of the work lies in such maneuvers as locating the problem in individual stories then aligning the client's story, reframing certain attitudes as strengths, and suggesting solutions.

Alternatively, a narrative perspective locates problems in cultural meaning and helps clients recognize the cultural underpinnings of their difficulties, thus allowing them to experience themselves as separate from the problem. This is a very different therapy, one that questions, even changes, the dominant cultural meanings that, if allowed to go unquestioned, can dictate the stories we live.

Authors' Response

by Joseph Eron and Thomas Lund

Thanks to Victoria Dickerson and James Coyne for their thoughtful comments about this case. Since our narrative solutions approach is an integration of narrative and strategic concepts, we were pleased to receive commentary from people representing these two approaches.

Victoria Dickerson's commentary emphasizes the impact of broad cultural influences on the development of Jerrine, Diane, and Frank's present predicament. She advocates an approach that helps family members locate their problems in cultural meanings and, in the process, separate themselves from these problems. James Coyne prefers directive interventions that waste no time in helping people solve problems. His outline of his own hypothetical treatment approach for this case demonstrates the forcefulness of strategic concepts and methods.

People dedicated to either of these schools of family therapy often attest to the effectiveness of one approach to the exclusion of the other. In his efforts to help people change, Coyne appears to have little confidence in the use of narrative concepts. In fact, he is concerned that our "immersion in the narrative frame of reference" might have slowed down therapy. Dickerson is equally confident about the helpfulness of the narrative metaphor in therapy but seems somewhat concerned about the use of terms like aligning and reframing that have a strategic ring.

A key assumption of both narrative and strategic therapies is that *meaning* (how people view their situation) and *action* (what people do about their situation) are inextricably linked. This assumption was the basis of the strategic technique of reframing, which involves therapists altering the way people view (or frame) their present circumstances in order to change what they do. Unfortunately, these principles were lost in strategic practice as reframing became almost exclusively a technique for getting people to go along with what the therapist wanted them to do, rather than help them think differently about their situation. Words like "aligning" and "reframing" may conjure up visions of techniques that now appear impositional and at times disrespectful. Yet, if one looks beyond the manipulative techniques that became the hallmark of strategic therapy, many of the ground breaking concepts of this approach remain useful.

Our approach to therapy developed while working within the basic assumption of the Mental Research Institute's brief therapy approach. For the past 14 years, we've looked critically at when our conversations with families work and when they do not. Our ideas about how problems start, persist, and resolve developed in this pragmatic way, as well as our thinking about what constitutes helpful conversations with families in distress. Our experience has shown that therapy is most effective when we combine the strategic emphasis on the therapist's responsibility to resolve the immediate presenting problem, along with the broader narrative influences that shape the stories that maintain the problem. ■

STUDY QUESTIONS

1. Why do Eron and Lund find the term *codependent* problematic? What is your opinion of the term?

2. What are Coyne's arguments against focusing exclusively on "strengths, competencies, and personal initiative"? What is your opinion about having such a focus as a clinician?

3. Why does Dickerson believe a discussion about gender would have been important for Diane and Jerrine? What do you think?

4. How did this case intervention demonstrate an integration of narrative therapy and strategic therapy?

IS THE CUSTOMER ALWAYS RIGHT?
MAYBE NOT, BUT IT'S A GOOD PLACE TO START

Barry L. Duncan, Scott D. Miller, and Mark A. Hubble

Many therapists today have abandoned a reliance on the Five Ds (diagnosis, disease, dysfunction, disorder, and deficit). They have stepped down from the throne of the exalted expert and learned to privilege the client's voice as the source of wisdom and solution. That's all fine and dandy until you are faced with clients who adhere to a pathological view of themselves despite your best efforts to highlight strengths. How do you avoid taking an expert stance when clients plead for advice and downplay their own abilities and expertise? How do you draw on the client's theory of change when it is so totally contrary to your core values?

Pat, a 37-year-old full-time mother of two children, was referred by the principal of a nearby school where I consult. She had worked her way through the helping professionals at the school, ruffling feathers along the way with her ardent concerns about her daughter Ann's "depression." The problem was that the school did not share her concerns—Ann was a hard-working student and a well-behaved 9-year-old, according to her teacher. The school counselor and school psychologist believed her to be remarkably well adjusted, despite a mother whom they described as a "certifiable nut" and "loose cannon waiting to go off."

My courtship of Pat began in the waiting room, when she said that she would like to smoke in my office and I agreed. As minor as it sounds, it helped us start off on the right foot. In the office, I chatted with her and Ann as welcomed guests. I got Pat an ashtray, laughed at her jokes, smiled, and was attentive. I asked Ann about her school and teachers, as well as her favorite television shows and CDs. Pat was an interesting character, full of extremes. She was charming and impeccably dressed in designer clothes, but spoke in a boisterous manner, emphasizing her points with sweeping gestures and intense eye contact. Ann looked like any 9-year-old, but predictably enough, wore an embarrassed expression that said she wanted to be somewhere else. She slumped in the chair and didn't look up as her mother opened the session: "Ann is so depressed." Pointing to her daughter, she said, "She complains about being bored and mopes around." She gestured broadly with her hands and continued, "I'm depressed, and I know that I have a chemical imbalance and will need to take antidepressants the rest of my life. I also take antipsychotics, because I had a psychotic break right after Ann was born—tried to kill myself and the whole nine yards. My mother is also depressed and takes antidepressants." She paused momentarily to take a drag from a cigarette, saying finally, "My doctor told me it was genetic, and I'm sure that Ann is just like my mother and me and probably needs to be on medication, too."

A more problematic script could not have been written for me. I though for a moment I was set up by those at the school who were sick of my impassioned railings about pathology and the *DSM* at team meetings. I heard a loud voice yelling in my head, " Privilege this!"

I was particularly concerned about Pat's statements in light of psychologists Seymour Fisher and Roger Greenberg's work highlighting the appalling lack of empirical support for drugging children. Pat not only wrapped herself in a cloak of psychiatric and psychopharmacological terminology, but wanted me to help her pass it along to her daughter. Sometimes, privileging the client's voice ain't so easy.

At times the art of therapy lies in forming alliances with those that others find difficult. Research confirms that the client's view of the relationship is the trump card in therapy outcome, second only to the winning hand of the client's strengths.

After Pat's opening assessment, I listened for her theory of change, her formula for a positive outcome. This becomes clear from a client's ideas, attitudes, and speculations about the future. It is important to join clients in exploring alternate routes on their own maps. I took note of Pat's exact words so I could honor her interpretations. I was careful not to enter into a needless clash of ideologies. This attitude of respectful attention ultimately provided the foothold into the relationship that enabled everything else to occur.

I then spent time with Pat and her daughter alone. Ann was quiet and sullen at first, but became animated and friendly when our conversation turned to the "mean" boys at school. She insisted that she was not depressed, that her only problem was that the boys teased her, which, she said, happened to all the girls in her class. Ann denied that the boys might really like her, but I remained skeptical. Our delightful banter left me no cause for concern. All she wanted was for her mom to stop asking whether she was depressed.

When I saw Pat alone, she conveyed her helplessness. She described how she tried to comfort Ann, and went to great lengths to monitor the "depression" and help her daughter overcome it. Her real fear, she said, was that Ann's "early signs" would worsen, damning her to the bouts of depression that had plagued two previous generations of women in the family.

When I asked her why she was seeing me instead of someone who could give Ann medication, she leaned forward with a frozen stare, forcefully stubbed out her cigarette and replied, "You're the expert. You tell me what to do about this genetic depression and how to help my daughter!"

Challenging Pat and her genetic-depression view would have only attached me to the conga line of failure. Ann's teacher, school counselor, and school psychologist had already attempted to persuade Pat that nothing was wrong, and had even asked her at length about times Ann wasn't depressed. Pat only perceived these efforts as belittling Ann's problems and subtly indicting her competence as a parent.

After the first session, the team believed that the task was to work within Pat's view of genetic depression, while trying to discover possible alternatives to medication. In the second session, I conveyed right off my acceptance of Pat's genetic-depression theory and validated her worry as understandable and appropriate, given the family history. I said it was an obvious expression of love and concern for her daughter. Surprised and relieved, Pat said, "Oh, you see it, too." She relaxed and I was then able to shift the conversation to what might help in the present situation. Validation of a client's viewpoint, even when it seems bizarre, often opens the conversation to new ideas and directions—ones we often never dreamed existed.

Staying with the genetic perspective of depression, I suggested in my most expert manner, tempered by a desire not to misrepresent my convictions, that while there was a strong familial predisposition to depression, the key to whether the depression actually appeared was what happened in Ann's environment. Straight textbook stuff. I proposed that perhaps Pat could help her daughter herself by dealing with the environmental aspects of Ann's depression.

All ears, Pat encouraged me to continue. It was at that moment that our collaboration began. We brainstormed about what the environmental contributions to Ann's depression could be and identified three areas: self-esteem, rewards and punishments, and family interactions. Pat reported that she was a "stroker" and often rewarded Ann in an attempt to build her self-esteem. We concluded that not much additional could be done here. Pat also extolled the virtues of her marriage and did not see any connection there to Ann's problems. She did think, however, that she needed to deal differently with Ann's negative feelings. She leaned forward when I said that parents sometimes discount a child's negative feelings out of love and hope for their children. "That's exactly what I do," she said with recognition. "I'm a stroker. I'm always upbeat and positive with her, always telling her how smart and pretty she is. I discount her feelings, and it's not helping. I need to support her feelings, even if they are negative."

By the end of the session, Pat agreed to encourage and validate Ann's complaints, and to occasionally exaggerate them "as a way of helping Ann learn to cope with her depressive tendencies." This latter idea really struck a chord with Pat. She said, "When you say exaggerate, I'm thinking that when she criticizes herself, how about if I exaggerate it to the point of ridiculousness? Like if she says she's ugly, I'll say, 'Yeah, you're so ugly I've had to replace three broken mirrors because you looked at them,' instead of trying to convince her how pretty she is?" This approach addressed both Pat's desire to help and Ann's wish for her mom to back off. We agreed that medication remained an option if environmental efforts failed.

Pat's husband, Chris, attended the next session because she wanted him to hear what we had discussed. He shared Pat's concerns about Ann's complaints and worried about the family history of "mental problems." Courting Chris's favor wasn't easy. He had a patronizing attitude toward Pat, continually emphasizing her illness. Nevertheless, Pat seemed in total awe of her husband. Once again, I followed the client's lead despite my uneasiness and Chris agreed to join Pat in her plans to help Ann.

Pat returned for two more meetings. She reported that Ann was smiling more and complaining less. Pat had altered the proposed suggestions to fit her sense of humor and strengths, so her exaggerations of Ann's complaints were funny instead of the serious fare I had suggested. Pat laughed as she recounted her exchanges with Ann and their giggling together. Pat also reported that although it was difficult for her, she was not attempting to rescue Ann from her depression. She concluded that perhaps her daughter was only mildly predisposed to depression.

By our final session, Pat was satisfied that antidepressant medication was not needed. This was music to my ears. Adopting her theory of change had opened the door to other options—other means for accomplishing the same end. Pat's theory of change only required that someone take her fears of genetic depression seriously, not that they embrace them absolutely.

Pat contacted me six months later because she wanted to go off her antipsychotic medication. I supported her decision, consulted her psychiatrist, and Pat discontinued that medication. Ann continued to do well.

Despite our commitment to collaboration, clients will hold beliefs and values that at times can be like sharp fingernails on a chalkboard to us. Women oppressed by male chauvinism sometimes embrace a subservient position. Clients disempowered by victim- or deficit-based views sometimes persist in seeing themselves as damaged goods. Clients deceived by the medical model and wanting to see us as experts sometimes don't see the value of collaboration. These are the cases—like Pat's—that test our mettle as therapists. Here is where we really see if we can embrace multiple perspectives.

CASE COMMENTARY
BY LEE COMBRINCK-GRAHAM

I liked how this case turned out. The therapist did a fine job of joining with the mother, and helping her use her devotion to her daughter in a more constructive way. I was also glad to see that Pat began to challenge her use of antipsychotic medication. Nevertheless, this case raises several questions for me as a family systems-oriented child and adolescent psychiatrist.

I was puzzled by the therapist's initial perplexity about Pat's insistence that her daughter has an inherited, biologically based depression. Why should he find this so unusual? Doesn't he read *The New York Times?* Doesn't he know that the lay public is being systematically trained in the "medicalization of social deviance"? All of us in the mental health field implicitly encourage a view of our own and our children's flaws as probably diagnoseable and fixable with psychotherapy or, with luck, some medication. Instead of discussing this or addressing this directly with Pat, the therapist sticks with his approach to "privilege the client's voice"—that would be Pat's voice—and "honor her interpretations," which comes across as patronizing. He describes himself as going out of his way to accommodate her by allowing her to smoke in his office and laughing at her jokes. When he later describes the patronizing attitude of Chris toward his wife, Pat, I wondered if the therapist was aware that he had assumed a similar role with Pat. Such unrecognized replication of interpersonal patterns by the therapist tends to maintain interpersonal patterns rather than change them. We know that Pat's strategy for coping with her daughter's "depressive" expressions changed, but what about the interactions in the family?

When a mother has concerns about her child, who has the problem? Here, the therapist assumes that it is the mother. In contrast, a family-systems therapist would ask a larger question, assessing the role of all the people involved with Ann in defining and maintaining the problem. For example, the principal and other school authorities have a problem: They tried to dispel Pat's concerns and then to dismiss her. The therapist has a problem with Pat's insistence on Ann's having a problem. Pat, herself, carries the burden of a genetic disorder and her personal history around it, a "breakdown," and psychotropic medication, and whatever grief she may have suffered in the relationship with her similarly affected mother. Ann, about whom her mother worries, has a problem with her mother's worrying. Chris shares his wife's concerns about Ann, but also has a parental attitude toward Pat (is this a problem?). And there is another child, not described or included in the therapy. By seeing his task as finding a way to get Pat to abandon her campaign to have her daughter declared "depressed," the therapist is like many others who do incidental work with children, identifying the source of their problems as their parents. This long tradition, from Little Hans through Kanner's Refrigerator Mothers, to the current and persistent practice of mother blaming seems to stem from adult therapists' unfamiliarity or discomfort with children, as well as a prevailing view of children as innocent, dependent, and not accountable.

Some therapists work through the parents because they don't want to intrude themselves ambiguously into the power structure of the family—they don't want the children to feel, somehow, that the parents can't be effective without the therapist's telling them what to do. But I believe that children make essential contributions to family change. In this case, my first step would have been to invite the whole family to come in. In this session, Pat might have stated her concerns; Chris might have agreed in a patronizing way; Ann might have shrugged off their concern but lost her voice, not daring to confront her mother; and the other child might have been annoyed and disgusted with all the attention Ann was getting, and wondered why he had to be there, anyway. Whatever might have transpired, the session would have revealed the cycle of family interactions that maintain Pat's conviction that her child is depressed, as well as how Pat's concern for her daughter generates another chain of responses within the family. It is very likely, for example, that when Pat expresses concern, Ann withdraws, and then withdraws further when Chris joins with Pat in his scrutiny of his daughter's moods. Wouldn't this withdrawal look like depression to the parents? Pat isn't crazy: Ann's behavior with her mother probably does look like depression. Instead of viewing Ann as a passive symptom bearer of mother or parents' dysfunction, I would view Ann as an active player in the therapy—she would have to play a significant role in changing her mother's view of her, if she doesn't want to be labeled depressed. She would have to learn how to tell her mother about her worries, and Pat would have to learn how to respond without scaring her daughter away.

Would the outcome have been any better had the therapist used a family-systems focus? We can't know, of course. But certainly, the therapist would have formed a clearer picture of how other members of the family fared in the treatment. Here we have only Pat's outcome. We can guess that the school personnel were happier now that Pat was no longer bothering them. We don't know whether Ann's ability to speak honestly and openly with her mother improved, although we do know her mother was better at talking to her. We have no idea, at all, how Pat's increasing comfort with herself affected Chris and her other child.

When the whole family is involved in treatment, individuals' difficulties are recognized as parts of familiar patterns that can be changed, transforming everyone's view of the situation and the possibilities. At the very least, family members can learn how they can be helpful to one another. When the family is not involved in treatment, undue responsibility falls on the therapist.

AUTHORS' RESPONSE

BY BARRY L. DUNCAN, SCOTT D. MILLER, AND MARK A. HUBBLE

Lee Combrinck-Graham's thoughtful commentary cites the differences between our approach and her family-systems perspective, which is based on the idea that the whole family must be involved for real change to occur. Our response is to emphasize again that 40 years of research have not demonstrated the superiority of any one therapeutic model over another. Psychoanalytic, solution-focused, cognitive-behavioral, family systems—it simply doesn't matter what brand the therapist uses.

What does matter, the data affirms, is the client: the client's resources, participation, evaluation of the alliance, and perceptions of the problem and its resolution. Therapists' theories are only helpful if the clients see them as relevant and credible. We, therefore, elevate clients' perceptions and experiences above theory, and look to them to direct therapeutic choices. Consequently, in this case we did not take on the task of "finding a way to get Pat to abandon her campaign to have her daughter declared depressed," as Combrinck-Graham suggests. On the contrary, we accepted Pat's declaration of Ann's depression and worked within that perspective to accomplish Pat's goals for therapy.

Combrinck-Graham believes that her family-systems map of the therapeutic territory gives her a "clearer picture." Her map tells her who must be seen, who has the problem and what it is, what they might do in session, what the patterns of interaction likely are at home, and what they must do for problem resolution. In addition, her map led her to assume that she understood the exact attitude and role that the therapists adopted with Pat. In contrast, we try to illuminate the client's map of the therapeutic territory. Our "clearer picture" evolves from exploring the landscape of the client's theory of change, the client's own routes of restoration. We privilege the client's voice not only about what destination is desired from the therapeutic journey, but also what paths may be followed to get there. While Combrinck-Graham's suggestions are, no doubt, useful for some clients, we believe, based on our direct experience with Pat, that they wouldn't have been a good fit here.

Historically, mental-health professions have relegated clients to playing nameless, faceless parts in therapeutic change, like interchangeable, cardboard cutouts fitting into a theory of therapy. We agree with renowned scholar Jerome Frank who said, "therapists should select for each patient the therapy that accords, or can be brought to accord, with the patient's personal characteristics and view of the problem." Such a selection requires a shift in view from the omnipotence of the therapist's theory of therapy to the prominence of the client's theory of change. ■

STUDY QUESTIONS

1. How did Duncan "form an alliance" with Pat, and how did he address her theory of change?

2. Who do you think was the client in this case? Do you agree with the therapist's decision about who to treat in this case, or do you agree with Combrinck-Graham that a family intervention would have been more helpful? Why or why not?

3. The author of the case says that the model of therapy doesn't make any measurable difference. In your opinion, what are the factors that lead to successful outcomes in therapy?

CONSULTATION CORNER

ONE STEP FORWARD, TWO STEPS BACK

Treating the Unmotivated Client

EDITED BY H. CHARLES FISHMAN

Family therapy's pioneers seemed to believe the family approach was the key to overcoming previously untreatable psychiatric problems. Today's family therapists, however, are more likely to see family work as one component in a coordinated treatment approach with the chronically mentally ill. The following case raises the question of the advisability of family involvement in the therapy of a young man, living on disability, with questionable coping skills and few family resources. The case commentators focus on the issue of when to involve families in such cases, as well as the pitfalls of working with seemingly unmotivated clients.

H.C.F.

Steve, an intelligent, heavy-set, 38-year-old man, was referred to me when his previous therapist was about to leave our family-oriented agency. At our first meeting, he didn't make much eye contact with me and smiled at inappropriate times. His clothes didn't match and his hair was uncombed. He told me he was on psychotropic medications to diminish his paranoia and depression, and he hadn't held a steady job in seven years, although he sometimes picked up a little money doing odd jobs.

Steve was uncomfortable in most social situations and he had only one friend outside his family. He told me he had been in and out of institutions and therapy for 12 years because of alcohol problems, fears of working in crowds of people, and what he called "paranoid, crazy thoughts" that other people were out to kill or harm him.

In 1989, he told me, a psychiatrist assessed him and told him that he suffered from "schizotypal personality disorder." He said that the

(Continued)

294

(Continued)

diagnosis perfectly described his paranoia and his fears—that someone had finally understood him.

Steve also told me that before he was first hospitalized, at the age
of 26, he had completed three years of college, studying mathematics.
Since then, he had quit school and worked only sporadically. He left
his last full-time job when he was 31, after a painful incident in which
fellow workers jokingly threatened to kill him. Since then, he'd lived
alone in an efficiency apartment in a poor neighborhood, and was on
federal and state disability and health insurance.

I spent our first sessions establishing rapport, finding out about previous therapy and taking a family history. Steve told me that he had a
brother and a sister, both of whom held down full-time jobs, were
married and had children. Both lived a couple of hours' drive away.
His sister, a physical therapist who was in AA, treated him decently,
but only called him twice a year. His brother, whom he described as a
son-of-a-bitch, called once a month to find out how he was doing, but
then badgered him and screamed at him for not pulling himself up by
his bootstraps and getting his life together.

Steve said his father had a "nervous condition" and an alcohol
problem, and had left the family when Steve was 11. Steve's mother,
who had been hospitalized 12 times when he was growing up and was
diagnosed as schizophrenic, had been dangerously violent toward
Steve when he was a child. Now she lived in a retirement home and
frequently called Steve on the phone and screamed at him. At the
same time, she told him that he was her main source of support, that
they shared a bond because they both had biologically based mental
illnesses, and she often asked him to take her out of the retirement
home for the weekend. Then, whether or not he felt like it, Steve
would bring her to his apartment, where she would spend hours doing
housecleaning, and sometimes leave him money or food to supple-
ment his meager benefits.

Steve also got distressing phone calls from his maternal grandmother,
who had not spoken to Steve's mother (her daughter) in 12 years. They
had stopped speaking after his mother's final hospitalization, which

(Continued)

(Continued)

occurred after an episode during which she had been particularly brutal to Steve. Steve was caught between these two women. His mother would say Steve was her only support, and talk about how mean and hostile Steve's grandmother was. The grandmother, meanwhile, told Steve he was her favorite grandchild, and not at all like his mother. But she accused him of being lazy and not really sick.

Steve also told me that he had gone to AA meetings about a year ago for six weeks and had stopped drinking. But he quit AA after his sponsor suggested that his mother and grandmother were "making him crazy" and he should cut off contact with them. Since then, he told me, he'd stayed sober, on his own, except for one day of drunkenness.

Previous therapists, Steve said, had helped him when they got him connected to AA, but the outcome wasn't as positive when they addressed his paranoia. He felt they didn't understand that he was sick, and he worried that if he got better he would lose his federal disability benefits.

When I asked Steve to talk more about his paranoid thoughts and feelings, a pattern emerged. In weeks that Steve had little contact with his mother and grandmother, he was less paranoid. The more he talked to them, the more paranoid his thoughts became, usually beginning a day or two after the phone call. He would imagine that schoolchildren in the park where he walked were going to come after him and hurt him; another time, he thought that a street sweeper outside his house was planning to kill him.

As I asked him questions about the patterns of his bouts of paranoia, Steve, too, saw the connection to phone calls from his mother and grandmother. We found that his paranoia was considerably reduced when *he* took the initiative, called his mother, and suggested a much more limited outing—with no overnight visit. He also thought of getting an answering machine, but didn't do so. Most of the time, he said, he simply couldn't end a conversation with her or set limits on her visits.

I thought that Steve's paranoia, even if it were biologically based, was exacerbated by his position between his mother and

(Continued)

(Continued)

grandmother. Hoping to change these relationship patterns and the effect they had on Steve, I asked him to bring other members of his family into therapy. I didn't want to cut Steve off from his family, and I hoped that if he and his mother replayed their relationship in therapy, Steve might learn to set better boundaries with her—to tell her, for example, that how he kept his apartment was his own business. I wanted Steve to find some areas where he was competent and amplify them; I hoped he might find his own voice and express that competence in front of his mother and me. It seemed to me that staying sick was part of the price Steve had to pay to stay close to his mother and grandmother. I hoped that family therapy might give him a chance to be more independent and more autonomous.

When I suggested family therapy, Steve told me that his sister lived too far away and that his brother wouldn't listen to anybody. He was eager to bring his mother or grandmother in, and both agreed. But his mother's own paranoid thoughts would rise shortly before scheduled sessions, and she would cancel at the last moment. His grandmother reported a succession of physical ailments that ultimately kept her from coming in.

Since then, Steve has expressed that, on the one hand, he loves being diagnosed as schizotypal, and, on the other hand, he would like to go to AA meetings, get a job, and deal with his mother in a different way. He says he wants to get better, but his behavior doesn't confirm this. I have made many phone calls attempting to find him a nurturing, nonconfrontational AA meeting, to connect him with his old sponsor, or to arrange career counseling. He never follows up. Steve himself even set up an interview for an $11-an-hour telephone job that would have allowed him to use his mathematics skills, but he never made it to the interview.

More recently, Steve has begun to express his fears that we at the agency don't see him as sick. He fears that the agency director will not recertify him as handicapped and that he will lose his disability benefits. I see this as a realistic fear.

(Continued)

(Continued)

At this point, my questions are: How might I help Steve find a motivation for getting better when staying sick guarantees him a low but secure income? Is my relationship with Steve strong enough to warrant bringing in other family members, or am I pushing too hard and too fast to get them involved? And if I decide to wait for a while, how will I know when it's time to bring other family members in?

COMMENTARY 1

A Challenge Model Approach

STEVEN J. WOLIN

Not all clients can be treated immediately with family therapy. Sometimes, therapists need to work with the individual before involving the whole family, and this case is one of those times.

When he entered therapy, Steve had already been identified as having a schizotypal personality disorder. While his therapist acknowledges this diagnosis, he seems to be missing its full implications. People with schizotypal personalities have disturbed thoughts including paranoid ideation, excessive anxiety in social situations, odd behavior and physical appearance, few, if any, close relationships, and inappropriate affect. They are highly suggestible, regress easily, and have fragile egos with a limited, fluctuating ability to observe themselves. So, it is not surprising that Steve cannot limit his contact with his mother and grandmother simply by getting an answering machine, and that he is unable to keep a vocational counseling appointment or reconnect with AA despite his best intentions.

Rather than seeing Steve's failure to act in his own interest as the main, underlying problem, his therapist seems to view it as something to get out of the way so that he can get on with the real thing—family therapy. Accordingly, he develops an agenda of immediate goals that he expects Steve to achieve. He wants to get Steve back to work, to find him an acceptable AA sponsor, and to have him bring his mother, grandmother, and siblings into treatment. Then he compensates for Steve's inaction by taking over and acting for him by making many phone calls on Steve's behalf and setting up sessions for the family. At the same time, he presses forward on the long-term and grander goals—to help Steve become more independent, to develop personal boundaries and self-confidence in his relationship with his mother, and to relieve his paranoia by limiting his contact both with her and his grandmother. In answer to the question this therapist poses at the end of the case description—yes, you are pushing too hard. You are not taking Steve's serious limitations into account, and you, not your client, are the source of your own frustration.

Schizotypal clients *can* change, but slowly. I have found that therapy is most effective when I do not get ahead of these clients, when I set small goals and remind them of the distortions in their perceptions of reality. Drawing from a psychoeducational model, I would spend some time preparing Steve for new and threatening encounters. I would give him the opportunity to practice in role plays and I would provide information that he lacks or has distorted. For instance, he should know that his disability status can be renewed if he starts but cannot continue working, or that he could seek employment through vocational rehabilitation and not lose his disability payments until he had demonstrated that he can stay on the job.

A family session should be held only after the two of you have defined the challenges that are likely to occur, set goals, practiced responses that will achieve those goals, and agreed that Steve is ready. Structure the session so that Steve can borrow ego strength from you if he begins to falter. Tell the family that you are going to interrupt the meeting midway through so you can talk to Steve alone. When the others have left, debrief Steve. Ask him how things are going. Remind him of your original goals and the challenges he is facing. Help him make adjustments if necessary; then return to finish the session with Steve. For follow-up sessions, repeat the same routine. Practice. Reach an agreement on the right time for a family appointment. Allow time for a break so that you can support Steve while the session is in progress.

A *US News and World Report* review of the effectiveness of psychotherapy describes a study done by psychologist Kenneth Howard at Northwestern University. Howard charted a "dose response" to psychotherapy similar to the graphs used to track variations in responses to drugs. After collecting data on 2,400 patients during a 30-year period, Howard found that the number of sessions required for patients to improve was related to their diagnosis. While problems such as anxiety and depression abated relatively quickly, more severe conditions required considerable clinical patience. The personality-disordered clients who participated in the study began to show improvement only at the one-year mark.

There is an important lesson here for overly eager family therapists. Toward the end of my psychiatry training, a fellow resident asked, "How do you know what kind of therapy to prescribe for different types of patients?" Our teacher's response was wry. "You'd be surprised," he said, "Everyone will need *exactly* what you have available." Family therapists should know better. While understanding the family's powerful influence, Steve's therapist should also hone his skills for treating individuals.

COMMENTARY 2

A Social-Constructionist Approach

LEE COMBRINCK-GRAHAM

It appears that being a psychiatric patient is Steve's career; he is afraid to get better because he might lose his only means of support. While Steve is an intelligent and insightful person who knows how to look after his own interests, he doesn't seem ready to change his career. Nevertheless, change might be possible if his situation were framed in terms other than "mental illness" and "family dysfunction" and if the therapist expressed less interest in Steve's deficits and more interest in his choices—the ones he has made as well as the ones he may have rejected or not yet considered.

For this to happen, the therapist would have to show an interest in Steve as a person rather than a patient; he would need to be genuinely curious about how Steve makes decisions and respect the considerations that lead him to one choice over another. Taking this approach, I imagine a beginning conversation with Steve might go something like this:

THERAPIST: Hello. I see you have been in therapy for 12 years or so. What would you like to do with me? [Begins by emphasizing that Steve is choosing to be in therapy.]

STEVE: Well, a psychiatrist once told me I have schizotypal personality disorder. I take medicine for my paranoia and depression.

THERAPIST: Yes, I see that in your record. What would you like to do in therapy? [Doesn't focus on psychopathology.]

STEVE: What do you mean? I have a mental illness, don't I?

THERAPIST: Do you think so?

STEVE: Don't you think so?

THERAPIST: I don't know. I just want to know what you'd like to do with all of this. [Is curious about Steve's opinion.]

STEVE: You tell me; you're the doctor.

THERAPIST: I can't really tell you, because I don't know what goes on in your head. I don't know the circumstances of your life. I don't know what you dream about and wish for in your life. Only you know that. [Does not presume to know who or what Steve is.]

STEVE: I thought therapists were trained to know what people want and how they feel. You're just playing with my mind. I think I'm getting paranoid.

THERAPIST: What do you mean, "getting paranoid?" [Doesn't take jargon for granted.]

STEVE: I feel weird, like you're not telling the truth, like you're trying to manipulate me or something.

THERAPIST: That's interesting. Can you tell me why I would want to manipulate you? [Accepts the validity of Steve's suspiciousness. It's based on Steve's reality, and not necessarily irrational and pathological.]

STEVE: Maybe to take away my disability or something.

THERAPIST: Your disability? Is that what you live on? [Getting to nitty-gritty.]

STEVE: Yes.

THERAPIST: I certainly wouldn't want to take away your living. By the way, how is disability as a living? Can you make ends meet?

[More nitty-gritty. Curiosity about lifestyle: hints that there might be alternatives.]

STEVE: Yeah. I mean with the supplements for housing and a little bit of cash from odd jobs, I make ends meet. But it's not easy. If I'd finished college, I could have gone on to graduate school and I could have some security as a college professor or something.

THERAPIST: So you're on disability instead? [Implies this is Steve's choice.]

STEVE: I didn't choose to be on disability, you know.

THERAPIST: You didn't? How did it happen? [Invites Steve to review his story in different terms.]

The therapist maintains an interest in Steve and Steve's description of his experience, while downplaying his diagnosis and symptoms as definers of who Steve is. The focus of the therapy would be to put aside the therapist's agenda and have Steve define himself rather than be defined by other people's stories about him. Given this kind of therapeutic conversation, Steve's story about his family might unfold differently. Here's one possibility:

STEVE: Doctors keep telling me that my problems are caused by my family. I'm confused, because some people tell me I have a "biologically based mental illness," like my mother, and others seem to imply that if I could just get out from being triangulated between my mother and grandmother, I would be better off. [Steve is thinking in the terms he has learned in his conversations with prior therapists. His use of the word "triangulated" comes from this experience.]

THERAPIST: Are there other ways that you think about your problems? [Encouraging Steve to explore his own theories.]

STEVE: Well, I worry that I have the same condition as my mother. Or maybe the "nervous condition" they say my father had. My grandmother says I'm lazy and not really sick, and then she tells me I'm her favorite.

THERAPIST: So you worry that you're like your mother or your father. And you wonder what your grandmother means. Let's take these worries one by one. In what ways are you like your mother? And in what ways are you not like your mother? [Suggesting an avenue for examining the conflicting messages he has been getting from previous therapists.]

STEVE: I guess I'm like my mother because I'm emotionally unstable and paranoid. But I don't get violent, the way she did. So maybe I don't have the same condition she has. I thought I might be like my father, so I started drinking. Then I went to AA and stopped drinking. He never did that. So I guess I'm not like my father. My grandmother doesn't really understand what it's like to live the way I do. She calls me lazy, but she would call me worse names if I got involved with something and didn't take care of Mother.

THERAPIST: What do you mean? [The therapist keeps communicating curiosity.]

STEVE: I'm not sure. Sometimes I think that my brother and sister have skipped town and left me holding the bag. Then they call in now and then to make sure I'm still holding it.

THERAPIST: You mean staying close to your mother? [Just keeping the conversation flowing.]

STEVE: Yeah. They used to get out of the way when Mother was in her psychotic rages, and leave me to get beaten up. But she can't help herself, and she really tries to make up for it by helping me out, in her own way.

THERAPIST: So you forgive your mother.

STEVE: Yes. I think it's my brother and sister I can't forgive. Somehow I think they're the ones that are plotting to do me in . . . really . . .

There are an infinite number of avenues Steve can take to make sense of his own family; this is just one way his story could unfold. The important point is that the therapist is simply a facilitator of Steve's own explorations and does not offer his or her own interpretation or pursue information about Steve's family according to his or her personal agenda.

In this scenario, Steve could accept more responsibility for experimenting with change. A decision to invite his mother into a therapy session, for example, would have to come from him rather than the therapist. It would happen if Steve recognized that he has trouble following through with his plans when he sees her alone, and wanted some help in changing that. The advantage of having the invitation actually come from Steve would be that he'd be far more likely to see that she actually comes in.

Similarly, if Steve became interested in his relationship with his siblings, he might decide he wanted to change his usual interactions with them, perhaps using the therapist as a coach. He could first role-play new possibilities—like calling his sister once a month to ask her how *she* is doing—to see whether he wants these changes or not.

Helped to clarify his own choices, Steve might get a yen to try a different job, return to school, or get some other kind of training. And maybe he wouldn't. The point is that it would be up to him. But suppose Steve decided that he really is not interested in using therapy to change. In that case, it's the therapist's job to avoid pretending that there is a therapeutic contract when there isn't:

THERAPIST: Now that we've talked for a while, it seems to me that you've pretty much decided not to rock the boat, to keep things pretty much the way they are. [Broaches the subject of Steve not wishing to use therapy to make any changes in his life.]

STEVE: What do you mean? I want to get better.

THERAPIST: Well, yes, certainly part of you wants to get well. But as we've talked, it's become clear that a part of you is very aware of some of the negative consequences of getting well—you would lose your disability benefits and have to support yourself. Right now, it doesn't seem to me you want to face that. [Considering the question in terms of Steve's own decision.]

STEVE: Yeah, I see what you mean. But what about my disability? Don't I have to be in therapy to keep getting it?

THERAPIST: You have to check in with your doctor to get your prescriptions renewed and to see how you're doing. He'll sign your disability forms. [Reassuring Steve that his familiar supports are not being taken away.]

THERAPIST: And Steve, always remember that if you decide you want to give something a try, you can come back and we can talk about what you have in mind. But for now, I can see that talking about this stuff kind of puts you on the defensive. I don't think that's helpful, do you? [Offering reassurance that the therapist is not unavailable.]

STEVE: I see what you're saying. But what will I do? Who will I talk to? Where will I go if I get into a bind with my mother or something?

THERAPIST: You can always come in and talk through some ideas you have. I'm sure you would use that time productively. [Continues to focus on Steve's intentions.]

STEVE: Will I be able to see you?

THERAPIST: For as long as I'm available. Of course, if I'm on vacation or tied up, we would want to make sure that you'd have someone to see when you need to. [Making no promises he or she can't keep.]

Once the therapist places the responsibility for setting the course of therapy on Steve, the case becomes less confusing and frustrating. Even if Steve chooses not to be in therapy, he is still entitled to continued access to care and certification of his continued disability. That is Steve's decision, but his experience with a therapist who is respectful of his right to make his own choices in life will make Steve's future contacts with the mental-health system, whatever they are, more productive than they are now. ■

STUDY QUESTIONS

1. The therapist in this case sees family therapy as the best way to help Steve move forward in his life, but Wolin argues for a more individual approach. Do you think family therapy is appropriate for every case and every situation? Why or why not?

2. Combrinck-Graham says she would have deemphasized the client's psychopathology to allow Steve to define himself. What do you think are the strengths and weaknesses of her proposed approach?

3. In what ways might clinical diagnoses both help and hinder therapy?

CASE STUDIES

HERMAN WEPT
OR, THE BATTLE OF NARRATIVES

Michael J. Murphy

In the age of deinstitutionalization, conflicting narratives collide. The mental-health administrators, legislative budgetary committees, and civil-rights lawyers who advocate the closure of state-funded mental hospitals tell one story about patients poised at the gates of institutions, eager to slam their doors behind them. Those who want to keep the hospitals open—the families of the mentally ill, community leaders, and lawyers who might file suit if a released patient hurts himself or anyone else in the community—subscribe to a very different description. And in the middle, of course, are the patients.

Herman was one such patient, caught in a no-man's-land between these two narratives. In the autumn of 1992, he was one of 20 patients remaining at Greystone, a state hospital in rural New England. He and the other patients were the only barrier remaining to the hospital's closure, and the state mental-health bureaucracy was being pushed hard to find them placements and save the state millions of dollars a year.

Herman was not a particularly difficult patient; he was something worse—an enigma. In his two years at Greystone, he had never assaulted a staff member or another patient or attempted to escape. Despite the fact that he shaved every morning, dressed in a suit on visiting days, and was sometimes mistaken for a doctor, he had never been issued a single pass to the hospital grounds.

Herman's admission to Greystone, and his behavior inside it, did not conform to any of the usual pathways in or out of a state mental hospital. He did not show the symptoms of decompensated schizophrenia or any other major mental illness, and so he could not be categorized, put on medication, taught better coping skills, and released. He had been committed because, while trying to kill himself, he had set his apartment building on fire and endangered many lives. His wife, who had left him some months before, told clinicians that he had sexually abused

306

one daughter and beaten the other children. He had no memory of the fire or his suicide attempt, and he showed no remorse, grief, or insight into it, despite repeated but gentle questioning by Greystone's clinicians. And so he was stuck at Greystone, categorized as a psychopath and a con artist who had failed to exhibit the human responses that could have opened a pathway to his release.

When the narrative describing Herman-as-psychopath met the governor's directive to close Greystone, the state mental-health director for the region came to our community care center. He was in a terrible bind: Herman's behavior was still impeccable, but a local forensic psychologist had recently interviewed him and confirmed his diagnosis as a dangerous psychopath. Yet Herman had to go—and soon. The state department of mental health wanted us to design a program for Herman so they could shut down Greystone without risking becoming the subjects of an incompetent-state-facility-releases-dangerous-psychopath story on "60 Minutes."

The state administrators tried to transfer their quandary to us; now we were in a parallel bind. We obviously could not supply as much security as a state hospital, and yet we could not afford to offend the state administrators who were the source of half of our operating budget. As the clinic director and I discussed the matter with state administrators, I realized that all of us, community mental-health staff, state administrators, and Herman were stuck together in a narrative that seemed to offer no way out.

After much discussion, the director and I agreed to interview Herman for a place in our community support program. The state administrators wanted it to be a routine interview preliminary to discharge, but because our program was voluntary and we had to find out whether we could all get along and work together productively, we insisted on reserving judgment until we met Herman.

Two weeks later, I sat in my office waiting for Herman. As the community care center's forensic psychologist, I faced a crucial decision: Would I define the interview as a formal forensic evaluation, assessing Herman's dangerousness for later submission to the state? Or could it be an informal, confidential encounter in which we got to know each other as two people who might work closely together in the future?

At the last minute—as I greeted Herman in the waiting room—I decided to be informal. I told him about my choice as he settled himself into a chair in my office. He seemed pleased with my decision. I began gently urging him to tell me his story as I completed a family genogram.

About half an hour later, Herman was telling me about the Christmas holiday just before he tried to kill himself. His wife and family had left him, and he was working hard at restoring an apartment in a building he owned.

As he talked, I noticed a change in Herman's usually facile manner and self-possessed face. It was as if a sudden wind had blown in, darkening his features. "I really hoped that somehow they would come back and spend Christmas with me," he said, standing staunch in the growing gale. I leaned forward and rolled my chair a little closer to him. I don't remember exactly what I said, but it was something like, "It sounds like that really means a lot to you."

Herman tried to contain his grief, but it overcame him. He wept, and we sat together for a couple of minutes. Then he collected himself. "Hmmn," he said, dabbing at his eyes with a tissue. "Well, I'll be damned. I don't know where that came from."

He may not have known where it came from, but his tears sure made sense to me. He had shown himself to be a human being with feelings, capable of taking part in a relationship. I decided that Herman would do okay in our community support program. At the same time, I knew that by choosing to believe in a narrative of hope and recovery rather than one of pathology, I was taking a risk.

A week later, Herman left the state hospital. His wife and family obtained restraining orders against him, and we made agreements to notify the local police when Herman planned visits to the town where they lived. He moved into a supervised apartment shared with another patient and began making his way in the world. You might say that his tears had formed a river that carried him to a new definition of himself, but it was really a lot more complicated than that. His tears solved our agency's problem as well as his own.

I struggled to comprehend what had happened and began to understand that together we had created a new narrative, a new story. As long as he remained within the old definition of Herman-as-dangerous-psychopath, we were all stuck. We had to participate with Herman in the development of an alternative story that provided a new pathway. His long-suppressed tears were the bridge to this new story.

The new story, which unfolded as the weeks went on, depicted Herman as a man who had lost a great deal in his life; a man who, with his last shred of pride, had maintained himself in rigid isolation in the state hospital to avoid being categorized as a mental patient. To break down and show his grief would have assuaged the anxieties of administrators, but for Herman it would have meant joining a club to which he did not choose to belong. He felt he had been unfairly imprisoned, and had spent two long years in a marathon effort to maintain his integrity.

Later, I met with the community support staff who were to deal with Herman every day. I presented them with the two narratives—Herman as psychopath and Herman as a man choosing to grieve his losses in his own way—and suggested that while at any given moment either one might appear to have greater truth, in a constructivist universe they should not marry either one. Rather, they should allow Herman to define himself in his new situation, to create a new story.

Herman returned weekly for therapy with me for a couple of months, and he now comes in about once every three weeks. He keeps himself busy, takes excellent care of his supervised apartment, and cooks elaborate meals for himself and his roommate, a patient with a lower level of daily functioning. He talks about getting a job someday. In four months, he has not attempted to contact his family or been in trouble with the law.

As a humanistically oriented family therapist, I was intrigued to note that it was Herman's grief that provided the bridge to a new narrative. Had he not had the courage to show his feelings, our impasse could have continued indefinitely. What I had supplied was the open space within which a new narrative could be invented. My willful ignorance allowed us to encounter each other as two people who needed to define themselves anew.

As Herman gets more established, he is settling into a fairly rigid approach to life. No miracles have happened, but, to the relief of the state administrators, his new narrative is beginning to have real veracity, and most importantly, it is offering Herman the chance at a new life.

CASE COMMENTARY 1
BY DAVID DAN

Michael Murphy tells a story whose importance revolves around two elements: First, he gives voice to a combination of social forces that I, as a community mental-health center director, struggle with almost daily; and second, he describes this struggle as a battle of narratives, thereby highlighting the crucial role that language plays in constructing our realities.

The real hero of this case history is the process of psychotherapy, which is to me what is both most winning and most problematic about the story. The dilemma caused by conflicting external pressures—economics versus public safety—is brought to Murphy's doorstep as an unresolvable problem; there is no way out. And yet the therapeutic encounter saves the day. The patient consciously experiences his grief, apparently for the first time. A new narrative emerges—his tears solved our agency's problem as well as his own.

It is not clear, however, what Murphy wishes us to learn from his clinical success. Does he mean for us to view Herman as an exceptional case, or is he suggesting that there is something in his approach to treatment that can be applied by hundreds of clinicians who will have to evaluate thousands of Hermans now under pressure to leave state hospitals? If the latter, which of the many factors involved in his intervention are salient? The informality, or the self-disclosure inspired by it? The genogram he drew, or his empathic mirroring in language he does not exactly remember? Why did Herman respond to Murphy's "open space" when the "gentle questioning" of the hospital staff had long gotten nowhere? Or was it perhaps the fact of Herman's being off-grounds? Was the patient aware of his impending release? Could Herman's changed behavior be a response to his own conscious political decision rather than to a clinical technique?

One thing is clear; this clinical encounter seems to have resolved a terrible dilemma that many of us face: the struggle to maintain clinical integrity in the face of pressure from administrators we cannot afford to offend. In this case, Murphy is spared what might have been his own grief at having to sacrifice the first to the second. His story thus illustrates and celebrates a foundational myth, or meta-narrative, of our subculture of psychotherapy: that the one-to-one, personal therapeutic encounter can resolve the demands of conflicting external social pressures.

In the battle of narratives described by Murphy, it is this *meta*narrative that emerges victorious. Once the patient weeps, Murphy never returns to the social and political narratives (so wonderfully described early on) that have given the story its context.

This resolution through clinical intervention also marks a change in the narrative structure of the story: A variety of perspectives and substantial tensions gives way to a coherent, univocal presentation with a clear meaning. What is that meaning? "As a humanistically oriented family therapist," Murphy was "intrigued" to note the significance of the patient's grief. (I wondered if this was disingenuous. Could a constructivist truly be intrigued by finding confirmed in practice what he believed in theory?) Murphy's point seems to be that a humanistic approach to therapy here created an open space for the expression of grief, which in turn allowed a new narrative to emerge. This is unarguable and well within the canon of accomplished practice. But it suggests that the author's purpose in writing this piece was not as much to characterize the dilemmas posed by the conflicting political narratives in community mental health as to illustrate the clinical principles he believes in. Is he offering these principles as a solution to a systemic problem, or has he simply lost track of the systemic forces that will inevitably re-create the same conflicts for himself, his center, and others?

By the end of the story, Herman and Murphy have switched places. At the beginning, Herman's narrative is characterized by a denial of conflict and implacable detachment; he becomes more human as a new narrative, richly endowed with feelings of grief, desire, and regret emerge. The author, on the other hand, begins with a tumultuous conflict, which by the story's end has been resolved into a simple, straightforward parable about the efficacy of individual psychotherapy. All the loose ends have been neatly tied. I would have preferred less tying and more unraveling—but that, of course, is my story.

CASE COMMENTARY 2

BY CARLOS SLUZKI

Reading this vignette about a man caught in at least a double—and perhaps a triple—bind, I was reminded of a trip I took to a Latin American country earlier this year. I had been sent as a representative of the commission on Human Rights of the American Psychiatric Association investigating alleged human-rights abuses in a local psychiatric hospital, an institution of last resort for some 500 patients with chronic psychiatric disorders.

The point of entry to the first pavilion at the institution was a large, dirt courtyard, criss-crossed by tiled pathways, in which some 50 men (the vast majority of them stark naked or wearing only a small T-shirt) were sitting, lying on the floor in a fetal position, walking in circles, or standing up and endlessly rocking. Some patients were profoundly mentally retarded, some showed visible signs of head injuries and some behaved in the best tradition of chronic psychiatric patients seen in the back wards of large psychiatric hospitals some 30 years ago, before the deinstitutionalization revolution. Several asked for cigarettes with gestures and grunts, and three or four ran toward me and shook my hand profusely.

As I entered the building proper, the picture didn't change much except that this time the patients were lying on cement beds, some of them completely covered by blankets, some of them stark naked. The stench was overwhelming. I had the sense of having been transported in a time capsule to peek into a Cro-Magnon cave, at the dawn of the human race.

I later visited the forensic ward, where the experience was less alien. While definitely overcrowded, it lacked the ferocious stench of the other ward, and most of the inmates were at least dressed in pajamas.

In each pavilion, I was able to establish reasonably lengthy dialogues with deviant characters. In the first one, I was approached by a 50-year-old man dressed in pants, shirt, shoes, and peasant hat, who invited me for a tour of his vegetable garden. This turned out to be a self-generated project for which he had lassoed in as an additional labor force three mentally retarded inmates; he had also enlisted the support of an assistant administrator of the hospital who got some gardening tools for him and the authorization to cultivate a parcel of the otherwise barren land inside the hospital walls. We engaged in a friendly conversation, mainly about gardening—he contributed his products to the hospital kitchen—and the difficulties derived from having had his garden tools stolen four times. Nothing in the conversation differentiated him from a bona fide gardener; everything differentiated him from the average naked refugee from society who otherwise seemed to inhabit that ward.

The second exchange was with a patient in the forensic ward. When I first met him, I thought he was a member of the staff; he was well spoken and properly dressed. The conversation started when, after greeting me, he mentioned, with a twinkle in his eye, that the authorities of the hospital somehow must have received word that a snooping visitor was to be expected, because the day before they had cleaned and painted many walls of that ward. We then discussed politics and institutions. He mentioned in passing that he had been a union representative caught in a political confrontation that led to his commitment to that hospital.

In each case I inquired of a ward orderly why those specific people were still there. In the first case, the answer was that the man didn't have any family to generate the request for his release, and also that "he seemed to like it here." The second man had been involved in a labor dispute, and as union representative, he had physically confronted and threatened some authorities with political connections. Now, he was considered "too dangerous to be released."

Both of these men reminded me of Herman. Like him, their predicament was one of the unavoidable effects of using psychiatry as a form of social control, a use that inevitably dehumanizes patients. The psychiatric label robs people of their history, or at least drastically prunes, selectively minimalizes, and trivializes their story to justify the label and, hence, the need for social control. Individuals caught in that trap frequently end up forgetting their own story, or create a rigid character of their former self in an effort to avoid being subsumed under the description applied to them by the institution. Herman was able to reconnect with, and reroot himself in his own history of competence and responsibility when Michael established a humane, informal conversation with him that validated a narrative placing him in a locus that was historically, socially, and personally appropriate.

For me, the most attractive feature of this powerful vignette is Michael's lucid, introspective account of the therapeutic process; it locates the beginning of the transformation in *the mind-in-action of the therapist.* As the biases and beliefs of Herman's new therapist allowed him to resonate with the *persona* that Herman had kept very private—perhaps to safeguard and preserve it from psychiatric incursions—Herman began to act (and thus to think) differently.

Where is Herman's new/renewed, rehabilitated, budding identity located? In the interpersonal realm of the narrative validated by Michael, and subsequently by all those who concurred with it and acted accordingly. Of course, that new reality will be reconstituted and anchored by Herman's daily activities in his new contexts, and by the dialogue that he will maintain every now and then with his therapist.

More than anything else, this vignette is for me a reminder of the moral power of responsible clinical practice.

AUTHOR'S RESPONSE
BY MICHAEL J. MURPHY

The point of the story, as David Dan accurately presents, is that Herman's situation presented a neat confluence of at least three systemic factors: how the human service bureaucracies we inhabit are rendered immobile by conflicting agendas; how these agendas assume the form of complementary narratives or stories; and how movement between these narratives is facilitated by some mysterious human process, which appears to come from nowhere and tears us from our narrative moorings, hurling us from one interpretive structure to another like airborne Buicks in a Texas tornado.

Unfortunately (perhaps), the whole experience has much less internal consistency than Dan's critique implies it should have. As far as I can see (just up to the next corner), there is no great lesson from the Herman story, no approach that can be applied in hundreds of similar situations. Indeed the very concepts of *approach* and *similarity* rendered the system stuck in the first place, imposing, as they do, uniform responses on millions of utterly unique human situations. No, Herman's story was merely special, revealed to me for God knows what reason, and I wanted to share its elegance and pathos with others.

Maybe it was because Herman appeared to be imprisoned within the mental-health system's narrative as securely as Carlos Sluzki's wonderful Latin American forensic gardener was kept behind his asylum's walls. As Robert Frost said, "Something there is that loves a wall"; but something *else* there is, particularly in psychotherapists, that hates a wall, and yearns, perhaps perversely, for the open, unwalled space of freedom, uncertainty, and terror. Almost as if he was speaking to this very subject, Nietzsche described, much better than I, the characteristics of the man who lives in the metaland, outside the grounding myths, superstitious and narrative themes of our culture: "Bravery, patience, no turning back, no haste to go forward."

Better lessons for the narrative-switching psychotherapist could not be sought. In a similar vein, the humorist did not know he was defining our existential task when he mouthed the punch line: "Don't do something, just stand there!" ■

STUDY QUESTIONS

1. David Dan writes about the "crucial role language plays in constructing our realities." How did the therapist in this case use the concept of narratives to find a solution to the problem of what to do with Herman?

2. Based on Murphy's description of his work with Herman, how would you define a humanistically oriented family therapy?

3. Some clinicians, like Sluzki, worry about how psychiatry can become a form of social control. Discuss what this means. Do you think Herman was subjected to psychiatry as a form of social control? Why or why not?